Experimental Trans

Practice as Research

The Goldsmiths Press Practice as Research series celebrates and explores the multiplicity of practice research and the ways in which it is published. The series is committed to pushing the boundaries of doing and disseminating research.

Experimental Translation

The Work of Translation in the Age of Algorithmic Production

Lily Robert-Foley

Goldsmiths
Press

Goldsmiths
UNIVERSITY OF LONDON

Contents

Introduction   1

1. *Emprunt*   39

2. The Calque   77

3. Literal Translation   107

4. Transpose   135

5. Modulated   167

6. *Equivalencias*   187

7.   205

Notes   219
Bibliography   227
Index   245

Introduction

"The vodka is good but the meat is lousy." So goes a back-translation of one of the first machine translations from English into Russian of the proverb "The spirit is willing but the flesh is weak" (Matthew 26:41, in English translation). It was the Cold War, and the first frenzy over the dream that machines might solve for the luxury of the world's costly multilingualism was sending off sparks, generating human beings' first encounter with the odd errancies of machine translation (MT). Since then, the bemused, sometimes astonished, sometimes disdainful human reactions to MT have become a trope of machinic fallibility and potential: the menacing, exciting question of whether machines can close the gap of language difference.

But that's impossible, isn't it? Machines can't translate meaning; they don't have a sense of sense, some humans might say (Bellos). They'll translate the wrong meaning of a word, translating an accidental homonym (Poibeau), or miming syntax to the point of absurdity. Or they translate overliterally and can't get "humour, irony, metaphors, similes and wordplay" (Youdale 9), cultural reference, or prosody: rhyme, rhythm and music in language. Or they make grammatical mistakes, especially in longer sentences when questions of coherence and anaphora are concerned (Hofstadter). Or the streamlining and standardizing of language and content eclipses the material context, the specificity of texts and languages in translation (Larsonneur).

Machine translation has come a long way since the Cold War, when Warren Weaver and his associates at MIT attempted to nail down the rules of language that would reveal its deep nature as a universal code (spoiler alert: this doesn't work). Statistical machine translation (SMT) in the 1990s got much better results calculating the frequency and thus the likelihood of a translation for a given segment by relying on large data-banks of human translations made possible by the internet. And now, neural machine translation (NMT) translates not words but values produced through natural language processing (NLP) matrices, which enable languages to meet in complex calculations and translate through encoding and decoding.

So let's see how a translation of the phrase "The spirit is willing but the flesh is weak" holds up on June 23, 2022, when it passes consecutively through all the languages of what is probably today's most accurate free online machine translator into English, DeepL:

Bulgarian: Духът е готов, но плътта е слаба.
Chinese (simplified): 心甘情愿，肉体不坚
Czech: Srdce je ochotné, tělo není silné.
Danish: Hjertet er villigt, men kroppen er ikke stærk.
Dutch: Het hart is gewillig, maar het lichaam is niet sterk.
Estonian: Süda on valmis, kuid keha ei ole tugev.
Finnish: Sydän on valmis, mutta ruumis ei ole vahva.
French: Le cœur est prêt, mais le corps n'est pas fort.
German: Das Herz ist bereit, aber der Körper ist nicht stark.
Greek: Η καρδιά είναι έτοιμη, αλλά το σώμα δεν είναι δυνατό.
Hungarian: A szív készen áll, de a test nem erős.
Indonesian: Hati sudah siap, tetapi tubuh tidak kuat.
Italian: Il cuore è pronto, ma il corpo no.
Japanese: 心はできているが、体はできていない。
Latvian: Prāts ir gatavs, bet ķermenis nav.
Lithuanian: Protas pasiruošęs, bet kūnas—ne.
Polish: Umysł jest gotowy, ale ciało nie.
Portugese: A mente está pronta, mas o corpo não está.
Romanian: Mintea este pregătită, dar corpul nu este.
Russian: Ум готов, а тело—нет.
Slovak: Myseľ je pripravená, ale telo nie.
Slovenian: Um je pripravljen, telo pa ne.

Spanish: La mente está preparada, pero el cuerpo no.
Swedish: Sinnet är redo, men inte kroppen.
Turkish: Zihin hazırdır ama beden hazır değildir.
English: The mind is ready, but the body is not.

If I had no idea of the procedure implemented in order to reach the final translation in this series—that is, if someone presented the first and last sentence of this experiment to me and said the result were a back translation of a translation arrived at by a human between a single language pair, I might not think this was entirely wrong. I might imagine that the translator had a good reason for translating in this way, a reason based on linguistic constraints or context, or a particular translational approach or ethics that made them think the receiving public could not fully get the English-language notion of spirit, or that the communicative line would be cut or blocked or twisted with the reference to the relationship of domination between spirit and body. The idea (and the word) of spirit, after all, can change radically from culture to culture, and modulates in the above translations to something closer to heart (introduced with the translation from Bulgarian to Chinese) and, from there, something closer to mind (in the passage between Italian and Japanese). And couldn't the move from "willing" to "ready" in the passage from Dutch to Estonian betray a kind of revisiting of the notion of will, which, rather than an inner failing, could be seen as a set of affective circumstances coming together in the right way at the right time? And what about weakness, which modulates into "not strong" (passing from Bulgarian to Chinese), and finally loses its adjective, so that it opposes "not ready," rather than "strong": the body is not weak, it just isn't quite ready. Is there a universe in which this last translation, "The mind is ready, but the body is not," could be read simply as a softer, gentler, more forgiving variant of the original?

And what if the machine's translation *is* meaningful? What if the machine did *intend* to translate in that way? After all, there are people who are claiming today that machines are sentient, and also people saying that humans are less sentient than we think we are, driven by our programming. But how do we know? How do we know how much sense the machine is making in translation, or how much the meaning of sense is suspended, suspected, surrendered in these processes? The "intention" in my imagined anthropomorphized reading of the proverb in the above experiment happens on the level of language difference, that "irreducible strangeness" (Waldrop), in lexical and grammatical slippages and changes in perspective, for example between a negative formulation and a positive one. How much "sense" is there in language simply performing itself, produced by the incalculable calculations of NMT?

This is the question that Mónica de la Torre, as well as many other poets and experimental language artists working today with machine translators and other translation technologies (voice recognition apps, online dictionaries, crowd sourcing, subtitling, etc.), asks herself when she includes Google translations of her own bilingual poem "Equivalencies/ *Equivalencias*" in her book *Repetition Nineteen*. What are the limits of language in the age of algorithmic production? What does it mean for the translator that language can't help making sense, even when it has been translated by a machine that "doesn't deal with meaning" (Bellos 154)? What does machine translation mean for the literary arts, for translation in general and for human language?

De la Torre translates her poem not once but twenty-five times, using different procedures she refers to by number in her translation key (T1, T2, T3, etc.). Versions T4, T6, T7, T9, T14 and T15 use Google Translate or the Google Translate voice recognition app for smartphone. T15 uses the autocorrect function in SMS. And she is not the only one. In *Pink Noise* (2007), Hsia Yü uses collaged English- and French-language fragments from the internet to create poems and then machine translate them into Chinese. In *Eighty-Four Doors*, Baiden Pailthorpe uses Google Translate to generate fifty-eight versions of the beginning of Orwell's *1984* to create an art exhibit and film version from the results (2012). Annie Abrahams uses Google Translate and voice recognition software for collaborative, performed writing experiments, passing back and forth between multiple languages and technologies (2014). L'Indéprimeuse in France has produced a Google Translation of Hamlet, *Jambonlaissé* (2018), that is regularly performed in theaters. In "Deep Dante" (2021), Camille Bloomfield uses the dropdown menu feature on DeepL to compose a stuttering, proliferating meditation on l.142 of Dante's *Inferno*, "E caddi, come corpo morto cade."

But surely this is just whimsical play. Machines can't *really* translate literature, can they? Warren Weaver himself, the English language "father" of machine translation, wrote in 1955, in one of the first scientific articles devoted to machine translation: "No reasonable person thinks that a machine translation can ever achieve elegance and style. Pushkin need not shudder" (cited in Poibeau 171). Jean-Paul Vinay and Jean Darbelnet, from whom I appropriate the seven translation procedures that I hijack in the seven chapters (including the conclusion) of this book, likewise imply in the introduction to their *Comparative Stylistics of French and English* (translated by Juan C. Sager and Marie-José Hamel) that machine translation is suitable only for texts that can be "reduced to an unambiguous transfer from SL to TL" and do not require any "special stylistic procedures" (34). What then to make of this explosion of the use of MT in poetic and language art practices?

First of all, machines have been writing poetry for at least sixty years, if one takes Theo Lutz's *Stochastische Texte* (1959) as a starting point. Practices that use automatic writing, such as the Oulipo, and language art that use various types of electronic or technological tools, such as can be found on the Electronic Literature Organization's (ELO) website,[1] have a rich, diverse history that is both fundamental and undeniable in any thinking of literature in our contemporary historical moment. And if machines (or humans imitating machines) can write literature, why shouldn't they translate it? Avery Slater, in an article on "Machine Translation and the Poetics of Automation" that has been crucial for my thinking in this book, writes: "What transformation is underway once the work of art in the age of mechanical (re)production is replaced, as a problematic, with the work of art *in the age of its computational generativity*?" This quote is situated in Slater's discussion of Avant-Garde and Dada practices of absurd and automatic writing, carrying through to the Oulipo, as responding to both language mechanization and the structural linguistics that accompanied it as a tool and a response to the technological experimentation. Slater analyses this with regard to developments in machine translation, much like I am intending to do here. She formulates the question thusly: "If structuralism gave us, famously, the death of the author, has it also given us the death of the translator?" From the paradigm of the death of the author, it does not matter if the machine makes meaning or not, since meaning does not reside in the text, but in the "intertextuality that is multiply constructed by the reader" (Robinson, *Experimental Translator* 22, citing Arrojo 138–139). And if machine translation can make meaning and can pass a translational Turing test, if it can develop to the point of being indistinguishable from human translation, does this mean the human translator is dead? What is the space left over for humans to translate in?

Slater also posits literature as the limit and litmus test of machine translation, a gauge for the way that machines are changing the way humans translate, and therefore the way they write and live in language. What I am proposing to do here, in this inventory, analysis and creative critical experimentation of what I will call "experimental translation" (although it has been known by many names), is to push this litmus and limit to the extreme, and to suggest that this practice of experimental translation is a way to respond to and interrogate, to seek to understand, but also to resist and oppose in many cases what machine translation is doing to language, that most "human" of language productions. Although not all of these experiments with translation begin with literature (many start with language-learning manuals, for example), when texts get taken up in this kind of experimentation, they often end up somewhere in the wastes and wilds of what one might call literature, and frequently poetry, if only because "poetry" is the moniker that is often given to uncategorizable experiments in writing.

There is a strand of thought in the history of translation studies that suggests that the division between signifier and signified, the construction of the sign itself in metareflection on language, only happens because of translation, through translation. If a word (for example) does not come up against its untranslatability in another language, how can one know that there is breakage, static on the line between the materiality of a word and what it represents, or between a word and the sum total of what it can represent in the potential infinity of its iterations? It is only by seeing that a word in translation might not mean the same thing, or that a meaning in translation can be broken and splintered into many words, that one can operate the split between signifier and signified in what can at least sometimes be uttered and received as a felt totality in one single language (if such a thing exists). This is one reading of the famous allegory of the Tower of Babel. Walter Benjamin, in "The Task of the Translator," called this the "foreignness of languages," represented in his figure of the fragmented vessel glued back together (Benjamin/Zohn 78), and in his idea that any act of translation is striving toward the truth of language itself. In Paul de Man's reading of Benjamin's famously equivocal essay, this truth is the structure and deconstruction of signification itself, in language. We see this carried through in postcolonial thinking about hybridity, for example in Homi K. Bhabha, where the process of translation, which aligns with "a theory of culture," serves as a "motif or trope for the activity of displacement within the linguistic sign" (Rutherford and Bhabha 210).

But in MT, and especially NMT, the sign is dead. If translation is fundamental to the thinking of the sign in language, what does it mean that "the sign is gone," to quote Rita Raley in her responses to questions after her talk at *What's the Matter in Translation?/Traduction et matérialité*, a conference I co-organized during the writing of this book. No longer can writers and translation and language scholars rely on the signifier/signified model in any work that seeks to take on the contemporary discourse and practice of translation. And yet, this thinking is so embedded, so inescapably anchored into the fabric of reflections on language that it is almost impossible to conceive of language in any other way.

In NMT, there is no signifier or signified, but tokens, numerical values that represent linguistic segments in a given corpus. You can think of a token as a word, although they are not words, since it is not always possible to strictly define what a word is. How many words is "didn't"? Or "machine translation"—is that one word or two? What about "hot dog"? There's a whole science to breaking that down.[2] Those tokens are then calculated for their vector embedding, a complex set of calculations that represents the relationship of a token to other tokens in the corpus, based on their likelihood of appearing together in the same "word window," usually between three and fifteen tokens. Each vector is multidimensional, since it is looking not only at one token's or one word window's relationship to another's (this is already a kind of linear vector), but also that token's relationship to many others, and each of those to many others. Vectors can also show word similarity, so that the machine knows that dogs and cats are animals or red and blue and purple are all colors, and therefore might find themselves in similar situations in parallel word windows. This means that the machine is tapping into something like syntagmatic and paradigmatic models for signification, without any recourse to a binary signifier/signified model. In machine translation, this massive, imaginary, multidimensional matrix of tokens encoded for their vector value—called vector space—in one language is decoded into the vector space of another language.

What is absolutely crazy about this is that the machinations of word vectors end up giving us something like meaning. One example[3] that crops up regularly is:

$$king - man + woman = queen$$

In other words, if you take the vector associated with the word "king," subtract the vector "man" and add that of "woman," you get "queen." Allison Parrish uses colors to show the same principle, adding vectors for red and blue together to get purple.[4] This blows up any model for language that is thinking of the meaning of language as a relationship of referents to an external (or internal) reality, since meaning is produced by vector space: the plotting of tokens on a matrix according to where they fall in language use—and not in relation to what they represent. But language still represents, and organic bodies are still feeling it in space-times other than vector space, and what do you do with that?

There is a quiet crisis going on about how meaning happens in language. It is not dissimilar to the crisis that occurred in art with the advent of photography that Benjamin wrote of in "The Work of Art in the Age of Mechanical Reproduction" (from which this book takes its name), in which he wonders "whether the very invention of photography had not transformed the entire nature of art" (Benjamin/Zohn 229). Many theorists, as well as artists, have posited this technological rupture as the impetus for the Avant-Garde (Scheunemann 2005). And experimental translation shares much with the Avant-Garde: its critique of the institutions that frame it and give it its identity, as well as the crisis of originality, the aura of authenticity and authorship, the questioning of the regime of mimesis in representation—which includes an experimentation with the fracture and disruption of the sign (for example, in the Avant-Garde practice of montage).

And like the Avant-Garde, what I will be positing in the pages that follow as a practice of experimental translation is translation that opposes itself to translational norms, and, by opposing these norms, interrogates them, "helps readers understand translation in transformative ways" (Robinson, *Experimental Translator* 32). So why not simply use this term, Avant-Garde, as I have done elsewhere ("To Erre Is Calque"), and call this a practice of Avant-Garde translation rather than experimental translation?

My reasons have to do with the specific relationship of experimental translation to translation technology, but also the way that translation is situated within literary and linguistic institutions. For Peter Bürger, who first advanced the now well-known theory of the Avant-Garde, it was precisely because the effect of photography could not be transferred to the literary sphere that Bürger discounted Benjamin's locating of photography as the impetus of the Avant-Garde:

Because the advent of photography makes possible the precise mechanical reproduction of reality, the mimetic function of the fine arts withers. But the limits of this explanatory model become clear when one calls to mind that it cannot be transferred to literature. For in literature, there is no technical innovation that could have produced an effect comparable to that of photography in the fine arts. (Bürger/ Shaw 32)

Although experimental translation shares cultural, institutional and formal elements with the Avant-Garde, its story is different, precisely because it is located in relation to a very different set of techno-cultural apparatuses. When Bürger's book appeared in German in 1974, MT already existed as a viable cultural project and as a series of prominent and well-funded scientific and mathematical experiments. In 1977, one of the first MT systems, TAUM-METEO, would be put into place to translate Canada's weather reports (Poibeau 64). Two years after that, also in Canada, in 1979, bpNichol would publish his *Translating Translating Apollinaire*, a series of "translations" based on an original poem he wrote in response to his translation of Baudelaire's poem "Zone" (more on this a bit later).

But Bürger was operating on an assumption of the literary institution as monolingual and thus based on models of nation-state linguistic identities, and so missed the very fact of translation as part of what the word "literature" might mean.

But also, translation never had the status of autonomy (as somehow beyond or outside social life, labor and class) against which Bürger sets up his critique of modern art. And experimental translation, as a kind of Avant-Garde, is responding to the specific practice and institution of translation. It is interrogating, challenging, resisting and opposing the norms of translational practice, and thereby also delineating them. This is embodied in its relationship to language difference, and also its critique of originality and authorship, which happens on the level of challenging the law of fidelity in translation. The question of aura in the Benjaminian sense is articulated in a totally different way in the institution of translation, since no translation intends to be the original—it is in fact the very condition of possibility of a translation that it is *not* the original. In fact, to conceive of a translation as a perfect reproduction—a photograph—of an original is not a point of rupture, but rather the traditional regime that is here begging to be ruptured. Likewise, the critique of art as an institution, and its relationship to lived reality and to labor that is harnessed by the Avant-Garde, is completely discombobulated in a critique of the institution of translation, which, on the contrary, has struggled to assert itself as an art form, and is rather a form of labor, paid by the sign, word, or page. In fact, read in this way, translation was always and already a kind of Avant-Garde.

But still, Avant-Garde studies have done an excellent job evolving with the times and adapting to the specific circumstances of art practices and the cultural contexts in which they occur. And certainly, one could call experimental translation "Avant-Garde translation" or "Neo-Avant-Garde translation," just as others have called it "creative translation" (Santiago Artozqui), "poetic translation" (Tim Atkins), "potential translation" (Pablo Martín Ruiz and Irène Gayraud), "translucinación" (Vincent Broqua by way of Andrès Ajens by way of Jena Osman and Juliana Spahr), "transcreation" (Haroldo de Campos), "transelation" (Erín Moure), "perverse translation" (Sherry Simon), "queer translation" (Allison Grimaldi-Donahue and Amanda Murphy) and "performative translation" (Delphine Grass).

The real reason I settled on the word "experimental" is because of what Vincent Broqua calls its "fallible force," the potential of meaning that comes from the difficulty the word "experimental" encounters to fix on one single definition. This happens first of all in the translation of the word. As Broqua remarks, the word "experiment" as we hear it in English does not exist in nominal form in French (the language in which Broqua writes his article), and in its verbal form, *expérimenter*, it is actually a *faux-ami*, a false friend or false cognate, and back-translates from French as "experience." *Expérience*, on the other hand, in French, means "experiment" in English. But it is also a question of temporality and periodicity: "The experimental has the particularity of being neither modern, nor contemporary, nor Avant-Garde, nor postmodern... It is what tests, resists and pushes history and temporality to their edge. It is perhaps also for this reason that it is impossible to stabilise the experimental in a permanent definition" ("Temporalités de l'expérimental" 5).[5]

This interrogation of periodicity is not to be confused with an immunity to temporal, ideological virtues, but is rather a testing, a pushing of translational norms, as they are fixed by a certain, specific, translational climate: historically, culturally, linguistically and technologically. The critique of norms in experimental translation is profoundly situated, in its language and in its cultural and historical specificity.

A first critique of translational norms that happens in experimental translation is of the presumption that translation is a transparent transfer of meaning, which likewise relies on a sense model of translation (that one translates meanings rather than materiality, in language or other sign systems). This joins with another common discourse surrounding translation, that of the inherent goodness of translating everything—the idea that translation can and should cross all borders and thereby solve for the problems of cultural difference and conflict. Tiphaine Samoyault, in her book *Traduction et violence*, has analyzed this discourse as part of the "vocabulary of democratic consensus in neoliberal societies" (24). "Setting the language of translation in the vocabulary of democratic consensus does not happen without paradox or difficulty: it implies a reduction, a weakening, even a complete denial, of all the conflicts inscribed within it [and] comes at the price of a reduction of the difference between one (or oneself) and another, of belief—likely false—in the reciprocity of empathy" (11).[6]

Samoyault compares this discourse with the promise of MT, not only as that which will provide mathematical solutions to the ambiguities of human communication, but also that which will provide total access, all the time, to information in any language. Michael Cronin too has critiqued this aspect of translation technology as promising the "ultimate translatability of all content to the binary code of machine language" (Cronin 105). This in turn is connected to the "cult or transparency" (107), which is not just universal accessibility but also universal surveillance, and also universal, unregulated access of capital. Free-flowing data also means free-flowing capital. The power of capital to cross borders freely can thus be read as tangential to the discourse that translation crosses borders freely. One might also compare this to a presumption of mathematical or monetary equivalence that infuses certain practices and discourses of translation—the injunction of equal value between a translation and its original.

The critique of ultimate translatability or translation as presumed neoliberal consensus in the algorithmic era is the continuation of a critique that has existed in translation studies since Tejaswini Niranjana's *Siting Translation*, which critiques the philosophy of the transcendental signified as pretence to a universal meaning that is in fact the heritage of European colonial metaphysics.

As Barbara Johnson points out, translation "has always been the translation of meaning" (Johnson, *Difference in Translation* 145). The idea that signified and signifier can be separated informs the classical conception of philosophy as well as translation. Derrida has long contended that translatability as transfer of meaning is the very *thesis* of philosophy. The notion of the transcendental signified that for him is a founding concept of Western metaphysics "[takes] shape within the horizon of an absolutely pure, transparent, and unequivocal translatability" (Derrida, *Positions* 20). The concept of translation that grounds Western metaphysics is the same one that presides over the beginnings of Orientalism. Neither is prepared to acknowledge, in its humanism and universalism, the heterogeneity that contaminates "pure meaning" from the start, occluding the project of translation. (Niranjana 55)

A first norm of translation that is challenged in experimental translation, then, is the presumption of sense, of meaning-driven translations—a presumption that is both reified and put into question in the age of NMT and algorithmic production. This does not mean that experimental translation does not translate meaning or is somehow *against* the translation of meaning. To critique does not mean to throw the baby out with the bathwater. Of course there is something called meaning, and of course sometimes we translate that, and sometimes it makes sense to translate it. Experimental translation does not forbid the translation of meaning: it wonders about it, probes and tests its limits.

The same may be said of fidelity. The law of fidelity, which is perhaps the first law of translation in the popular imaginary and in translation classrooms (in France, at least, students are deducted points for straying too far from the original or changing its meaning), also stems from European colonial discourses of meaning that privilege the transcendental signified, in a trifecta of patriarchal apparatuses that structure the translational norms that experimental translation questions: God, State and Capital. In all three, it is a fidelity to the transcendental signified that is required. The first of these is embodied in the injunction to be faithful to the divine word of God, and is inherited from biblical translation, embodied in the legend of the Septuagint in which scribes translating separately all produced the same word-for-word translations, inspired by an "invisible prompter" (which Douglas Robinson compares to the "MT earbud" [*Experimental Translator* 42]). The second can be identified in the figure of the translator as traitor, but also insofar as the stabilization of the very notion of translation as we think of it today is dependent on the separation of national languages as distinct entities and thus on nation-state boundaries (Berman; Sakai). The last relates first of all to the idea that a text is property, owned by an author or a publisher, and thus subject to copyright law, which also connects the state to capital (Venuti). The translator is never the owner of a translation.

The concept of norms and the identification and mobilization of norms in translation studies is not new, of course. Gideon Toury's *Descriptive Translation Studies* (1995) hinged on the identifying and analyzing of translational norms on the level of translation policies (what gets translated and by whom and for whom), as well as methodologies—both those embodied in the departure text and the conventions regulating the language and culture of the arrival text, but also operations that happen in the process of translation and govern decision-making. This likewise led to a field of study devoted to the identification of translation universals, or translation processes that traverse all instances of translation (Mauranen and Kujamäki). Norms can also be *prescriptive* and code for an evaluation (tacit or explicit) of their correctness, as Theo Hermans has pointed out. This is another way in which experimental translation questions and opposes translational norms: by erring (see chapter 2 especially).

Hermans also refers to the profoundly situated nature of norms, as determined by linguistic, cultural and temporal context. This is perhaps nowhere more evident than in the translation of the word "translation" itself, which is not transparent at all. A very frequently cited example of this in translation studies is the Hindi/Marathi terms for translation, *anuvad*, meaning "speaking after or following," and *rupantar*, which means "change of form," which do not at all imply obedience to the law of fidelity (Mukherjee 80; Pym, *Exploring Translation Theories* 63; Bassnett and Trivedi 9; Palekar 17). This works temporally as well, as the word "translation" only appeared in English in the fourteenth century, which reflects the more fluid textual practices of the medieval period in Europe and points to the instability of the idea of translation as a fixed category. It was a frequent practice in medieval translations to appropriate, cut, add, interpolate, interpret, provide commentary or translate without citing the original.

This is another way in which the practices of experimental translation that I will describe do more than simply come along to oppose contemporary norms of translation inherited from European colonial discourse and practices, and which is related to what Broqua says about the experimental, insofar as these practices can adopt translational norms that do not belong to the context in which they are situated: appropriating, cutting, adding, interpolating, interpreting, providing commentary, translating without citing the original. These practices translate using a historical and cultural thickness of procedures and methodologies to test, resist and push history and temporality to their edge. These norms are also undone even in our contemporary moment, and in the context of the English language in which I am writing—a language with a thick and complex colonial history, present and future.

These norms are a lot less fixed than they might first appear—which is one of the reasons I will not attempt a typology of translational norms, as Toury does, but rather lean into practices of experimental translation to see what they can reveal about these norms, through their dialogue with them. To do so, I will be adopting Delphine Grass's creative-critical approach, which critiques the theory/practice divide that has haunted translation studies since its beginnings, for example, as Grass shows in Holmes's division between "pure" (meaning theoretical, metareflexive) and "applied" translation studies. For Grass, the "here and now of translation" is a form of critical inquiry, in a creative mode: "Since the process of translation requires both critical distantiation from and artistic engagement with its source text, literary translation is naturally at the crossroads of creative writing and criticism" (8).[7] The practices she studies, some of which can be found in these pages as well, ask the question of "what translation as a form of practice-led and embodied research might look and *think* like" (8). For Grass, this is also an entry into a critique of translational norms, moving "away from a communicative model of translation in order to reframe and rethink the regime of translation which naturalizes ... differences" (12).

I will also be looking at the examples of experimental translation in these pages as forms of research in their own right, to show the way translational practice deconstructs and interrogates the discourse surrounding it. Indeed, much of what might be considered translational norms by the mainstream imaginary, norms like fidelity, equivalence and accuracy, are actually norms that have rarely existed in actual translation practices but exist as a kind of metareflexive ideal—sometimes a pedagogical one (in the case of the French *concours d'agrégation*, which requires a translation examination of almost absurd literality, fidelity and "correctness"). In the translation of literature, prosodic and narrative features that do not transfer between languages or cultures are often adapted or rewritten to suit stylistic or editorial needs. In legal, medical and technical translations, the translations of directives and information need to be tailored to the extralinguistic systems in which they are situated. In audiovisual translation, translations need to be made to fit formal requirements like time and space constraints, or visual elements—and of course cultural taboos. In the translation of news articles or online content, translations are often cut up and collaged together or interpolated with new material to suit the framework. In the translation of advertising and marketing, practices like localization and transcreation fall over into creation. With all these examples, one might begin to wonder where norms like fidelity, equivalence and accuracy even come from (God, State and Capital).

These are the norms that humans have programmed into the machine, and that the machine does its best to produce, along with what Slater has identified as a trifecta of new norms of translation: "the navigable, the productive, and the predictive," which joins with the discussion above about the continuity between critiques of humanist translation projects which aim for transcendent signifieds that cross borders unimpeded, and the data flows of machine translation. It is not for nothing that the experiments of the "modernist translators" (Venuti; Baillehache) such as Pound, the Zukofskys and Klossowski emerged at the same time as the first experiments with machine translation. The fixing and encoding of these norms engendered a resistant response in the form of poetic experimentation. These poetic experiments evolved and expanded into the experimental translations of the algorithmic age that I will be treating in this book. But cultural norms themselves, the norms of translation practice as they are really happening and resisting commonly held beliefs about what translation is and should be, are also opposing machine translation norms, as humans take up the place of what is left over by the machine, adapting to their own planned obsolescence. Experimental translation, then, in a way, also accompanies those changing practices. Its opposition is complex, both resisting and also responding and dialoguing, trying to understand.

And again, these norms are not static or isolated, they are "grown from the logic of enlightenment transparency" (Slater). In the above paragraph, I cite Pound, the Zukofskys and Klossowski as the forebearers of this practice or experimental translation, but I could also cite practices of transcreation, beginning with Haroldo de Campos. Many of the procedures of experimental translation I outline, such as collage, language hybridization and calque, can be found in de Campos's "transillumination" or "transparadisation" of Faust, his "transhelenziation" of the *Iliad* and his "reimagination" of classical Chinese poetry. De Campos's experiments with "cannibalizing" canonical Western texts embody the logic of hijacking that is the basis for this very book, in the hijacking of Vinay and Darbelnet's seven translation procedures (which I'll get to in a minute). It is by situating itself as a continuation of de Campos's experiments that experimental translation stakes its claim as a challenge to patriarchal structures. Transcreation is a "parricidal dis-memory" (Ribeiro Pires Vieira 109, citing de Campos) that challenges not only the direction of European colonial domination but also its attending signifying regimes, such as the one in which translation is perceived as a copy of content, not as a motor for meaning through matter (which, for de Campos, would not be separable from meaning). Anthropophagic appropriation is a potent critique of "the colonial matrix of power, with its accompanying regime of language and capitalist consumption" (20–21), writes Rachel Galvin in an article where she deploys the theoretical armatures of transcreation to read contemporary authors in the age of algorithmic production, including two central figures to the practice of experimental translation that I lay out in this book: M. NourbeSe Philip and Mónica de la Torre.

But appropriation is also the logic of capitalism (which is another good reason to hijack it), and "transcreation" has itself been hacked in the algorithmic age, as David Katan shows in the genealogy of the term he gives in his study on the "transcreational turn" in the translation profession. Transcreation now refers to marketing strategies for companies wishing to expand across borders and also tells us something about how translational norms are changing (I return to this in the conclusion). And this is another way that experimental translation tests, resists and pushes history and temporality to their edge: through the time of performative obsolescence that is accompanying the writing of this book. As I am writing these words, they are becoming obsolete, as though their very writing were rendering them so. That is the temporality of techno-capitalism, that it should always be exceeding itself to create a surplus of innovation and capital. Over the two years that it took me to write this book, I had to constantly return to amend and rethink the relationship between experimental translation and technology, as NMT advanced past what I had come to understand of it. By the time this book was ready to go to press for example, the transformer algorithms of ChatGPT had already enabled it to surpass DeepL, which was my online machine translator of reference for writing this book.

This points to perhaps the most classic definition of "experimental," which Broqua has critiqued as the "legend" of the experimental, going back to John Cage's "an act the outcome of which is unknown" (Cage 7–13). In the word "experimental" and even more so in the word *expérimental*, as Broqua points out, there is a connection to the experiments of the hard sciences. It is the word that is used by machine translation scholars to refer to the tests they run on new models. Experimental translation too is testing new models, as a form of creative-critical, practice-based research. The outcomes of these experiments is always unknown, even after testing them out, as I have done. And this highlights the specificity of the term "experimental" as it adapts to the human sciences and to the intersecting fields of translation studies and creative writing, as I am practicing them, namely, that a known outcome can become unknown as it transfers to a new ecology, a new actor, a new receiver, in a new situation.

And as much as I want to posit experimental translation as *testing* the limits of periodicity, experimentation or the moniker "experimental" by no means fall outside the bounds of historical periodization. Experimental writing, and therefore experimental translation, express what Natalia Cecire has referred to as "epistemic virtues." Epistemic virtues, as the name implies, are ethical values that are also codes for how thinking is done and how truth is measured. For Cecire, the word "experimental" is tied up with the epistemic values of modernity, and, in particular, science: "The performance of epistemic virtue works to bring specific practices under the sign of science (that is, knowledge with a privileged purchase on reality)" (ix). The aesthetic values of experimental writing are tied to the epistemic virtues of modernity such as "flash," "objectivity," "precision" and "contact." These virtues are bound to scientific and technological modernity—neither is autonomous. Experimental translation, then, is a creative-critical, practice-based research interrogating translational norms and epistemic virtues, in their relationship to experimentation in the hard sciences, and in particular to developments in MT. It is not because experimental translation falls outside the bounds of periodicity that it questions the epistemic virtues of translation, but rather because it doesn't.

For all these reasons, I have hesitantly chosen the moniker "experimental" in spite of the fact that Erín Moure, an experimental translator of crucial importance to my thinking, does not like the word.

Today, reading an online Scandinavian litmag of "experimental work" I realized that I'm so uninterested in this construct continually dug up by other people in which "lyric" is split off and set up against "experiment." I can't even be bothered to protest it, for protest would just give it credence, in a way. I am interested in the signature and the mouth and throat. I am interested in how ear and throat receive language. [...]

What's strange to me I guess is how that false dichotomy only looks interesting (perhaps this is it, I am only guessing) from the interior of monolingualism. Once other languages are part of the foment, the dichotomy does not hold at all; there is but opening, opening. This opening is where we meet as poet-beings. And we get on with our work, which lets us both meet so richly, ever and repeatedly anew. This "getting on with the work of language" is both lyric, and experiment. Deeply both. Yours, E. (*O Resplandor* 142)

This false opposition between lyrical and experimental, funnily enough, also emerges in the question of machine translation, as the machine is what might be considered to be deeply conceptual as opposed to lyrical, if the lyric is what embodies a human (and one might include animal) voice or experience. Moure solves for this dichotomy by "getting on with the work of language," which can only happen in language difference. For Moure, the division between experimental and lyrical is an affair of monolingualism. When languages meet, there is an opening, where the poet's voice meets the voice of language as conceptual device, as I proposed above in the reading of the multitiered DeepL translation of "the spirit is willing but the flesh is weak." Moure also says, in another text: "Experiment is always translation, and translation is always experiment" ("Paradox" 23).

One thing that experimental translation does is it makes the translator, and their voice, more visible, in its opposition to the translational norm embodied in the "translator's invisibility," as per the well-known title of

Lawrence Venuti's book. But another thing that it does, which is related but perhaps even more important, is make language difference visible. This perhaps accompanies a heightened attention in the humanities to the agonisms of linguistic and cultural difference and politics, along with a critique of the way that machine translation seeks to flatten these agonisms out.

It is not insignificant then that in writing this book, which I intended as a reflection, inventory and practical guide to experimental translation as a global phenomenon, I realized at a certain point that on some level I was not writing a book about global languages in translation, but about global English. Perhaps any book is in a way about the language it is written in, and any work of translation studies (or any work on language or literature, ideally) must by necessity be situated in the languages known by its author. But I think this also relates to the specificity of the English language itself, as a language of hegemony and linguistic privilege, the language that, like MT, pretends to be able to cross all borders and turn borders transparent. English-language privilege, like other forms of privilege, allows its speakers a certain blindness to its positionality. It is in this way that English travels as *not a language*, the way that masculinity has traveled as *not a gender*, or whiteness as *not a race* (although of course I do not wish to conflate the structures or injustices of these prejudices). As Sara Ahmed writes: "What makes a privilege a privilege: the experiences you are protected from having; the thoughts you do not have to think" (238).

This is also why I have been so insistent on language difference— as the differences between languages as political entities spoken[8] by peoples—and, at least in this work, have tended to stray away from the idea of experimental translation as translating between sign systems, such as with intersemiotic or multimodal translation, or with translations of or between animal or plant communication systems. It is not because I do not think sign systems other than spoken human languages as political entities defined in relation to the nation-state (either as national or as nonnational languages) cannot undergo processes of experimental translation, as I discuss in the conclusion. It is not because I do not think it is possible that animals or plants have language or that language does not happen in gesture, dance, painting, film, music or other semiotic systems. It is because it was important to me to recenter the question of translation on the agonisms of spoken human language difference, in order for English not to be invisibilized as a hegemonic arm of privilege. That said, I would be lying if I didn't say this choice was not also made of convenience, as a way of drawing a line, of delimiting and limiting what gets treated in the book, as any book must do, if it wants to end.

But it is also because the invisible language of the machine is English, as Slater and Raley have pointed out. It is the language of computer code and programming languages (although there are attempts now to do programming in other languages besides English, as I discuss in chapter 4). It is also often used as a hinge language in machine translation, meaning that two languages that do not have enough respective data between them to create neural nets and train a machine translation model will pass first through a translation into English and then out again (Poibeau 140). In this way, the structures of English contaminate many other languages—and the smaller the language, the more vulnerable it is.

Code, thus, is imbued with the structures of English, and it is likely that vestiges will remain in programming languages long after the English language has become obsolete. But the poetics of code have likewise infiltrated the structures of English, as Raley writes: "As English becomes computer languages, as it moves into new codes, and becomes in a sense post-English, it both transforms itself and reveals in different guise its instrumental functional, performative aspects. What allows English to spread in such a particular way, then, is its functionality" ("Global English" 305).

This functionality of "both Global English and machine translation abide by the principle of instrumental rationality and exist in the technocratic mode" (307). This sits quite well into the critique of the translational norms defined by Slater as the "productive, predictive and the navigable" as it is carried out in experimental translation, which, significantly, serves no real "purpose," at least in the rational and technocratic sense. It is a question I often receive from students and colleagues, as well as people outside the academic institution when I present them with this idea and practice of experimental translation: Why? What purpose does this serve, how is it useful? Well, it is not useful, not in the sense given to utility in the regime of "post"colonial, post-Enlightenment technocapitalist hegemony. As

Robinson writes: "Experimental hypercyborg translators... experiment as part of an interconnected gift exchange that does not fully participate in bio-capitalist circulations" (*Experimental Translator* 62). But therein, perhaps, lies its usefulness: to critique the injunction to instrumental functionality.

Likewise, the English language, like all hegemonic structures, also has a way of undoing itself from within. This happens primarily through the fact that English has become so big, so multinational, that the majority of its speakers are no longer native speakers, which makes English the least monolingual language in the world, at the same time as its monolingual ideologies are producing and reproducing events of linguistic oppression all over the globe. English may not be *not a language* but it also is not *one* language. This too is a motor for experimental translation, as I discuss with reference to Nicoline van Harskamp's work in chapter 4.

But to return to the presumption of English as a universal, which accompanied the quest for a deep structure of language in the context of the first experiments with machine translation, I quote a letter written by Warren Weaver to Norbert Wiener in March 1947 that is often cited in work on MT in the humanities (Weaver 18; cited in Raley "Global English" 295; Slater; Poibeau 41):

Also knowing nothing official about, but having guessed and inferred consider-able about, powerful new mechanized methods in cryptography—methods which I believe succeed even when one does not know what language has been coded—one naturally wonders if the problem of translation could conceivably be treated as a problem in cryptography. When I look at an article in Russian, I say "This is really written in English, but it has been coded in some strange symbols. I will now proceed to decode."

This is reflective of the early thinking on machine translation, which was rule based, and grounded in military cryptography, searching for an Ur-code of linguistic rules and structures that would solve the problem of language difference. The elision here between this Ur-code and the English language (although Weaver did not really believe this code would be in English) is also significant for thinking about the relationship of machine translation to poetic experimentation. Early examples of experimental translation do the same thing. The best example of this is bpNichol's *Translating Translating*

Apollinaire (1979), which is not a translation at all, but the application of a set of constraints, in English, onto an original poem, written in English, with the exception perhaps of the line "*soleil cou coupé*," which also happens to be the title of a collection by Aimé Césaire (1948), which bpNichol does not reference. bpNichol's "translations" are in dialogue with the experiments of the Oulipo, who also confounded interlinguistic (translating between languages) and intralinguistic ("translating" within one single language) translation, to use Roman Jakobson's vocabulary (429).

But rule-based MT did not work, because there is no Ur-code that solves for language difference that all language can code into and out of. There are no ultimate rules of language. There are, however, algorithms that are based on habit, that can calculate for the likelihood that one thing will be translated by another (SMT), which work quite a bit better. And there are also algorithms that can calculate and encode the differential relationships of tokens to one another within a single language using word vectors, and then decode those relationships into a parallel set of data in another language that has been treated by the same or similar algorithms. We call that NMT, and it takes place not in a simple decoding of the "strange symbols" of a foreign language but in a set of sophisticated operations happening within one language that can allow them to enter into dialogue with complex operations happening in another, in the "spacey emptiness" (202), to quote Gayatri Spivak, between languages. The practices of experimental translation that I will be treating in the pages that follow seek to contend with that, to understand and critique it, but also to understand and critique what has happened in technology, linguistics and geopolitical culture that brought us to this point.

The first experiments in MT, as I mention above, happened in dialogue with structural linguistics, which both made the idea of machine translation conceivable and was also impacted by it, developed in order to provide the conceptual tools necessary to advance technological and production aims.

It is not irrelevant, then, that translation studies, as a formal field, tradition and a school of thought (although we might not want to say discipline) began at the same time as these first experiments in machine translation. There was a need to codify the norms of translation in order to tell the machine what to do. Eugene Nida founded his journal *The Bible Translator* in 1949. In Russia, Andrei Fedorov's *Introduction to the Theory of Translation* appeared in 1953. In China, Loh Dian-yang published *Translation: Its Principles and Techniques* in 1958,[9] the same year that Jean-Paul Vinay and Jean Darbelnet published their *Stylistique comparée du français et de l'anglais* in French.

It is the work of Vinay and Darbelnet (hereafter VD) that I have used as the architecture for the seven chapters (including the conclusion) of this book, namely, the seven translation procedures that lend their names to the chapter titles: *emprunt* (loan/borrowing), calque, literal translation, transposition, modulation, equivalence and adaptation. VD divide these procedures into "direct" and "oblique" translation strategies, where "direct" translation is what could be handled by a machine (*emprunt*, calque, literal translation), and "oblique" refers to more sophisticated stylistic intervention, metalinguistic knowledge or adaptation on the part of the translator. They also treat these figures on three levels: on a lexical level, on a structural level and on the level of the message or meaning. Here are some very reduced, baseline definitions of each procedure as they are used in VD:

1. *Emprunt:* a direct transfer of a linguistic item from one language into another, through linguistic loans or borrowing.
2. Calque: a literal translation of a linguistic unit or structure that does not exist in the arrival language, or the translation of a wrong meaning, or wrong word ordering.
3. Literal translation: a direct translation that makes adjustments only to preserve correctness regarding linguistic divergences between the two languages.
4. Transposition: a shift in grammatical category (from noun to verb or from verb to adjective, for example).
5. Modulation: a shift in perspective, such as in the shift between passive to active voice, or between affirmative and negative expressions of the same idea.

6. Equivalence: a translation of fixed idiomatic structures that fall outside the confines of simple grammatical or lexical exigencies.

7. Adaptation: translation of cultural references; translation of world.

As a key to how each of these procedures works, I have adapted my chapter headings so that they perform each operation:

1. *Emprunt*
2. The Calque
3. Literal Translation
4. Transpose
5. Modulated
6. *Equivalencias*
7. ⟲

Here is the table VD use in the book to provide examples between French and English:

TABLEAU GÉNÉRAL DES PROCÉDÉS DE TRADUCTION :

		Lexique	Agencement	Message
ORDRE DE DIFFICULTÉ CROISSANTE	1. Emprunt	F. Bulldozer	F. Science-fiction	F. Five o'Clock Tea.
		A. Fuselage	A. (Pie) à la mode	A. Bon voyage.
	2. Calque	F. Economiquement faible	F. Lutétia Palace	F. Compliments de la Saison
		A. Normal School	A. Governor General	A. Take it or leave it.
	3. Traduction littérale	F. ink	F. L'encre est sur la table	F. Quelle heure est-il ?
		A. encre	A. The ink is on the table	A. What time is it?
	4. Transposition . .	F. Expéditeur	F. Depuis la revalorisation du bois	F. Défense de fumer
		A. From:	A. As timber becomes more valuable	A. No smoking
	5. Modulation . . .	F. Peu profond	F. Donnez un peu de votre sang	F. Complet
		A. Shallow	A. Give a pint of your blood	A. No Vacancies
	6. Equivalence . . .	F. (Milit.) La soupe	F. Comme un chien dans un jeu de quilles	F. Château de cartes
		A. Br. (Milit.) Tea	A. Like a bull in a china shop	A. Hollow Triumph
	7. Adaptation . . .	F. Cyclisme A. Br. cricket A. U.S. baseball	F. En un clin d'œil A. Before you could say Jack Robinson	F. Bon appétit! A. U.S. Hi!

STYLISTIQUE COMPARÉE

55

Fig. 1. VD's general table of translation procedures (*Stylistique comparée* 55). © Jean-Paul Vinay and Jean Darbelnet. Reprinted with permission.

Already, there are some problems. For example, *science-fiction*, which is listed as an example of an *emprunt*, is given later in VD's explanations as an example of a *calque* (I explain why in detail in chapter 2). And, in fact, confusion and contamination of categories is present in all of VD's categories, which might be indicative of the slipperiness of language in translation, as much as or more than it is indicative of sloppiness in their method or its application, which also exists. *Défense de fumer* translated as "no smoking" is "at the same time a transposition, a modulation and an equivalence" (VD/Sager and Hamel 42), as VD point out in a similar example, "private" for *défense d'entrer*. Of course, one could probably make a similar argument for any system of classification, but at what point does a system of classification simply not hold? To quote Anthony Pym in his response to VD's "private"/*défense d'entrer* example: "If three categories explain the one phenomenon, do we really need all the categories? Or are there potentially as many categories as there are equivalents?" (*Exploring* 16). Michel Ballard in French has also critiqued VD for not distinguishing between fixed borrowings and borrowings that are the result of an individual translator's choice ("À propos des procédés" 4). Ballard also critiques the categories of equivalence and adaptation as covering the same activity, namely, translating extralinguistic material.

But the problems in VD go much deeper than sloppy labeling. To quote Pym again:

To produce that list, the French linguists made numerous assumptions about language and translation, and we nowadays find some of those assumptions questionable, if not entirely distasteful. The linguists, like most of those around them, unthinkingly accepted models that were essentialist: they never doubted that each phrase had a fixed meaning to be rendered by the translator. And their essentialism was implicitly nationalist: the linguists were sure the fixed meanings and acceptable turns of phrase had the same value for all citizens speaking the one language of a given nation. These days we are more inclined to accept that texts have multiple interpretations and that societies are linguistically segmented. This makes the old linguistics hard to read, let alone accept. And yet what Vinay and Darbelnet came up with, those seven major types of translation solutions, still have something to say in the context of current debates, most notably with respect to doubts about the meaning of the word 'translation' and the perennial question of whether humans translate in ways that machines do not. (*Translation Solutions* xii)

VD begin their story of setting out to write one of the first treatises of what would later come to fall under the name *traductologie* ("translation studies" in English), on a road trip from New York to Montreal. As they cross the border from the United States to Canada, they become increasingly perturbed by what they consider to be "cumbersome" translations of English-language road signs that "a monolingual French speaker would never have formed... spontaneously" (VD/Sager and Hamel 3), translations such as "slow" translated as *lentement* (as opposed to *ralentir*), or "slippery when wet" translated by *glissant si humide* (instead of *chaussée glissante*). They approach the Canadian translations with a great deal of disdain, as betraying the *génie* (which Sager and Hamel translate as "nature") of the French language. Their journey as told in the introduction ends happily back in France, where they are reunited with road signs as they would like to see them, and "find the situation in its pure state... Paris at last!" This introduction is the perfect allegory for what Pym critiques in the citation given above, namely, the ontological nationalism embodied in a prescriptivist and essentialized language model predicated on the purity of nature, or *génie*.

I agree with Pym that many scholars "nowadays find some of those assumptions questionable, if not entirely distasteful." I certainly am one of those scholars. Why then would I choose to reanimate these procedures that might seem to some not only irrelevant and old hat but harmful on both a practical and an ideological level? The first reason is because it is not so simple to get rid of inherited presumptions about language that are embodied in canonical scholarship, and VD's procedures can be found cropping up in translation studies across the globe.[10] So the first reason to return to these procedures is to put into question my own presumptions of what might be old hat, questionable or distasteful in translation studies, and to test that limit, since there are plenty of translation scholars who do not find VD's procedures to be questionable or distasteful at all. But also because, as Pym goes on to remark in the above citation, VD's procedures are still relevant in terms of figuring out what the word "translation" means, "and the perennial question of whether humans translate in ways that machines do not."

These procedures also continue to be widely used in translation class-rooms, in particular in France, where I live and teach. Students studying to be future teachers of English in France, for example, are expected to know these procedures and be able to do comparative analyses of their own translations using this vocabulary. In order to obtain my post at the Université Paul-Valéry Montpellier 3 and assimilate into the culture of the teaching of translation there, I had to learn and master these procedures, which have been an unending source of both frustration and curiosity for me and my students.

This frustration and curiosity is in large part also what has motivated the practice-based procedures you will find at the end of each chapter. These procedures seek to perform a creative-critical critique of VD's procedures, in Grass's sense, using creative process as a place to put "practice, social experience and theory into productive discussion." In the supplementary PDF to this book, the *Handbook of Translation Procedures* (housed on the Goldsmiths Press website), readers can find full, detailed, play-by-play renderings of these procedures as I carried them out in a wide variety of classroom, workshop and private settings in many languages.

I have not just adopted these procedures, I have hijacked them— *transcreated* them, perhaps. And in the pages that follow, you will not find rigorous analyses of VD's terms as they were intended to be used or a historical study of their sources or a comparison with other translation procedures or an account of their survival in the work of translation scholars like Peter Newmark, for example, whose foundational *Textbook of Translation* (1988) is deeply indebted to VD. Instead, what you will find is a kind of reappropriation of these categories as poetic figures, as material metaphors (to use Hayles's terminology in *Writing Machines*, 21–24) that in themselves generate meaning through the network of materiality in their uses.

This might seem kind of irresponsible at first (even to me), because in many senses I am decontextualizing the procedures from their original meaning, where they were of great value and made a considerable contribution to the nascent field of translation studies at the time, and to the visibilizing of translators, the work of translation and language difference. Much of what one might critique in VD now is simply the fact that they were working at a time and in a place where structural linguistics and national models of language were the primary mode of operation.

One of the reasons I can do this is because of Pym's work, to which I am deeply indebted. In both *Exploring Translation Theories* (2010/2014) and *Translation Solutions for Many Languages: Histories of a Flawed Dream* (2016), and elsewhere, Pym has conducted rigorous, insightful research and analysis into VD's procedures, as well as their influences, their contemporaries (known and unknown to VD) and the impact of their work on translation studies.

Pym's work has thus freed me, in a certain sense, to *womanhandle* (to borrow Barbara Godard's neologism for feminist translation) these terms as they translate into their contemporary materiality, in the context of the age of algorithmic production. The work of resituating these procedures as material figures finds itself in the continuum of what Karin Littau has termed the "material turn" of translation studies ("Translation and the Materialities of Communication"), which seeks to see the medium and technologies of translation as active agents in translation processes. This approach is opposed to an anthropocentric approach, which would see humans as in control over material tools serving as pure instruments. Rather, in Littau's work, these instruments not only influence but drive translation acts, networks, institutions and metareflection. From this perspective, the shift between oral and scribal culture invented the dichotomy between sense-for-sense (the operational mode of an oral translation culture) and word-for-word translation, which could only become conceivable once translations were written down (Littau, "Translation's Histories and Digital Futures"). Printing technologies also contributed to the rethinking of text as proprietary document and thus established the dichotomy between original and translation. As printing techniques sped up, this increased the necessity for translations to happen quickly and to be productive and cost-effective. The internet age has heightened this demand for rapidity and productivity at a low cost and seen the creation of fan-based and crowd-sourced translation, making translation more and more precarious. Online dictionaries and CAT technologies have profoundly affected the work of translation as a process, making it less paradigmatic and more syntagmatic, as translators search for and paste together translation solutions, rather than recalling and recording them (Pym, "What Technology Does to Translating"). And finally, we have the impact of MT, which is the impetus for the discussion of experimental translation that is the main focus of this book.

This is also related to what Samoyault has called the *tournant sensible* (literally: "the sensitive turn"), which connects the materiality of texts in translation and the work of translation to a rethinking that updates the "sense" model for translation to a model based on the senses, with an *s* (181). And as we will see, all of the experimental translation procedures and practices that I describe rely on the sensual, material, corporeal dimension to language and translation. This happens on the level of the letter or other linguistic units like the word, the token or the phrase, but also in the materiality of the structure of language, the materiality of its code and of code. It also happens on the level of the ecology in which the work is taking place and the texts are produced, translating through the material location and body of the translator in the world in which it is made, or operating material procedures on the physicality of the text and its medium. It is my contention, following Samoyault, that this tendency in experimental translation to translate through the materiality of the senses is connected to the material shifts in translation culture, and, in particular, with regards to the radical paradigm shifts that are happening to signification in language in the age of algorithmic production.

Each chapter thus picks up VD's figures in their full materiality, both as regards the translation procedures but also in terms of the materiality implicated by the particular figure itself, in its diffuse imaginary. This is not without prompting or precedent, since VD's figures are already highly materially metaphorical.

The figure of *emprunt*, which I treat in chapter 1, can be translated as both "borrowing" (Sager and Hamel) and "loan" (Pym), and calls up the figural landscape of debt, transaction, trade, exchange and monetary culture, which has changed considerably since VD first used the term to describe the translation procedure of transcribing a foreign word. What is the significance of the figures of loan and borrowing, of debt, in a context when there is no gold standard, and wealth is often signified by the transfer of data, numbers that are actually, in their materiality, signified through electrical pulses, the "flickering signifiers" (Hayles, *Posthuman* 25–49) of the machine? These digital signifiers might at first seem empty, as no external referent exists to prove, substantiate or secure them. But they are far from that, as the consequences in terms of wealth, access to resources and injustice are profoundly material. In this chapter, by analyzing texts that translate the letter, the shape or the sound of the word (rather than its sense)—in particular in M. NourbeSe Philip—I attempt to show that, in this culture of "dematerialized" transfers, the signifier, rather than emptying out, becomes thicker, more immediately symbolic, and that the weight of historical and ancestral debts is carried in the shape and sound of the letter itself.

In chapter 2, I hijack the figure of calque, which in VD refers to the literal translation of a borrowed meaning, like in the Spanish translation of basketball, *baloncesto* (literally, "ballbasket"). This can happen for the purposes of linguistic innovation, but also in instances of what VD refer to as "the most concrete expression of the abomination of desolation" (48, my translation). That biblical reference refers to language interference, to error, to the contamination of national language in its "pure state" (*génie*). Historically, the word *calque* in French refers to the technical and artistic practices of pressing, rubbing or tracing used for image reproduction. Metaphors for copying and reproduction, through physical contact or refraction, etc., are common in translation studies, as translations have often been seen as a copy or reproduction of an original. These metaphors can be used as a gauge for the way that material technologies have impacted the work of translation. Likewise, as translation has evolved, so too have the techniques of image reproduction, and the word *calque* in French now refers to the image layers in Photoshop: to collage rather than imitate. The practices of experimental translation I treat in this chapter thus approach translation as collage or montage, layering words, meanings, texts and languages together in erroneous ways.

Chapter 3 treats the figure of literal translation, which is difficult to separate from *calque* since the only real difference is that literal translation is normative, whereas *calque* is anomalous, inventive or faulty. Since experimental translation is, by definition, anomalous, inventive or faulty, the distinction between literal translation and calque is more or less moot in this context. It is also difficult because the term "literal" has referred to the letter (*littera*) but also to proper or natural meaning, as when we say that something "literally means" something. To solve this, I turn to Urayoán Noel's "litoral translation," which is not only a play on words but can be decomposed into lit-oral technologies. I look at the figure of transcription and experiments that use voice recognition software, but also transcription as the process by which linguistic data is transcribed into numerical data in machine translation, and set this into the story of the history of machine translation. Literal translation, after all, is what is considered by many scholars (including VD) to be the limit to what the machine can do, and machine translation is often taxed with being overly literal. This chapter thus ends with a history of the use of machine translation in poetic experiments, and the way in which poets have exploded the machine's "random acts of senseless beauty" (Julian Dibbel, cited in Raley, "Global English" 302).

Transposition is the fourth figure of VD's procedures, referring to shifts in grammatical categories, for example, between a noun and a verb or between a prepositional phrase and a noun phrase. However, transposition is also a type of code, and this is the chapter where I treat the question of code and to what extent translations between code and natural language can be considered experimental translation, namely, in the context of the translation of electronic literature. Grammar too has been treated as a code, a deep structure of language that submits language in translation to a series of constraints—and in such a way posits translation itself as a constraint—not only in experiments with electronic literature but also in language invention and in constraint-based writing and experimental translations of constraint-based writing. How can the grammar of a language be translated into a code of its own structures? How can codes and constraints serve as a baseline for the invention of a new language?

In chapter 5, on modulation, I turn away from machine-based practices to look at the lyrical, heteronymic and autotheoretical experiments of translators who have inserted interruptive subject positions into their translation work, like Erín Moure, Elisa Sampedrín, Douglas Robinson and Brandon Brown. Modulation, in VD, refers to a "change in perspective" and is undoubtedly the most nebulous of all of VD's procedures and requires the most creativity on the part of the translator. It also asks the question of where the writing, reading, translating subject is situated in language and grammar, and the multiplication of these situations in translation. Can the translator say "I"? What happens to the translator's body in translation? What of the translator's somatic affect, an integral part of the translation process (Robinson, *Translationality*) that is traditionally silenced? I also rely again here on my reading and collaboration with Grass for sussing out autotheoretical experiments in translation.

Chapter 6 turns to the problematic category of equivalence, a term that has been critiqued by Ballard and Pym as referring to the phenomenon of translation as a whole. VD's definition is inversely specific and refers to translation of idiomatic expressions or other language-specific markers of extralinguistic situations (like status or prestige markers, terms of endearment, etc.). Since this definition is both too narrow for me to do much with and perversely imploded when it meets contemporary uses of the word "equivalence" (and its translations), I have chosen to do precisely this with this figure as a node of experimental translation practices: perversely implode it. Following Pym's cheeky proposal in *Translation and Text Transfer* (1992/2010) to think of equivalence through mathematical symbols, I lean into the figure of equivalence to see how experimental translations implode or explode the idea of text and of quantity of text. I also treat collaborative translation (to some extent) and translations in serial, which is both a practice of experimental translation and a practical solution to real translation problems, as are many procedures for experimental translation (more on that in a moment).

The final chapter, which also doubles as the conclusion, is devoted to the procedure of adaptation, which in VD refers to the translation of extralinguistic realities, to the translation of the world, as when translations butt heads with untranslatable cultural realities. They give the example of cricket, which they suggest could be adapted with the Tour de France. I chose to multitask this chapter as both a conclusion and a reflection on the figure and procedure of adaptation because the figure of experimental translation comes up against another limit here. What separates translation from experimental translation is also what separates translation from adaptation: the norms of what is considered justified, faithful translation. It also comes up against the limit of the methodological line I drew for practical but also political reasons in order to restrict the figure of experimental translation to spoken human languages. Adaptation does not make that distinction, and the word "adaptation" can refer to text transfers that happen between natural languages as they can be used for transfers that adapt through multimodality (like in the transfer of a novel into film, for example), or using an intersemiotic transfer (for example, through an adaptation of music into gesture or dance).

Throughout these chapters and creative hijackings of VD's seven procedures, I am relying both on my own readings and translations of VD, as well as Pym's, but also on the very good translation into English of their *Comparative Stylistics* by Juan C. Sager and M.-J. Hamel. Their translation appeared in 1995 and has been of profound global impact (as is evidenced by the large number of works that cite the text in English). I am grateful to them for accompanying me in my reading of VD, and for the illuminations that have come from the creative tinkering that I am convinced occurs in any good translation. The one place I have chosen to significantly diverge from them is in their translation of *départ* and *arrivée* into "source" and "target" to distinguish original texts and languages (*départ*/source) from translated texts and languages (*arrivée*/target). Theirs is absolutely an accurate translation, and it is the way that the vast majority of translation scholars refer to original and translated texts and languages in English. However, this terminology is rooted in the militaristic context in which MT (and thus translation studies) first emerged. In order to distance myself and critique the military origins of translation studies, I have chosen instead a calque on VD's terms *départ* and *arrivée*: "departure" and "arrival." This imagery references the figural landscape of the voyage, which, like translation, can be beautiful and enlightening, a time of sharing and cultural encounter, but also painful and difficult, the site of violence and injustice.

For I am convinced that translation, experimental or not, is a site to carry out a negotiation of justice, for better or worse, just as translation plays a role in negotiations of justice and acts of injustice. And this is the one norm that escapes experimental translation's disobedience: the desire to "do justice" to an original, a phrase often heard in the mouths and seen on the pages (or screens) of translators and translation scholars. But what does it mean to do justice, how does one carry out justice to an original within the politics of injustice and disparity that accompany most textual and linguistic exchanges?

Samoyault theorizes this in terms of the discrepancy between the French word *justice*, a cognate of the English word, and the word *justesse*, which can mean accuracy, precision, correctness, but also the quality of being faithful or true. The sonic proximity in French between the two words tends toward a conflation of these two notions, in particular in translation, where the qualities of *justesse* are confused with that of *justice*. Fidelity in translation is not necessarily the best way to *do justice* to a translation. Being equivalent in a world marked by inequivalence is not always the most *just* translation. How best can a translator render, with justice, the conflicts and injustices inherent in the process of translation? Experimental translation opposes norms of *justesse*, but, for some reason that I can't quite explain, continues to try to do its own kind of *justice* to originals. *Justesse* does not always do *justice*.

This is also the way in which the tools of experimental translation that I elaborate here go beyond the bounds of their uses in experimental translation, first of all in their pedagogical uses. Sometimes, to explain a rule, it is valuable to do the opposite with students. But also, most students come to translation with a set of presumptions that are mostly false about real, contemporary practices of translation but perversely hold true in many of the uses of translation for language learning. As I mention above, the end of each chapter in this book includes a set of practical procedures that can be carried out at home, with friends, in the classroom, workshop, research seminar or elsewhere. Detailed, step-by-step instructions of how I did this, as well as the results, can be found in the supplementary *Handbook of Translation Procedures*.

One of the contexts in which I tested out several of these procedures is with the Outranspo,[11] an international group of experimental translators. We meet bimonthly in online meetings to share our personal projects, organize collective projects, geek out about translation and test out practical applications of our ideas: to play. We have also been working collaboratively for the past ten years on a list of constraints and procedures that have inspired many of the procedures you will find in the book, and also frequently come into play and dialogue with VD's procedures in the pages that follow.[12] But once again, these procedures are useful beyond the bounds of experimental translation, in pedagogy but also in the real, lived experience of translation work in the day-to-day. These procedures and the procedures I outline in the book serve a double role: to question, resist and oppose the norms of translation and interrogate the changing nature of translation in the age of algorithmic production, but also as tools to solve real problems in translation.

One excellent example of that is Ludivine Bouton-Kelly and Tiphaine Samoyault's retranslation into "French" of the end of book 1 of *Finnegan's Wake*, the section known as "Anna Livia Plurabelle." In their translation published in *Drunken Boat*,[13] they deploy outranspian constraints such as sonotranslation (translating sounds but not senses), paleotranslation (translating through etymological roots), neotranslation (translating to a language that doesn't exist) and many others, in order to produce a *just* translation, twisting the multilingual "nonsense" writing of *Finnegan's Wake* into French. The translation of *Io, Nessuno e Polifemo*, a play written in a mixture of Italian and Sicilian dialects by Emma Dante, was translated into French as *Moi, Personne et Polyphème* by the collective La Langue du Bourricot with a mixture of "pseudo-dialects" created out of "syntactic, rhythmic and phonetic calques" (27), contaminating the French with the structures and sonorities of the untranslatable mixture of dialects. I would also draw readers' attention to Samuel Millogo and Amadou Bissiri's invented language in their translation of Ken Saro-Wiwa's *Sozaboy* that I discuss in chapter 4, as well as the collective translation of Michel-Rolph Trouillot's poem "Imigrayson" that I discuss in chapter 6 as examples.

***

Before I move on, there are a few debts that I should pay. In addition to the many who are mentioned above (Outranspo, Abrahams, Grass, Samoyault, Broqua, de la Torre, my students in the master's translation program at Université Paul-Valéry Montpellier 3, and too many others to list), I am also indebted to the Expanded Translation Network, in particular Jennifer K. Dick, who suggested me as a member, and to Zoë Skoulding, who introduced me, among many other things, to Tim Atkins's translations of the Petrarch Sonnets and his classification of the

Seven Translation Procedures, which is a forerunner to my procedures here. My collaboration with Philip Terry in the network was also a major source of inspiration, and his *Exercises in Translation* applies many of the procedures I describe in this book to translate Queneau's *Exercises de Style*. I would also like to mention a "debt by anticipation" to Douglas Robinson, whose book *The Experimental Translator* I discovered as I was finishing my own. At first I was struck with horror that a world-renowned translation scholar was publishing a book with more or less the same title as my own at more or less the same time, but this horror quickly turned to delight as I read Robinson's book, and realized how wonderful it is when brilliant people wind up, through different paths, at some of the same destinations as oneself. I am deeply grateful to him, and to Craig Dworkin, for their attentive, encouraging, insightful readings of this book in its draft form.

The last and most ineluctable of these debts is to my early mentor, Stacy Doris, who was my teacher and master's thesis advisor in creative writing at San Francisco State University from 2004 to 2006. She was the first person to make me feel that the way I was thinking about translation and the experiments I was starting to do even then with translation were not entirely crazy (or if they were, that that could be a good thing). As I was writing this book, I continuously wondered when I would come round to writing about Doris and her work: her translation of prosodic forms in *Paramour*, or her translations of translations in *Conference*, or her visual and collage translations in *Cheerleader's Guide to the World: Council Book*, etc. But because I could have come round to it really at any point in the book, I somehow never managed to get straight to the point about it. And now, as I'm writing the final lines of this introduction, I am still stuck as to why this is. Is it because her work is so overwhelmingly pertinent that I could not find a point of entry to begin to dissect the different avenues, the different ways in which her work is relevant to this discussion? Is it because the way the procedures happen in Doris's work is so pervasive, but also very rarely overtly signaled, that it creates a nerve-wracking opacity that, as her student, made me feel too anxious to enter into? Was it because of the monumental status she plays in my own life, my own work, my own heart, even after her death? Or is it because, as Derrida said in response to the question of why he never wrote about Beckett, "[Doris] is an author to whom I feel very close, or to whom I would like to feel myself very close; but also too close. Precisely because of this proximity, it is too hard for me, too easy and too hard" (Derrida/Bennington and Bowlby 60). In other words, because of and in spite of the fact that she appears only this once, this book is in many ways about her work, in honor of her work.

1

Emprunt

M. NourbeSe Philip's *Zong!*, as told to the author by Setaey Adamu Boateng, tells a story that can't be told by ripping apart the text of the court decision of *Gregson v. Gilbert*, a case that treated the matter of whether insurance should be held liable for the deliberate drowning of 150 African slaves onboard the *Zong* in 1781. The reasoning behind the deliberate drowning was the captain's belief that the law did not provide for insurance to reimburse the cost should slaves die of natural causes, but that insurance was expected to cover the death of slaves in the event of rebellions, revolts or uprisings. It was thus financially more advantageous, theoretically, for the captain to throw the slaves overboard than to let them die from thirst or illness, which, due to the captain's navigational error that set them off course for many days, was what was happening onboard the *Zong*. And so he ordered the Africans to throw themselves or be thrown overboard. Whether or not the ship's underwriters actually received the insurance payment is unknown, and as Philip describes in the final *Notanda* section to her book, regardless of the outcome, the decision rests on the logic of whether or not the ship's underwriters can be reimbursed for a loss initiated by the captain, not on whether or not the Africans should be considered property or not.

"There is no telling this story; it must be told" (*Zong!* 189). And so Philip does not write it, she translates it out of pieces. Pieces taken from the words in the court decision. Pieces of the bones of Africans at the bottom of the sea. Starting with the very first poem, words dissected into letters are then stitched back together in different arrangements, and into different languages. *Zong!* is a work of recovery and memory. But as the poem tells what can't be told, it also remembers what can't be remembered, and one of those recoveries is language. In the *Notanda*, Philip records her reaction to a letter written by Granville Sharp, a British abolitionist: "Am unable to go on when he questions how many people would have understood English when the commands were given for them to jump or throw themselves overboard—cannot read on—too much for me" (*Zong!* 201). Here, language difference holds the space of the inability to read on, to tell the story, to make meaning. Indeed, Philip's entire project, composed of words, sounds, letters, floating, coming together, breaking apart in suspended separation, in fragments, strives to resist meaning making, while the relentless order of grammar, that "ordering mechanism, the mechanism of force" (*Zong!* 193), continues to try to impose it. This perpetual shattering of the original text is also an effort to remember what cannot be remembered: "How did they—the Africans onboard the *Zong* make meaning of what was happening to them?" (*Zong!* 194)—and because this language, the language that makes sense, English, is the same language that provided for the logic of the *Gregson v. Gilbert* court case to exist at all in the first place.

In this remembering through not telling, through the unmaking of sense, there are several instances of what I would call experimental translation. Many plays on words, or rather on letters, haunt the book, and return as a lyric chorus, a refrain. Indeed, *Zong!* is also a song, and has been performed all around the world in "durational readings," choral performances where the book is read and sung out in a polyphony of overlapping voices.[1] But even in its written form, all throughout the text of *Zong!*, we find other examples indicative of a theoretical, linguistic knot I am trying to unravel here: that of the *emprunt* as translation of the material of the letter, as a work of language difference in the body of phoneme and grapheme, the spaces between and their poetics of relation.

Running in a footnote under the body of the main text—"underwater" (*Zong!* 200)—you can find a list of African names, among whom is *Oba*. Of course the names of the Africans onboard the *Zong* were never recorded, and Philip's account of trying to recover these names from old documents is similar to the one of her facing the unspeakable language barriers onboard the *Zong*. A sales record from "one Thomas Case" tells the names of the purchasers, whereas the Africans are referred to as "negroe man," "negroe woman," or even "ditto man," "ditto woman" (*Zong!* 194). After some of these descriptors, she finds the addition "(meagre)": "Negro girl (meagre)";

"There are many 'meagre' girls, no 'meagre' boys. This description leaves me shaken—I want to weep. I leave the photocopied sheet of the ledger sitting on my old typewriter for days. I cannot approach the work for several days" (*Zong!* 194). Silence is an integral part of Philip's oeuvre, but also, for that reason, the need to make this silence speak. And so from the raw matter of the court case text, she makes the languages and the names speak.

Thus one of the recurring slips of the tongue that shift the sense of letters between languages and meanings is the play on "sobs" and "*oba.*" The third section of the text, *Sal*, begins on page 59 with the line "water parts" and a breath space below, "the *oba* sobs," which is repeated again at the bottom of page 60 (see Fig. 2).

The foreign languages in *Zong!* are often identified through the use of italics. I say often because can you always identify a foreign word? As Philip remarks, some words with the same spelling can mean different things in different languages, such as the word "auge" (*auge*), which in English refers to the body trembling in sickness, whereas it means "to fast" in Yoruba. And so foreignness in a text is most often an affair of the letter, of the graphic materiality of the word, not just in *Zong!* but in the common practice of italicizing foreign words, to separate them, identify them as meaning outside of the logos of the language the text is written in. It is the graphic surface of the text "towards a foreign likeness bent,"[2] to quote Shleiermacher's translated maxim on overliteral translation—translation that follows the letter too strictly, that follows the letter to the letter. A foreign *accent* written into the text. In *Zong!* the italics are a graphic mark of foreignness but also of orality, and of memory, as the italics also delineate the speech "heard" (that can never be heard) onboard the *Zong* by Setaey Adamu Boateng and recorded by Philip.

Oba is thus one of the names listed under the water of the main text in the first section of Philip's book, but it also means "king" or "ruler" in Yoruba, as you can read in the glossary, where Philip includes word lists in different languages that can be found in the book. But as is evident from the very first line, *oba* is a name and a word but also a letter; we find the traces of this word in the letters in the English word (and readily readable thus to the English speaker's eye) "sobs." "Sobs" shares the materiality of its meaning with *oba*. This is a translation not of meaning

Fig. 2. Extract from *Zong!* by M. NourbeSe Philip (*Zong!* 60).

but of letter, an experiment in meaning making through sound and print or code and light. Since the meaning cannot be recovered, lost in water, Philip makes it newly, through the material of this language whose meaning making she resists. The play on *oba*/sobs reoccurs like a drumbeat or a bell punctuating the pages of *Zong!*, as do some other refrains that can be read in this early passage, such as the play on *ifá* and "fall." At other places in the text, Philip also plays off the sonic proximity between *ifá* and the English "if," as *ifá* means "divination" in Yoruba, according to the glossary. And so *ifá* translates both the sense of "oracle" ("oh oracle" on the fourth line of the above passage), but also the sound of what cannot be told or perhaps foretold, the "*fá* fa fa fall ing over & over" of the Africans into the water. The "oh" is this first sigh or moan or plea of the oracle, which is also a homophone of the French *eau* (water), another one of the languages "heard" onboard the *Zong*. On page 82, we read "*omi omi l eau l eau* water," on page 96, "they dove *omi omi omi* oh my go oh d," and so on, flowing, draining, drowning through the text like bones (*os* in French), like an unheard SOS, onto the ocean floor:

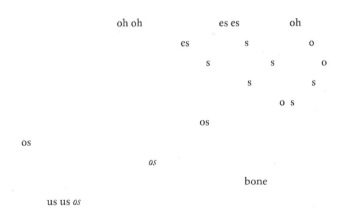

Fig. 3. Extract from *Zong!* by M. NourbeSe Philip (*Zong!* 63).

In telling the reader how she has gone about telling this story that can't be told but must be told, Philip quotes Stan Douglas speaking about his film *Inconsolable Memories*, a cut-up of Tomás Gutiérrez's 1968 film, *Memorias del Subdesarrollo* [*Memories of Underdevelopment*], where he speaks of his recombinant method as "'absolving' his work of 'authorial intention'"

(*Zong!* 204). Philip goes on to reflect upon the use of the word "absolving" in the context of her own cut-up method, but also "its connection with the idea of freeing from debt, blame, obligation, or guilt." But for Philip and the poetics of *Zong!*, it also "speaks to a relation and relationship of debt or obligation of spirit owed by later to earlier generations" (*Zong!* 205). It is this debt and obligation that I would like to reconsider in the context of the linguistic *emprunt* as it is used by Philip. For an *emprunt* creates a debt, though borrowing or a loan. And what Philip's text does is to make this debt speak, the very real symbolic and material debt that exists between languages and therefore peoples, that cannot be paid but must be paid.

Christina Sharpe has theorized Philip's work as belonging to what she calls "wake work," where the word and figure of the wake is mobilized in all its senses, as the wake of a ship, a wake of mourning, as well as wake as in being awake, to wake up. It is important, in this context, to understand that the phenomenon that Philip describes, of slaves jettisoned as cargo to preserve the inhuman mathematics of the transatlantic slave trade—"the key point in the beginning of global capital" (Sharpe 26)—was not an isolated phenomenon. Rather, it is what Sharpe refers to, quoting Philip, as the "ditto ditto of the archive," a part standing in for a whole. It is the job of wake work to "counter forgetting, erasure, the monumental, and that ditto ditto in the archives" (Sharpe 59). But wake work is not just about remembering a distant past, it is about waking up to the temporality of the wake: "In the wake, the past that is not past reappears, always, to rupture the present" (Sharpe 9):

In the wake, the semiotics of the slave ship continue from the forced movements of the enslaved to the forced movements of the migrant and the refugee, to the regulation of Black people in North American streets and neighborhoods, to those ongoing crossings of and drownings in the Mediterranean Sea, to the brutal colonial reimaginings of the slave ship and the ark; to the reappearance of the slave ship in every life in the form of the prison, the camp and the school. (Sharpe 21)

Philip's work mobilizes this temporality of the wake as she transforms the raw material of the *Gregson v. Gilbert* court case into the bones of her ancestors, floating through the water, entering into "the residence time of the wake," which is "the amount of time it takes for a substance to enter the ocean and then leave the ocean" (Sharpe 41).

The atoms of those people who were thrown overboard are out there in the ocean even today. They were eaten, organisms processed them, and those organisms were in turn eaten, processed, and the cycle continues [...] And what happens to the energy that is produced in the waters? It continues cycling like atoms in residence time. We, Black people, exist in the residence time of the wake, a time in which 'everything is now. It is all now' (Morrison 1987, 198)." (Sharpe 41)

In what follows, I will try to map what the wake work being done in Philip's *Zong!* means for the materiality of the letter in experimental translation and the way that something like a very real, material, historical debt (*emprunt*, borrowing, loan) can be housed in it, mobilized and potentially transformed—or reproduced—in full energetic, powerful and symbolic aliveness. I would also like to do so with respect to what remains opaque in this work to my own readership, and its instrumentalization in my reading of the figure of the *emprunt*. In many ways, when I place Philip's work under the rubric of experimental translation, I am appropriating it, relying on it to carry out my own ends, namely, to destabilize translational norms. This is because I do not want to deny or eclipse to what extent it has impacted—indeed, formed and sculpted—my thinking about translation. But Philip's work is much larger and escapes the use I am making of it here. As Philip writes, comparing the faulty translation of her work (which I discuss at the end of this chapter) to European modernism's appropriation of African aesthetics in masks and other artifacts: "the spirit inherent in the 'object' through ritual or ceremony was impossible to translate or appropriate" ("Dystranslation" 291). My sincerest hope and desire is to carry out my own work, deeply indebted as it is to Philip's, with respect and gratitude, never presuming that I have an "inherent right" (301) to it.

Translating *emprunt*

To get from VD to Philip and Sharpe, I will have to follow a somewhat circuitous path. This circuitous path starts in the letters of the word *emprunt* itself, and in its translation into English, which in the above section I have ambiguously glossed as both "loan" and "borrowing." So which is it? When one *emprunte*(s) a word, does one loan or does one borrow? The answer is both. Sager and Hamel translate it as "borrowing," whereas Anthony Pym, in his revisiting of VD's procedures, translates it as "loan" (*Translation Solutions* 23). So what's the difference? Is this just a needless terminological ambiguity?

Traditionally, linguists tend to distinguish between "borrowings" as referring to the process of a departure word imported into an arrival language and "loan" as the result of that process. To quote Denis Jamet's foreword to Aurélia Paulin and Jennifer Vince's special issue of *Lexis: Journal in English Lexicology* devoted to the *emprunt*: "borrowing refers to the process, whereas 'loan-word refers to the result; i.e. the linguistic material which has been borrowed from a foreign language. Yet, 'borrowing' is also frequently used to refer to the result of such a process, as in '*this word is a borrowing from Old Norse.*'"

In their nominalized forms, the words are more or less interchangeable, but they differ in their verbal forms. This difference also exists—but in a different way—in common definitions of the words "loan" and "borrowing" outside the context of linguistics. And it is this difference that is at the heart of my argument in this chapter, namely, that "to loan" is to give a loan, whereas "to borrow" is to receive it. In the bifurcation of *emprunt* into loan and borrow, a power differential erupts between those who have and those who need, or between those who take and those who are plundered. And although most linguists tend to gloss this difference in their deployment of the words, this bifurcation can also be found in the historicity of linguistics. According to a 2019 study by Shurooq Talab Jaafar, Dipima Buragohain and Harshita Aini Haroon, the word "borrowing" was first used by W. D. Whitney in 1875 and is much older than the term "loan," which was introduced in 1950 by Einar Haugen, as a calque of the German *lehnwert*. This distinction accompanies a shift in the research, as linguists up until Haugen were focused on the introduction of foreign elements into their native language, and it wasn't until Haugen that native elements were considered in a foreign context. Based on this evidence, Taleb Jaafar, Buragohain and Haroon propose to solve for the confusing ambiguity surrounding the terms "loan" and "borrowing" by using them to refer to the directionality of a translation. In other words, the word "loan" in their argument would be used when speaking of the importation of elements (sounds, words, parts of words, structures, meanings) from one's native language into a foreign one, and "borrowing" for foreign elements imported into one's native tongue. This makes sense as far as the words are concerned (loaning is giving words away, borrowing is receiving them), but it is the only article I have found that uses these words in this way. This is perhaps because of the multitude of situations in which it is very difficult or impossible to distinguish between "native" and "foreign," for example, in the case of multilingual texts, speakers, readerships, audiences or classrooms.

Loans and borrowings also depend upon where they sit in history. Hélène Chuquet and Michel Paillard, in their *Approche linguistique des problèmes de traduction*, jettison all of VD's procedures apart from transposition and modulation, starting with the *emprunt*, which for them is not a translation procedure, but rather is "generally integrated into a lexicon" (Chuquet and Paillard 10). Ballard has likewise critiqued VD for failing to make the distinction between an *emprunt*, which for Ballard is a "fact of society" ("À propos" 4), and what he calls (following Jean Delisle) a *report*, which is the individual act by a translator. An example of the difference between an *emprunt* and a *report* in Ballard: "Have you tried the soufflé?" (*emprunt*); "You called it the red belt back in the *front popu* days" (Queneau/Galvin 73) (*report*). *Front popu* is short for Front Populaire, a French left-wing political alliance.

I'm not actually sure such a critique is necessary, and actually I find that Ballard and especially Chuquet and Paillard end up downplaying or even erasing completely the profound role that translation plays in changing languages through *emprunt* (but not only). In my reading of VD, the distinction is clear (if not very sophisticated), first because of their inclusion of the *emprunt* into a list of translation procedures that are not intended to be descriptions of general linguistic phenomena, even if their reflections owe much to work that does that. But beyond that, they do distinguish between *emprunts* that are used by translators to fill a hole ("overcome a lacuna"), or those that are used for stylistic effect, and the fact that "some well-established, mainly older borrowings are so widely used that they are no longer considered as such and have become part of the respective TL lexicon" (VD/Sager and Hamel 32).

But actually that's not what they write, of course. What they write is: "*Il y a des emprunts anciens, qui n'en sont plus pour nous, puisqu'ils sont rentrés dans le lexique et deviennent des servitudes"* (VD, *Stylistique comparée* 47), which translates literally as: "There are old borrowings/loans, that are no longer considered as such, as they have entered into the lexicon and have become 'servitudes.'" As the translation of the word "servitude" shivers between French and English for me, it calls up the power games between loans and borrowings, and between languages, their degrees of indebtedness to one another. My first reading of this word, *servitude*, was that these foreign words have been dominated, indentured by the French language, assimilated to become part of it, losing their sense of foreignness. However, the word "servitude" in English captures only one sense of the meaning of *servitude* in French. It is actually an *emprunt* from old French and Latin, and in its passage from French to English it seems to have lost some of its homophony. The other meaning in French is as a constraint or a limitation, and this is the specific meaning employed by VD, for whom *servitude* is a theoretical tool included in the glossary at the beginning of the book, defining translation solutions for which the translator has no choice—for example, when translating according to the grammatical rules of the arrival language, or translating by a foreign word when that word has become a native word. And so *servitude* is not the domination of a foreign element by a native element, but refers to the servitude of the translator to constraints imposed by the language or texts.

But "servitude" does still exist in English as a word meaning to obey a certain constraint. I know this because Sager and Hamel use it to translate the entry on *servitude* in the glossary (they couldn't very well have created a glossary entry called "part of the respective TL lexicon"). But so then why? Why not translate *servitude* by "servitude" in the body of the text, so that it lines up with the glossary? Well, because it sounds odd, doesn't it? It feels foreign, it feels like an *emprunt*. And this is the way in which, paradoxically, an *emprunt*, which is not a translation, only has meaning in translation.

From the very beginning of reflections on the *emprunt*, it is apparent that identifying or defining a word as a borrowing is dependent on locating it in history. In Haugen's 1950 article where he initiates the term, he writes: "We know that great numbers of words in English which once were adopted are now quite indistinguishable from native words by any synchronic test" (Haugen 211). And according to Sara Thomason's *Language Contact: An Introduction*, "75% of English vocabulary comes from French and Latin."³ In other words, if you go back far enough, all languages are composed of an assemblage of *emprunts* from other languages, and no language is self-identical in a static sense of identity, rendering the very notion of an *emprunt* totally moot. Language is an *emprunt*, as it is through contact and borrowing, patching itself together from foreignness, that a language becomes able to differentiate itself from other languages and define itself in contrast to other languages—a contrast that is also an interdependence as a language relies on its difference from other languages to define itself.

But so, if you go back far enough, all language is *emprunt*—how then does one identify an *emprunt*? At what point does an *emprunt* cease to become an *emprunt*? Many accounts of linguistic borrowings will consider the frequency with which a word is used in order to calculate its foreignness: "Patterns of high frequency are certain not to sound 'queer' to native speakers; just how infrequent must a pattern be before it begins to 'feel foreign'?" (Haugen 230). As a word gets absorbed by a language and eventually becomes a word in that language, it is its potential to "sound queer" that will mark it out as an *emprunt*. And so Sager and Hamel translate *servitude* as "borrowings" that "have become part of the respective TL lexicon" and not as "servitude," as it has (not) become a part of the English language.

My critique of VD's *emprunt* has not so much to do with the fact that they fail to distinguish between *emprunt* as translator activity and *emprunt* as linguistic phenomenon (since they do do this), but rather starts (but does not end) with their overly simplistic vision of how *emprunt* is used to "overcome a lacuna" (VD/Sager and Hamel 31), which implies that there is an abstract and universal database of meanings out there that are waiting to be accessed by language—and that thus these meanings do not change when they get borrowed or loaned. This implies a profound separability between the matter of words and their meanings. The examples they give for *emprunt* are exclusively single words or short strings of words. For the servitudes, they give *alcool, redingote, paquebot* and *acajou* (*Stylistique comparée* 47). However, most of these words actually change meaning as they cross into French, and so do not so much import a meaning from a departure language as use the form of a departure word in order to create a meaning in the arrival language. The CNRTL (Centre National de Ressources Textuelles et Lexicales) website tells me that *alcool* comes from Arabic, referring originally to a fine powder or medicinal liquid. The word *redingote* comes from English, "riding coat," and referred to a man's long coat. As it integrates the French language, it gains in meaning, adapting to changing trends, and comes to refer to a style of a lady's dress, buttoned up to the top and gathered round the waist with a belled skirt. Tailored thus, it eventually returns to English, "redingote," to refer to a specific type of eighteenth-century long coat for men, or "a woman's lightweight coat open at the front."[4] Now, redingote or *redingote*, in both English and French, hesitating between gender identifications, but also across historical alterity, sounds very "queer" indeed.

But many servitudes, as VD remark, "enter a language through translation" (VD/Sager and Hamel 32), and the examples they give for *emprunt* as a translation procedure seem to be relatively transparent. They seem like they should be doing what VD want them to do: overcome a lacuna. But can a lacuna in an arrival language be exactly the same size and shape of a word in a departure language? For *emprunts* from English, they give two examples: "dollars" and "party." Since 1958, *party* has made its way into the French language as a servitude. Or rather, as a translation, in its naturalized spelling as *partie*, as in the now very kitsch (and probably very queer) "Merquez-partie"[5] by Les Musclés. This is my second critique of VD then: that their borrowing of the word *emprunt* shares not too much with its use in linguistics, but rather, not enough. VD's account treats the *emprunt* solely on the level of the lexis, the structure and the message (*lexique, agencement,* and *message* in the table reproduced in the introduction). Most linguistic accounts of borrowing are at least aware that borrowing can also happen on the level of the phoneme (that the sound of a word is often altered when it integrates an arrival language), or the grapheme, as is the case with the spelling of *partie*, or morphologically, for example, when French people say "*j'ai liké*" when responding to a post on Facebook. This is because in VD's lacuna-overcoming account of the *emprunt* the matter is secondary. It exists to represent a hole in the shape of a meaning, whereas in my reading of the *emprunt*, material is directly, concretely meaningful, but also unstable, because it exists in networks of unequal economies of exchange.

My last critique relates to their failure to situate themselves with regard to arrival and departure cultures. In the lacuna-overcoming account, it is possible for a word to integrate the context of an arrival language unchanged. Let's take the example of the "dollar," which should theoretically stay the "same" when employed by a translator of an English-language text. But on closer inspection, this sameness quickly breaks down, much like the distinction between loan and borrowing in translation. Putting aside the fact that "dollar" derives from an *emprunt* of a German place name,[6] it is not in any sense a *report* (to use Delisle and Ballard's distinction), but rather a "servitude" for which Le-dictionnaire.com gives the definition, in French, of the currency of Canada, the United States and Australia (but not Zimbabwe, Ethiopia, Puerto Rico, Ecuador, Panama, El Salvador, Guam or any of the other countries where the dollar is used). Finally, when the word is read or spoken aloud in French, whether it is a an *emprunt*, a *servitude* or a *report*, its pronunciation changes, its accentuation transferred from /ˈdɒl.ər/ to [dɔ.laʁ].

The materiality of the word "dollar" thus houses both a foreign meaning and a local one, the local interpretation of a foreign entity. It is in some sense a bit like Philip's "auge" or *auge*, which means two things at once in different languages. How then do we distinguish between the different instances of the dollar/*dollar*? How do we measure the meaning of a dollar as an *emprunt* rather than a servitude, in the hand of a Canadian, a Panamanian, an Ethiopian, and its meaning in the hand of a French person, a Mexican, a Uyghur? In the hand of a Canadian translated by a Mexican? In the hand of a Mexican translated by a Canadian? A dollar of course is more than just a word, it is a currency, and as a currency it is thus doubly representative of the economic value it represents. It is also material in the same way language is for the translator, in all the different senses of the word "material."

Meaningful tokens

To ask the question of what the word "dollar" or *dollar* means is also to ask the question of the value of a dollar, since a dollar, like language, is characterized by having an external referent. Or is it? Let's look at what Saussure, translated by Wade Baskin, says about the value of a dollar: "To determine what a five-franc piece is worth one must therefore know: (1) that it can be exchanged for a fixed quantity of a different thing, e.g. bread; and (2) that it can be compared with a similar value of the same system, e.g. a one-franc piece, or with coins of another system (a dollar, etc.)" (Saussure/Baskin, *Course in General Linguistics* 115).

In this passage, Saussure is using the allegory of monetary value in order to explicate the difference between "signification," which is a word's meaning in a given context, and "value," which is the sum total of meanings a word can take on across the ensemble of its iterations, in relation to other iterations, both syntagmatically (in relation to other signifiers in a sequence) and paradigmatically (in the meanings of words it can be defined in relation to, or that could potentially substitute for it in a sentence). These are the definitions that VD rely upon as well since they are writing in the Saussurian era of linguistics and rely on scholars who also rely on Saussure (Charles Bally, Alfred Malblanc, etc.[7]).

It is not at all uncommon to find monetary metaphors in studies on language and translation, and the model of currency exchange has also frequently found its way into translation studies to express the ways that "the same text operates in different modes of cultural currency," as Jan Walsh Hokenson and Marcella Munson write in their introduction to *The Bilingual Text: History and Theory of Literary Self-Translation* (5). They go on: "Florins, pounds, pesos, and deutschmarks are in this sense comparable divergences in functional correspondence" (5). Languages, like money, can be traded one for the other. Lydia Liu, on the other hand, has critiqued this scenario in Saussure and the presupposition of functional correspondence, which she calls reciprocity or hypothetical equivalence, in "The Question of Meaning-Value in the Political Economy of the Sign." In Saussure, the allegory of language and money is dependent upon a model whereby money as a signifier is distinct from its signified, where money "is not the metal in a coin which determines value" (Saussure, quoted in Liu 26). Or, as language scholar Lia Formigari writes, translated by William Dodd, "it is its capacity to abstract from the sensible world while maintaining its capacity to represent it that makes language resemble money" (quoted in Hokenson and Munson 5). This is an analogous model to one where an *emprunt* is something that "overcomes a lacuna," that fills a hole where a fixed meaning should be in a language.

Thus the monetary metaphor fits into the structural linguistics model whereby meaning is treated as "a fixed category a priori" (Liu 27). But in contemporary flows of capital, this is not how money works at all. To quote William Davies in his introduction to *Economic Science Fictions*, "Most money in twenty-first century capitalism is manufactured out of thin air by the private banking system, through the provision of credit to customers. Most of this money never attains any tangible form beyond its digital record." Credit and loans are represented by numbers shifting up in one column and down in another with no external referent. "Money is largely a leap of faith, backed up with machines of representation" (8).

My first instinct when I began thinking about updating the figure of the *emprunt* to take into account the model for monetary exchange described by Davies is to relate it to homophonic translation. Homophonic translation, also known as sound translation, traducson, or sonotranslation in Outranspo, empties out the material of the signifier of its corresponding meaning, translating only the sound. For example, "1-2-3-4" is translated as *"Oh Anne, tu cries fort."* This procedure—which is a procedure of experimental translation—has a very long history dating back to antiquity, and is a recurrent feature in the tradition of Dada and nonsense poetry, and also with the concrete and language poets in the United States such as Charles Bernstein, Ron Silliman, David Melnick, Robert Kelly, etc.[8] The Oulipo has also carried out many experiments with homophonic translation, particularly Marcel Benabou and François Le Lyonnais. Celia Zukofsky and Louis Zukofsky's translation of Catullus is another important reference for homophonic translation, and they are all part of the history of the Avant-Garde rupture that instigated the practice of experimental translation.

Because, in machine translation, like in the contemporary flows of capital as data that Davies describes above, there is no signified. (Or is there?) These are empty signifiers floating around, being exchanged for one another and defined solely on that exchange without any external referent. Isn't this what happens in homophonic translation? Isn't the word emptied of its meaning and only its signifier, its materiality, its sound remain to be exported in translation? As Dirk Weissmann puts it: "[Homophonic translation] seems to be the result of a distance taken from a certain tradition of literary translation, that is, from the widespread hierarchizing of sense (supposed to be immaterial) over formal and material aspects."[9] There is a shift away from meaning, from the "fixed quantity of a different thing, e.g. bread" to focus on an exchange of signifiers.

I wouldn't be the first person to consider theorizing a parallel, analogous shift from structural to poststructural linguistics as accompanying the loss of the gold standard.[10] Liu, on the other hand, situates the gold standard in a continuum with an exchange model that presupposes transparent value, presumed reciprocity, and "global translatability" inhabiting "universalistic aspirations" (Liu 15). She is less interested in allegorizing language and money than she is in introducing the real problems of translation into the "political economy of the sign" (Liu 19). Interestingly enough, in many of the quite different accounts Liu analyses that allegorize language and money (Marx, Saussure, Baudrillard, Bourdieu), what is left by the wayside or shoved under the rug are the agonisms of translation—much like in Chuquet and Paillard's jettisoning of the *emprunt* from the procedures of translation. Liu argues that this has to do with a disavowal of the thickness of cultural and political differentials that happen in the concrete and messy historical materialities of language exchange. More often than not, language exchange contains a presupposition of reciprocity, equivalence and equality that contradicts the way they actually go down. A shift to poststructural linguistics, along with the loss of the gold standard, is perhaps less significant (in this context) than the fact that the loss of the gold standard in the U.S. coincides almost exactly with the American Dutch poet and translation scholar James S. Holmes's coining of the term "translation studies." It is a critique of the transparency of translation that forms the basis of Liu's argument against Saussure's monetary model: "The study of meaning in the political economy of the sign needs to be grounded in the actual history of the global circulation of meaning value. That history is a history of colonialism whose exploitation of exotic difference has erected major obstacles against a historical understanding of difference" (Liu 19).

What Liu is arguing for is to think about how meaning and value happen in language as currency in and through translation, as concrete, material, site-specific, historically grounded circumstances of language exchange, in the fullness of their power differentials: "How does reciprocity become thinkable as an intellectual problem when predominantly unequal forms of global exchange characterize the material conditions of that exchange?" (Liu 14).

In thinking about how money relates to language in translation, a more direct line might be found in another analogy used by Saussure, also critiqued by Liu, again turning around the notion of value as common to both the field of linguistics and political economy: "Here as in political economy we are confronted with the notion of *value*: both sciences are concerned with a system for equating things of different orders—labor and wages in one and a signified and signifier in the other" (Saussure/Baskin, *Course in General Linguistics* 79). If one thinks about this in the context of the translator's lived reality, the analogy between wages and signifier is actually a really good one since translators are paid by the sign, the word or the page. And as translator contracts are negotiated, each word becomes a sign of potential and contested value both on a linguistic level and on an economic level.

In other words, the signifier in contemporary language models—as in contemporary flows of global capital—is not empty at all. It is thick and full, embodied and inhabited by histories and debts of unequal exchange. One of the things that Liu critiques in Saussure is the difficulty he encounters in distinguishing meaning (as a reference to a fixed external reality) and value (as the relationship between signifiers), which Saussure presents as distinct and autonomous but also dependent categories. "If value is different, can meaning remain the same? Why should meaning be a fixed category a priori when the sound pattern and other properties of language are subject to the law of differential relations?" (Liu 27). Likewise, NMT has shown us that meaning is less reference to an external fixed reality than it is produced in complex exchanges and relationalities between vectors that measure abstract distances between words syntagmatically and paradigmatically and machine learning whereby the machine calculates its translations in relation to a corpus. Meaning is not found, it is created, in networks of materialities. This is nowhere more evident than in homophonic translation, where, when the sound travels from one language to another, it does not lose meaning or empty out, but gains it tenfold, splaying out to the multiple potentialities of meanings and histories that inhabit linguistic signs.

Translating debt

I want to detour very briefly into what actually happens in contemporary social economics when money is loaned or borrowed, before relating this back to translation. For example, people pay taxes to the state under the narrative assumption that this tax money goes toward paying for essential services, such as healthcare, education and unemployment. In return, people are made to feel as though they owe a debt to the state, and to society. However, the reality could not be farther from the truth. To take the example of unemployment, these funds do not come from taxpayer money but rather are loaned, with interest, by the 1 percent. Taxpayer money actually goes toward paying the interest on that debt. In other words, when you pay taxes, you are not paying for services rendered, you are paying back a loan that you did not take out, to people who don't need your money.[11] This is also evident in higher education, where one could cite the 900 percent increase in costs that coincided with the development of debt-financed tuition as proof of profit for the rich motivating this theft.

Let's compare this with what Haugen says about the figures of loans and borrowing in linguistics and language exchange: "The metaphor implied is certainly absurd, since the borrowing takes place without the lender's consent or even awareness, and the borrower is under no obligation to repay the loan. One might well call it stealing, were it not that the owner is deprived of nothing and feels no urge to recover his goods" (Haugen 211).[12]

First of all, to consider a metaphor absurd implies to some extent a Platonic thinking about metaphor as something that represents a previously existing phenomenon, as opposed to metaphor as something that invents and creates the outline of a meaning. Part of the thrust of this book, of hijacking VD's procedures as figural topoi from which to rethink the materiality of translation, is the idea that a metaphor is performative and can be a motor for meaning. In this case, thinking about metaphors materially is also a way to call attention to the political thickness of language exchange, as Liu does in her critique of the language-money metaphor in Marx and Saussure. Haugen too is glossing something very important about what really happens when languages are exchanged.

In translation studies, there are a number of reasons why the term *emprunt* is actually quite well suited to perform the phenomenon it represents. First of all, it is because the rhetoric of loss and gain has permeated translation studies from the beginning. This remark by Haugen, who is a linguist and not a translation theorist (although the distinction did not exist at the time), recalls the famous metaphor of what is "lost" in translation. The mainstream imaginary, with its reverence for origins, loves to wax nostalgic over what is "lost" in translation, turning the set of signs in an original authored text into a kind of impenetrable, sacred store of assets. To invoke a metaphor of my own, consider the *emprunt* of the imperial English pint recalibrated into French. The word *pinte* (the French spelling of "pint"), metonym for a tall glass of beer, looks and tastes like a pint, but is only 50cl of beer, compared to the 66cl in an Anglophone pint. There is a very material, liquid loss for the English-speaking beer drinker who pays for their pint and receives 16cl less than what they expected. This loss is likewise often treated as a very material crime, as many translator contracts—such as the contract Karen Emmerich received to translate Vassilis Vassilikos's *Glafkos Thrassakis*—stipulate that the translator shall "neither omit anything from the original text nor add anything to it," whereas, as Emmerich comments, in a translation, "*all* the words are added, *all* the words are different" (7).

Of course, this addition and subtraction that relates to the material of the letters and words is not what the contract refers to, but Emmerich's argument is that most translations not only change all the letters and spaces in an original text but also substantially change the text in other ways. She is arguing for a more material relationship to text, which I am pushing to the extreme. If translation is exchange, it always goes two ways. If we focus on the materiality of the word "pint(*e*)," rather than the object it represents, it actually gains a letter. This might seem arbitrary, but it joins up with a number of critiques of the metaphor of loss in translation that invite us to see it as a gain. Looked at from the side of the lost, the supposedly "losing" text, the original actually gains in translation, as there would have been no loss possible without the translation; it gains its loss, at the very least. But things are not just lost in translation, they are also gained: sonorities, resonances, references and the poetics of the translator, who is not always less talented than the writer. Indeed, Pym has suggested that "to translate is to attempt improvement" (*Text Transfer* 170), and certain texts are actually held in higher regard in translation than in the original.[13] Finally, thinking of translation as a loss rather than a gain implies a closed outline to a text, whereas if a text is taken as a malleable, fluid entity, capable of variation, translation is always a gain, as it adds to the sum total of instances of a text, of interpretations and readership. Indeed, when a reader reads a translation, they are reading not just the original, but the translator's interpretation of that original, opening and expanding it. If an original is not a closed entity, a translation cannot be a simple copy of this original but is rather a creation transforming that original.

But what is it that is "lost" or "gained" in translation, presuming it's not actually 16cl of beer or the letter *e*? Is it a meaning, a metaphor, a word, a rhythm, a rhyme, a resonance, a joke, a cultural untranslatable? Speaking of the stuff of language in terms of loss and gain presents it as quantifiable, as discrete units lending themselves to tally, to accounts receivable and accounts payable. It presents the signifier and signified as abstract values. Translation scholars have often critiqued this vision of language as something calculable, for example, Kate Briggs meditating on what is "untallyable" (146) in translation, or Naoki Sakai, who argues against the exchange model for thinking of translation in his critique of monolingual ideologies in the construction of the nation-state that present languages as discrete entities.

On the other hand, in the context of machine translation, it is precisely the calculation of what NMT specialists refer to as "loss"—the difference between what the NMT model produced measured against preexisting translations (both human and machine)—in the training process that allows the machine to improve. In turn, the calculation of this loss is representative of the speculative value of the machine itself, and the corporation that finances it, its losses and gains in the marketplace of translation.

And again, human or computer-assisted translation is paid by the sign, word or page. If translation is untallyable, it is in resistance or relation to the fact that it is also, on a profound level, tallied; it is what is unequal in that tally that prompts scholars to make a claim for it being untallyable.

There are also metonymical reasons for why the metaphor of the *emprunt* is not necessarily ill-suited to the context of language exchange, as a lot of language contact and thus borrowing, loans and also translation happen through trade, as Michael Cronin lays out in his "3T paradigm," whereby trade, technology and translation "are inseparable in their development" (3). The transfers of goods and services find themselves in historical and cultural proximity to the process of translation, and not only influence but condition one another. To relate this back to linguistic borrowing (which, as I have critiqued, only makes sense as translation), Magdalena Bielenia-Grajewska, in "Linguistic Borrowing in the English Language of Economics," cites Greenough and Kittredge's *Words and Their Ways in English Speech* to support her claim about the importance of trade, which she aligns with colonial occupation, to linguistic borrowing: "The Enterprising spirit of the English people and their fondness for travel and colonization, as well as the great development of their commerce, have brought in miscellaneous words from every quarter of the world" (Greenough and Kittredge 108, cited in Bielenia-Grajewska 109).

That is one way to think of it; Liu invites us to think of the "enterprising spirit of the English" in a different light when she asks: "How does the circumstantial encounter of cultures produce and contest the reciprocity of meaning-value between their languages?" (Liu 14). As numerous translation scholars have shown, particularly in the postcolonial vein, language exchange is politically charged with very real, very concrete power differentials that impact lived experiences. As Philip writes, "Let us not forget that it was through the translation of the Bible into indigenous languages in Africa, for instance, that cultures were diminished and even destroyed. It was how people were made afraid of their own indigenous belief systems and came to see them as expressions of the devil. So, translation has a checkered history in all subjugated cultures" ("Dystranslation" 301). If I may invoke an example from my own country of birth, one might consider the *emprunt* of Native American toponyms or tribal names in U.S. place names, such as Ohio or the Dakotas, and what kind of outstanding loan might be expressed, for example, when a white person calls themself "the mayor of Sioux City."

If we relate this back to Haugen's comment on the metaphor of the *emprunt* where the actual operation of the *emprunt* as a procedure of linguistics is actually one of theft rather than exchange, it appears as though the metaphor is quite a good one with regard to the way that loans and borrowings actually go down, insofar as "one might well call it stealing."

Evidently, the resonance of what kinds of debts may be owed between languages is not part of VD's thinking of the notion of *emprunt*, since meaning, in the Saussurian model they ascribe to, is given an abstract, fixed meaning outside not only of language but of the political economy of the sign. They likewise suffer from the blindness of privilege regarding the extent to which unequal power differentials between languages are at play in their work and in the work of translation. For VD, when an *emprunt* is not imposed as a servitude, it can be deployed either to "overcome a lacuna," as I critique above, or "in order to create a stylistic effect. For instance, in order to introduce the flavour of the SL culture into a translation" (VD/Sager and Hamel 32). Sager and Hamel's translation is significantly more tactful than the original, and speaks perhaps to an increase in racial and cultural sensitivity—I hope. In the original French, the "flavour of the SL culture" is written as "*couleur locale*" or local color. If we set the discussion of *emprunt* into the thickness of power relations, the political value of the sign, this expression immediately begs the question: Local to whom? Colorful to whom? In VD, local means foreign, it refers to being situated in a place, instead of a non-situation in an abstract nowhere that is everywhere, that is also the space of the heritage of French universalist enlightenment thinking. In a word: Paris. Color is opposed to the neutrality of something colorless, the whiteness of the French visitor perhaps, who, in 1958, had no locality, no cultural specificity, as the French in 1958 (and, some might still think, today) had the authority on the universal. An *emprunt*, then, is a sign of specificity, of difference, of an unequal power relation.

This takes us right into the thick of debt, as part of the functioning of capitalism, and the extent to which it is racially motivated. For this I would like to mobilize Denise Ferreira da Silva's complex theorizing on "unpayable debt," which she uses as a "tool and a procedure designed to crack the circuitry, to expose, to crack open the racial dialectic and describe how it figures the liberal political architecture in its complexity" (*Unpayable Debt* 14). Unpayable debt describes a paradoxical debt that one owes but is not one's to pay. Such a debt is more than just the debt that a slave would owe if they wished to buy their own freedom (the paradox of not being the owner of one's own body or labor), but what Ferreira da Silva figures as "negative accumulation." Negative accumulation is what makes it possible for the dispossession of slave labor to lead not to reparations of that dispossession but rather to a compounding of that dispossession upon the descendants of slaves, by way of "a political-symbolic arsenal that attributed their economic dispossession to an inherent moral and intellectual defect" as well as "an accumulation of processes of economic exclusion and juridical alienation—slavery, segregation, mass incarceration—that have left a disproportional percentage of them economically dispossessed" (Ferreira da Silva "Reading Scenes of Value" 107).

Ferreira da Silva's unpayable debt functions using the lever of the figure of *the wounded captive body in the scene of subjugation* (italicized throughout the book), which she deploys to "re/de/compose" the most fundamental notions of Enlightenment and post-Enlightenment thinking, namely, "necessity and its onto-epistemological descriptors (formality and efficacy) and pillars (separability, determinacy and sequentiality)" (*Unpayable Debt* 214). Necessity, for Ferreira da Silva, can be "expressed in the armature of logic," in mathematical procedures that have grounded European philosophy, such as "the principle of non-contradiction (propositions *a* or *not-a* cannot both be true), the law of the excluded middle (either *a* or *not-a* is true, there is no mediating proposition between them) and the principle of identity (a = a)" (*Unpayable Debt* 57).

I am immediately tempted to dive into the way that translation comes into resonance with this critique, for translation certainly is the place where *a* both = and ≠ *a*, and where *a* and *not-a* are both true and exist in a kind of contaminated middle ground between departure and arrival texts and languages. Experimental translation also seeks to challenge principles of equivalence, which rely on determinacy, separability between languages and same identity in meaning, but also of efficacy, of the logic of what is most productive, and actions leading logically to ends, signifiers leading logically to transparent signifieds. One of the motifs of Ferreira da Silva's argument is the critique of the *transparent I* in philosophers like Kant and Hegel, which I might like to put into relation with a critique of transparency in language or of meaning.

But I do not want to, by evoking that resonance, lead the thrust of Ferreira da Silva's argument too far astray from its central figure of the *wounded captive body at the scene of subjugation*. I would rather lead it back into resonance with Philip's *Zong!*, which I read as doing something very similar in its re/de/composition of the *Gregson v. Gilbert* court case. Philip also reflects on negative accumulation, although not in the same terms, when she quotes Lindon Barret in the *Notanda*: "The continued exclusion of African Americans (I would say New World Africans) from systems of value, Lindon Barrett argues, creates a need to 'pursue novel or original access to meaning, voice, value and authority.' In its cacophonous representation of the babel that was the *Zong*, *Zong!* attempts and tempts just such access to meaning" (*Zong!* 207).

How then does Philip re/de/compose the archive to rewrite systems of value? This happens first of all through a re/de/composition of separability, of texts, of words and of languages, as embodied in the *os* of the SOS, which means "bone" in French, "the" or "them," both plural article and pronoun in Portuguese, and "mouth" in Latin, for starters. There is no strict division between languages here, which is the ground upon which is built the fiction of reciprocity, of equal exchange between languages but also money, insofar as that allegory relies on the fixity of an external referent, and divisions between national currencies. If an *emprunt* is that which fills a lacuna, the distinction between signifier and signified is profoundly dependent on the distinction between languages as national entities. Signifier and signified are thus also national affairs. But in Philip, instead of that strict division of languages that relies on that strict division between linguistic materiality and external referent, we have homophonic (and homographic) translation, and an exchange of signifiers generating a surplus of meaning. The referent is matter that matters.

This critique of separability also happens in the way that *Zong!* is dealing with the raw matter of the archive. One of Ferreira da Silva's very powerful critiques that she carries out in her work on *Unpayable Debt* is a critique of Marx's constituting of the value in labor on paid labor, excluding unpaid labor. A worker cannot sell labor she[14] does not own. Instead, in Marx, slave labor is figured along with the raw material of primitive accumulation, along with horses and cotton. Ferreira da Silva asks: What happens if we take labor not as the abstract principle of the laborer's time that can be sold, but as the vital force of her body, her flesh? In doing so, Ferreira da Silva returns labor to the slave, as something that generates wealth. This is part of her larger project of using the figure of the *wounded captive body at the scene of subjugation* to ask: What if—in opposition to the heritage of Enlightenment thinking—we consider the slave as a human? How does that end up unwriting or rewriting the tenets of Enlightenment and post-Enlightenment descriptions and interpretations of what a human is? Among other things, it explodes the determination and separability of raw material, of what she refers to as *elementa*.

What if the basis of our ethical program was simply that everything that exists, has existed or may come to exist is made of the same raw material, the same *elementa*, the quantic things (particle-wave emanations) whose re/de/composition allows us to say anything about their existence? If we begin, as I do, by concurring with this question, such a point of departure for thinking troubles the very notion of value. (*Unpayable Debt* 73)

For Ferreira da Silva, it is the notion of value as it appears in Marx, as exchange value and use value dependent upon the worker being able to sell her labor (which is dependent upon the worker being both free and, on some profound level, equal to the person they are selling their labor to) that is being troubled. But if one puts this into dialogue with Saussure's notion of value, through what Philip does in *Zong!*, not only is the distinction between meaning and value collapsed, but so is the whole veneer of representation in language, of the import of matter. Recall Sharpe's "residence time" evoked at the beginning of this chapter, which puts the temporality of the wake into an oceanic circuit of re/de/composition where atoms and elements break down into separability. The re/de/composition of the raw material of the archive in *ZONG!* then goes way beyond an appropriation of the abstract sounds or meanings represented by letters, and into conversion of the physical material of this archive, and not only this archive, but elementa "at the molecular and atomic levels" (*Unpayable Debt* 246): "Infinite and undeterminable (that is, at once all and nothing), everything possible and actual and forever virtual, an existent (elementa entering into the constitution of other things across spacetime, in spite of spacetime, and despite spacetime), she is neither Object nor Other—even if, as elementa, she composes today's dearest commodities" (*Unpayable Debt* 270).

If we place Philip's *Zong!* in the critical procedures of *Unpayable Debt*, the letters re/de/composing from the archive and falling down the page are not signifiers or metaphors for the bones of her ancestors falling through the water, they *are* those bones, re/de/composed into the notebooks Philip used in her writing process, the electricity that was used to power the machines that processed and printed the text, the carbon and water in the pages and ink with which the book is printed, the tissues, blood, bones and voices of the people who performed it in collective readings across the globe, the electronic transfer of capital as you swipe your card to pay for the book. Philip herself reads this materiality of words on the page not in terms of bones, but rather in terms of breath, in what she refers to as the "pneumatic function" of the spacing between the words as they appear on the page, meaning that no word must be printed directly above or below another, in order to allow space for the words to breathe, as her ancestors could not: "the text must breathe and live in the breaths of those who died and for whom we now breathe .... In our reading of the text, which can be said to be arranged pneumatically, we are carrying out the act of breathing for those who couldn't breathe at an earlier time" ("Dystranslation" 298). The importance of this breathing space cannot be overstated.

Signs of value

The nineteenth poem in Mónica de la Torre's *Repetition Nineteen* is written using the constraint "T19: Version of the poem including only words with Anglo-Saxon roots" (72) and is entitled "On 'A Big Beautiful Wall' " (47). In the corresponding commentary she gives of her translation procedure in the third section of the book, she relates this to where she was when she was working on her translations, in residency at the Montalvo Arts Center in Saratoga, California. The Montalvo Center, first of all, is in the heart of Silicon Valley, "less than twenty-five miles away from Googleplex, Google's corporate headquarters, and less than ten miles away from Apple's in Cupertino" (*Repetition* 115). This geographical location relates interestingly to the use of Google software in de la Torre's poems, in the way that the materiality of place and situation can be generative of practice.

But the Montalvo Center was also founded by white supremacist James D. Phelan. Her translation in T19 using only Anglo-Saxon words hijacks this politics of racial supremacy through language experimentation. But de la Torre's translation is a critique of the legacy of white supremacy not only with regards to the place where she physically wrote her translations, but also of the time in which she wrote them:

That it is a platitude to state that indeed history is repeating itself in America does not make this fact less true, less demoralizing, or less alarming. As I was working on my translation in the summer of 2018, the Trump administration implemented a "zero tolerance" approach to migrant families detained at the border, which resulted in the separation of families and the unprecedented detention of more than 2,600 children in government shelters. (*Repetition* 117)

The critique of separability and sequentiality found in Ferreiro da Silva can also be found in this operation of inscribing the stratified presence of racism in the poetic practice, critiquing a post-racist teleology of progress that pretends to lead us out of racism but instead blinds us to its continuing practices. In Ferreira da Silva, it is the materiality of history that enables this critique; in de la Torre, as in Philip, it is the materiality of language too, in the translation using Anglo-Saxon words, but also in her use of homophonic translation and her experiments with Google translation using speakers with varying degrees of linguistic abilities, privileges and access to the opacity of a departure language.

I also read this in de la Torre's play with homophonic translation, across the spine of the book in the bilingual poem "Unlike *nostos, algo* is unspecified" (4-6) in the section preceding de la Torre's serial translations in *Repetition Nineteen*. The contamination of languages mobilizes the charge of power in the political economy of the sign to resist monolingual ideologies that are also norms of translation (in Google translate, you always translate between two distinct languages). The complex political position of the *emprunt,* as theft and reappropriation, pain and liberation, violence and reparation, is embodied in de la Torre's translation of "*ay*"/ "I," a homophonic translation nearing the end of the poem. The meaning of the sound of pain is mimicked in its phonetic displacement into the construction of the subject in the English pronoun. This conflicted displacement happens within the body of the signifier in translation, its matter:

ay, interjección para expresar muchos y muy diversos moviemientos del ánimo, y más ordinariamente aflicción
o dolor

ay, pronounced *I,* interjection used to express a range of mood shifts, and more commonly affliction
or pain

[...]

I, pronunciado *ay,* primera persona singular en inglés

I, pronounced *ay,* first person singular.

In the phrases "pronounced *I*" and "*en inglés,*" there is excess, surplus. This visualizes a translation remainder that is already present in the phoneme I/*ay,* first of all as it is overflowed with the graphic difference it carries. In Norma Cole's "nines and tens" in the volume *towards a foreign likeness bent* mentioned above, mathematical discrepancy or incalculability is directly related to the translation between sound into writing—a mathematics that also carries a political charge in the way that written literature historically has been set as superior to oral literatures. There is also an excess of meaning showing the extent to which matter and meaning are entangled. This excess of meaning in the I/*ay* sound is proliferative as it creates more new meanings in the third text, in the onomatopoetic expression of pain in the enunciation of "I" in a foreign language. But of course, a foreign language is never just any foreign language. Writing in the borderlands between English and Spanish is a deeply situated practice in de la Torre, as we saw in poem 19, deconstructing Trump's "big beautiful wall."

English is also a fraught linguistic location for Philip, both in her re/de/composition in *Zong!* and in her other work as well. For example, in Philip's "Discourse on the Logic of Language," English

> is a foreign lan lan lang
> language
> l/anguish
>   anguish
> a foreign anguish
> is english—
>
> (*She Tries Her Tongue* 32)

In this poem, we hear a resonance with de la Torre's I/*ay*, the pain of speaking English where the legacy of English supremacy is so heavy. For Philip this has less to do with the immigration policies and racism between the U.S. and Mexico and more to do with the colonial heritage in Philip's own history in Trinidad and Tobago. In *She Tries Her Tongue, Her Silence Softly Breaks*, where one finds "Discourse on the Logic of Language," Philip mixes formal English with what she calls "Caribbean demotic," embracing a historical thickness and the disruption of English hegemony that began through the layering and interruption of African languages. Philip transforms this history into a poetics:

In the vortex of New World slavery, the African forged new and different words, developed strategies to impress her experience on the language. The formal standard language was subverted, turned upside down, inside out, and even sometimes erased. Nouns become strangers to verbs and vice versa; tonal accentuation took the place of several words at a time; rhythms held sway. Many of these "techniques" are rooted in African languages; their collective impact on the English language would result in the latter being, at times, unrecognizable as English. Bad English. Broken English. Patois. Dialect. (*She Tries Her Tongue* 85)

This too is a kind of negative accumulation, beginning with the initial violence of being punished for speaking one's own language. "Discourse on the Logic of Language" mixes different registers and addresses, one of which is hijacked legal language in the form of two "edicts" printed in italics and inserted in the right-hand margin of the poem. Edict II reads: "Every slave caught speaking his native language shall be severely punished. Where necessary, removal of the tongue is recommended. The offending organ, when removed, should be hung on high in a central place so that all may see and tremble" (*She Tries Her Tongue* 32). This violent prohibition to speak one's own tongue is combined with the obligation to speak in a language in which one's own reality is not imaginable: "In whose language / Am I / If not in yours / Beautiful?" ends another poem in the book. English is the language of colonization, abduction, expropriation, enslavement: total violence (to use Ferreira da Silva's term). It is the language of *Gregson v. Gilbert*. And today, speaking in Caribbean demotic or the other linguistic variants Philip cites ("Bad English. Broken English. Patois. Dialect.") could keep you from getting a job, from succeeding in school, could impact the truth value accorded to a legal testimony. Philip's power comes from using "language in such a way that the historical realities are not erased or obliterated, so that English is revealed as the tainted tongue it truly is. Only in so doing will English be redeemed" (*She Tries Her Tongue* 85).

Saying things the wrong way, speaking the wrong language, or speaking with traces from the wrong language can kill you. This is the driving force behind Caroline Bergvall's "Say Parsley," an installation, poetic performance and later text based on the massacre in the Dominican Republic under the Trujillo dictatorship of tens of thousands of Creole Haitians who failed to roll the *r* in the Spanish word for "parsley": *perejil*. For the installation, Bergvall used a homophonic translation that was also a metacommentary on the linguistic form the shibboleth took: the utterance "rolling hills," where "hill" is the homophonic translation of the Spanish *jil* and "rolling" the metacommentary on the injunction to roll the *r*. She then made recordings of people speaking this short phrase on the streets of London, with all the phonetic, inflectional, accentual, regional, multilingual resonances that were bound to be represented. A complex psychoacoustic sound environment was created in collaboration with Irish composer Ciarán Maher that further increased the polyphonic and poly-lingual resonances of these recordings as they were played during the installation and performance. On one of the walls of the exhibit, a speech by the British home secretary in 2002 was fastidiously recopied, in which he enjoins bilingual families to "SPEAK ENGLISH AT HOME."[15]

The question of the shibboleth in this context raises some interesting questions about the power plays at stake in the *emprunt*, in-between loan and borrowing, as the mark of the native tongue becomes the sign of the foreign, identifies a speaker as foreign. There is a critique here of the password, of the sign that puts one within or outside of something, in this case, the monolingualism of the nation-state. At what point do two dialects become native and foreign languages, same and other, self and enemy? In the case of *Say Parsley*, debt, as the heritage of violence, is materialized in the language, in the form of an accent, which, according to Haugen and the linguists that followed him, is a case of borrowing, although translation scholars do not treat the accent as *emprunt*, except in very rare cases where a translator is called upon to translate one. And how do you do that?

These experimental translation practices are or could be, sometimes must be, put to use in "faithful" translations of experimental texts, which sometimes call for their own experimental translations. This is the case in an experiment carried out by Amanda Murphy in her article on the heterolingual writing of Katalin Molnár. Molnár's work is its own example of experimental translation, as the author's book of life writing, *Quant à je (kantaje)*, is written in a kind of personal French tortured by the author's Hungarian accent. This is evident even from the title, which is written both in standard French spelling (if not in standard French)—*Quant à je*—and in the author's phonetic writing as *kantaje*. Murphy gives a deep reading of the title before attempting to translate it, tracing the syntagm from "*Quant à moi*" to "*kantaje*" and beyond, to homophonic invention:

Quant à moi → Quant à je → Quant à je (kantaje) → Quant à je (contagieux)

Figure 5 Le mouvement de la traduction à l'intérieur de la langue molnárienne

Fig. 4. The movement of translation from within Molnarian language (Murphy).

Figure 6 Le mouvement de la traduction de la langue molnárienne vers l'anglais

Fig. 5. The movement of translation from Molnarian language into English (Murphy).

Murphy's translation experiment thus reproduces Molnár's, translating first the grammatical mistake in Molnár's use of *je* instead of *moi* (as "as for I" instead of "as for me"), and then rewriting this mistake in a kind of invented, personal phonetics. But she does not stop there; she unwinds the phonetic version to make new words: "as foray." She then goes on in the article to translate "as foray" back into French as *"Comme pour moi (comme incursion),"* a kind of calque on "as foray," and then homophonically, passing through a deformation of the English pronunciation to get to *"Demande quatre œil (as forêt),"* which is literally "ask four eye (ace/ has forest)." She calls this "the continued variation of queer translation" (*"la variation continue de la traduction queere"*). This translation, like the original, is made possible by the slippage at the point between speech and writing that actually makes homophonic translation possible, the writing of "as" as "ask" or "for" as "four," "I" as "eye," etc.

Murphy also comments upon the way that Molnár's unique phonetic transcription of her Hungarian accent performs a critique of the violence of linguistic normalizing practices and the way they reinforce the division between those who feel at home within the culture of a given nation and those who are excluded by it. Molnár's writing testifies to the shame and humiliation of the foreign accent, that material linguistic debt of difference, embodying asymmetries as of course different accents are perceived in different lights according to the politics of the identity of the speaker.

Molnár transcribes her accent, the oral and aural difference that marks her as a foreigner into writing, making it visible. The surface of the text is disturbed, troubled by foreignness, interrupting the clean stability of monolingual orthographical conventions. Bergvall does this as well, to write out a historical debt, for example with her use of Old English and Old Norse letters such as Þ or ð in her work *Drift*, which experimentally translates the *Seafarer*. *Drift*, and indeed all of Bergvall's works, invokes the nonsequential model of history, layering together texts, historical languages and alphabets. *Drift* drifts, as the *Seafarer* finds itself translated in the heart of the book by a report printed in white ink on black paper from *Forensic Oceanography: Report on the Left-to-Die Boat* concerning a boat with seventy-two migrants who had been left to float adrift and unaided between Tripoli and Lampedusa.

Bergvall's work does something similar to de la Torre and Philip, but from a different position, showing the extent to which experimental translation can manifest a practice of situating and deconstructing the politics of language difference. She uses the report to appropriate the *Seafarer*, to unwrite and rewrite it. Like de la Torre, she summons Anglo-Saxon language roots to interrupt fluency in the surface of English, and to resituate it and the text in the materiality of history. Like Philip, she hijacks an unreadable report, but in this case, the report is the most readable thing in the text, and it is everything else that surrounds it that brings in an opacity, an incomprehensibility that attempts to tell the affective resonances of a story of which Bergvall is not a part. Specifically, the drift is also a linguistic drift embodied in Bergvall's poetic inquiry into the Old Norse thorn rune Þ in a text at the end of the book entitled NOÞING. Þ was carried over into Old English, where it marked the difference from the ð as voiced and Þ as the voiceless fricative of the [th] sound; both of these letters as well as others from the *Seafarer*'s alphabet replace sounds in Bergvall's own English writing. Bergvall traces this loss historically and also technologically as no Þ was cast into the first German letterpresses; Bergvall associates this with a move toward greater simplicity and standardization of languages. The book also contains drawings of the thorn rune repeated over and over again, blurring, overlapping and erasing, rendered opaque in the materiality of their writing, as perhaps a reader of the "Left to Die" report might be struck dumb trying to fathom the depths of power inequalities that could allow the migrants to be ignored by the multitude of vessels that could have provided assistance.

But I have to wonder if Bergvall's text doesn't also do something else, in spite of its undoubtedly good intentions. Because when you mobilize the materiality of the signifier, you don't always just mobilize what you intend, since signifiers bring with them the complexity of their historical agonisms, the circuitry of elementa in atoms, electricity, sound, ink, paper, data. For me the thickness of the Þ overwriting itself, blurring, erasing its specificity in contaminated blocks of ink, is mimetic of another kind of erasing that happens in the text of the residence time. Sharpe also writes, reaches across the density, the synchronous stratification of history in the wake, to make a connection between the unnamed boat that came to be known as the "left-to-die" and another story of a ship lost at sea: the *Zong*. Commenting on the use of the expression "human cargo" as it was used in news reports of the event, Sharpe writes:

> Two hundred thirty years after the crew on board the slave ship *Zong* threw over-board those living Africans, that word *cargo* repeats, and so do the horrors of the holding, the throwing, the beating. African migrants are exposed "to inhuman levels of violence," stabbed and thrown overboard, shot and thrown overboard, migrants shut in the "dark and suffocating hold," while others are packed on deck—standing on the door to the hold; the perils are not now, and have never been, evenly distributed (Sharpe 55).

Read through the optic of residence time, I am compelled to ask the question of the politics of appropriating the "left-to-die" story in the con-text of an experimental translation of the *Seafarer*. When Murphy trans-lates Molnár's homophonic writing as a form of practice-based research, she carries the poetic intention forward, into translation, but she does not erase it or conflate it with another set of circumstances that are not appro-priate to it. Is the story of the migrants really Bergvall's for the taking—or for the borrowing? As I hope to have shown, the gesture of the *emprunt*, when one complicates the distinction between matter and meaning, car-ries with it the full material force of historical violence. What kind of politi-cal history is Bergvall reenacting when she inserts the report—the most readable, accessible section—into the center of her book?

Occlusion

How do you translate an *emprunt*? Others have treated the problem exten-sively (Raguet-Bouvart, Suchet), and I will try not to linger too long on the various strategies translators have adopted over the years to overcome these obstacles: carrying over the *emprunt*, transcribing it in a foreign alphabet, transliterating it, adapting it phonetically or graphically, marking it with italics, erasing it, naturalizing it, generalizing it, specifying it, explicating it, calquing it or supplementing it with prefacing, footnoting or glossaries (although some of these strategies will be tackled in latter chapters).

The most obvious way to translate an *emprunt* is not to. Experimental translators, however, sometimes push this to the extreme, not only conserving *emprunts* or other heterolingual markers but adding them. John Felstiner's translations of Paul Celan in his biography of the poet, *Paul Celan: Poet, Survivor, Jew,* do this by *not* translating everything. In his translation, certain words or passages are left in the original German (Samoyault 58-60; Suchet 200-203). In Felstiner's English translations, the German is not a point of entry, but an intentional opacity, meant to translate an untranslatable foreignness that exists in the giving text. As Samoyault comments in her reading of the poem, "this return to German in the English is not a non-translation nor a return to the original: it carries out a difference that exists within the poem and is embodied in the German, both the language of death and the language of the poet, both oppression and resistance" (Samoyault 59).[16] As Samoyault comments, Celan himself was a renowned translator, and his German is marked by this work. His German is strange, as though written through with a foreign tongue. This unreadability, opacity, is a poetics of unspeakability, as Celan was "writing in a language sullied by criminality (Celan's parents both died in Nazi camps in addition to his own internment in 1943), seeking to write as though translating into German, singular to the extreme point of seeming at times unrecognizable" (Samoyault 60).[17] The unspeakable materiality of history, its impossibility to be told, is translated through the material of the letter, the inscription of opaque foreign words on a page.

In the middle of a talk given at the 2010 Columbia University conference on *Rethinking Poetics*, de la Torre switched to Spanish in a room full of English speakers. Instead of creating transparency, or an illusion of transparency, in the metaphysics of mimesis, she performed opacity, the very real, material opacity of cultural difference that can also be a critique of the violence of representation. It is for this reason as well that not everything should be translated. Sophie Collins's edited volume *Currently & Emotion* includes examples not only of experimental translation but translations of marginalized voices, aligning the two in what she proposes as their shared capacity to interrupt textual flows, canons and corpuses in a way similar to how experimental translation might interrupt the hegemony of certain languages.[18] However, these texts do not simply exist in order to disrupt Westnorthern textual power centers. They have their own paths to carve out, and sometimes it is best to preserve these trajectories through a politics of opacity rather than transparency in opposition to a translational norm that implies that everything should be accessible and translation is always good. As Philip writes, "there is no 'right' to translation, particularly as it relates to Black and African descended people" ("Dystranslation" 301), but rather, a "right to opacity" (300), she writes, referencing Edouard Glissant.

Because translation is dangerous. And as much as there is great potential for doing justice in translation, there is also a great risk of doing wrong, specifically when the very real, material debts housed in signifiers are not handled with adequate attention.

This is in fact what happened with a recent translation into Italian of Philip's *Zong!*, which in many ways reeancts the violence the original so powerfully critiques. One way it does this is through the material conditions of the translation as they were carried out by the different actors (all white) involved in the publication of the translation, including the translator, the publishers at Benway, the original publishing house (Wesleyan), who sold the translation rights for $150 without consent or even notification of the author, and the members of the Canada Council, who funded the translation to the tune of $13,000. Another way is through the disrespect of the material elementa of the text as it appears on the page. As I quote above, the "pneumatic function" of the text is far more than an aesthetic choice for Philip, it is its "spiritual architecture," "spaces of potentiality, spaces of the future, spaces that represent the erasure of the past, spaces that function as musical rests, as spaces of fugal amnesia—all that and more" ("Dystranslation" 294). To disrespect this guiding principle of the text, as the Italian translation did, is a disrespect for the spirit of and in the work, for the breath of Philip's ancestors, something "much larger than the physical form itself" ("Dystranslation" 291).

When Philip signaled the gravity of the disrespect to the translator and publishers, she was met with dismissal and disdain, as well as accusations of "racial essentialism, tribalism, authoritarianism & totalitarianism, North American privilege and colonialsm," as she explains on her blog, where the record of the full correspondence can be found.[19] They also used legal language—the same kind used in *Gregson v. Gilbert*—to justify their tampering.

To summarize, what the publishers and the translator did regarding the so-called translation of the text was a reprise of that age-old colonial strategy of theft and appropriation under cover of law, which Benway Series also used to justify this travesty. I say under the guise of law because in one of their emails, they write that: "[t]he Italian edition of *Zong!* is the object of a publishing agreement between Benway, who bought the rights, and Wesleyan, who sold them." The echoes of contract law of insurance, which the ship's owners used to justify the massacre of the "cargo" of enslaved Africans on board the Zong, are almost too loud to hear. ("Dystranslation" 291)

In the word "cargo," I am reminded of Sharpe's comments on the use of the word in the news reports of the "left-to-die" boat. It is significant too that the translator's justification for the changes made to the text in Italian was that she saw the words as the bodies of migrants floating in the Mediterranean that helicopter pilots use to give coordinates to rescue teams. This reads like a profoundly undigested understanding of Sharpe's "wake time," which is not intended to be used as an excuse to conflate situations of enormous difference, or to appropriate texts from the specificity of their context and instrumentalize them for ends that erase their original import. The same should be said for all practices of translation— experimental and otherwise—and can be read in the danger that accompanies uses and abuses of *emprunt* as a material marker of debt between languages, cultures and peoples. As Philip writes of *Zong!*:

What if the "language" in which it is written comprises more than the words and more than the weight of inference and resonance than words already carry? What if that is what I'm gesturing towards when I talk about the placement of the words on the page being linked to the events of the massacre—the drownings? And further, what if the "more than words" is actually akin to the opacity that Glissant talks of and insists that we have a right to? What if that opacity, that I think is more than the sum of its parts, is untranslatable? ("Dystranslation" 303)

PROCEDURES

1.1 The *Traduit Partouze* (or: "translation orgy")

A text is chosen, and a group of players assembled. One player reads out lines from the original, segment by segment, while the other players carry out a collective homophonic translation. A scribe records the results, and rereads periodically throughout and at the end.

1.2 Recouperation

A text for hijacking, ideally in a language different from the one(s) the players will be assembling their poems in. Each player, hovering eyes at a slight remove from the page, allows words to emerge from the letters, chopping, recombining, collapsing the spaces between the words in the original and allowing new ones to appear. As the words appear, players transcribe them onto a new sheet of paper. Share and discuss.

1.3 Mess(e)

Beginning with a text or a single word, players translate experimentally in turn, each time uttering the word aloud (all kinds of utterances should be encouraged: speaking, whispering, singing, yelling, crying, growling, etc.). Players can prepare these translations before the mess(e) or it can be done spontaneously. To aid groups with little musical aplomb, a workshop guide can repeat the start word continuously as a rhythmic undertone. The other players are likewise encouraged to give a rhythmic/melodic aspect to their translations, as well as to repeat them, and other players' translations, embracing interruption, polyphony and layering. The goal is cacophony.

See the supplementary *Handbook of Translation Procedures* for full, detailed instructions and creative results.

2

The Calque

It's definitely not my day of chance
I'd better get back to bed and achieve my book
That only never deceives me
  — "A sympathetic day: snob poem," Camille Bloomfield
  (Co-founder of Outranspo)

In Camille Bloomfield's snob poem, part of her series of "Poems for Brexitees," English *emprunts* are brought back home to the English language. Words like *"brushing"* (blow-dry), *"dressing"* (wardrobe), *"baskets"* (sneakers), *"addition"* (bill), *"baby-foot"* (table-football) pepper the poem in English. These are borrowings that, through their integration into the French, have undergone a semantic change. The morphologies have been borrowed but the meanings have changed. They are now what are called "false cognates," or "false friends": words that look the same but mean different things. This is why Bloomfield calls it a snob poem, because the reader has to be a bilingual French speaker in order to understand the meaning of the poem (and because *"snob"* is another borrowing into French). She also uses false friends such as "achieve" (*achever* in French means "to finish") and "deceive" (*décevoir* in French means "to disappoint"). Both *achever* and *décevoir* derive from Old French, but they have slipped and slid in their English meanings and now mean something different. The French and English meanings are slightly to the side of one another, like the vision produced by crossed eyes, rather than one on top of the other in parallax. In a sense, Bloomfield's intruders perform an anachronistic back translation, or a time-traveling translation, translating past or future meanings in foreign languages into a text-time-space continuum where they do not belong. She also uses false friends with common third-language roots, such as "*liquide*" (cash), or "sympathetic" for "*sympathique*" ("nice"— ironic in Bloomfield's poem, which tells the story of a bad day), reenacting the correspondences told by root etymologies. Bloomfield uses these words in the French meanings rather than their English ones in the context of the poem in English, importing the word's meaning with its matter, where it's not supposed to be. The two meanings layer on top of each other, like a collage or a palimpsest.

She also translates French expressions literally into English. The idiomatic translation for "lucky day" in French is a *jour de chance*, which is translated in the above expression "day of chance" ("Brexitees" 78). In this case, what Bloomfield has done is borrowed the individual words of the syntagm "*jour de chance*" and translated them literally into English, for use in her English-language poem. This is why, for this chapter on calque, I am focusing on the unit of the word, because in calque, often, words get translated in the place of syntagm, a phrase gets broken down, a whole translated by smaller fragments. Or, the sound or the meaning of a word gets translated without its corresponding meaning or sound, respectively. Or, parts of words get translated instead of the word as a whole: a morpheme or morphosyntactic (grammatical) marker. In any case, it is the unit of the word that is at stake. The meanings of the French words, but also their construction, their order, are seeping through the surface of the English language. It is also where the English teacher in a language-learning classroom in France would reach for their red pen to hastily scribble the word "calque," and deduct a point from the total grade. Because calques are strange, alien and out of place: wrong. They err, or *errent*, are errant. It is as though the ghost of French was hanging oddly in Bloomfield's poem, out of time and out of space.

This is also the driving poetic intention behind Bloomfield's "RIP Motivation: Entente cordiale poem" in the same series of poems:

Pain? bizarre.
Chat? impatient.
Bras sale? impossible.
Main sale? banal.

☞

> MINCE EMOTION
> SINGE SENSATION
> POUR SATISFACTION...
> RIP MOTIVATION.
>
> ("Brexitees" 76)[1]

This poem can be read directly in English, but it can also be read in French. And an English (calqued) translation of the French poem clinging to the English, seeping through it like an image through tracing paper reads as:

Bread? weird.
Cat? restless.
Dirty arm? unbearable.
Dirty hand? unremarkable.

☞

> THIN AFFECT
> APES FEELING
> FOR SATISFACTION
> GOODBYE CHUTZPAH
>
> (my translation, with author input)

This inhabiting of two languages within the same lexeme can also be found in another poem for Brexitees, "Étonnante Athena" ("Brexitees" 74). This poem is bestrewn with what Outranspians call *aubergines* (a term coined by Ludivine Bouton-Kelly), which refers to words that contain both original and translation in one. The original and translation cohabiting in the same space do not necessarily (and perhaps preferably do not) coincide with the meaning of the word as a whole. *Aubergine*, the name used to denote the phenomenon, is one such example: *auberge* is the French equivalent of the English "inn," thus *aubergine* (playing off a French pronunciation of "inn"). In Bloomfield's poem (written in French) we find aubergines like "**fourmill***ant*," "*born-***nés**," "*bar***bar**es" or indeed, "*At*hena." These words are bilingual assemblages, two words from two languages collaged together to make a third with an entirely different meaning.

Barbaric likeness

Paolo Bellomo's article on calque tells that *calque* first arrived in the French language as a material process. It is actually an *emprunt*, from Italian: *calco, calcare* and refers to technical processes of reproduction, such as pressing or tracing, but also of casting or modeling. When it is borrowed (or calqued?) into French, it loses the sense of casting and moulding, of taking the bidimensional or tridimensional shape of something, since French already has words for these things (*moulage*, "casting, moulding," or *empreinte*, "imprint"). It retains primarily the sense of tracing, as in tracing a deep image through to a surface image, or of creating a rubbing from an engraving. For Bellomo, it is the aspect of *pression* that remains primordial, a French word that means pressure, that is found in the word for printing, *impression*. It is the materials pressing together, their proximity, that creates the reproduction.

For Bellomo, this *pression* also explains the uncanniness of *calque*, for it reveals the extent to which the act of translation is material, which disturbs the idea of languages as sign systems,[2] both in terms of the division of signifier and signified and also of languages as distinct from one another. This is because of the way in which the division of signifier and signified is related to the monolingual, ideological and national division of languages into pure, standardized, distinct entities. This distinction between sign systems is also where the classification and division of *calque* as separate from *emprunt* and *traduction littérale* runs into trouble. VD situate *calque* halfway between a borrowing and a literal translation. This is evident from the definition they give of calque in the glossary: "A **borrowing** of a foreign syntagm whose elements have undergone **literal translation**" (VD/Sager and Hamel 340). If a calque is a literal translation of a borrowing, how can we tell them all apart?

A different way to describe a calque is to say it is a literal translation where no literal translation exists. VD propose this as another way to fill a lacuna "without having to use an actual borrowing" (VD/Sager and Hamel 33). This is the sense of *calque* as linguistic innovation (for example, *gratte-ciel*, which is a literal translation of "skyscraper"). However, calques can also be "awkward," which is the translation we find in Sager and Hamel for VD's description of unacceptable calques as *"l'expression la plus concrète de l'abomination de la désolation"* (*Stylistique comparée* 48): the most concrete expression of the abomination of desolation. This is a pretty extreme condemnation of linguistic interference, to say the least. Bellomo shows that it is a biblical expression from the book of Daniel used to condemn the introduction of Greek statues into Judaic temples in 168 BC.[3] It describes the heresy of foreign elements in a sacred space. Sager and Hamel's translation operates a purge of its own, diminishing the force of VD's moralizing. But in the original, it reveals the ideological pulse that drives VD's injunction to keep the languages distinct. It is an ideological pulse that still inflects linguistic policies to this day, especially in the classroom. As I mentioned above, a calque makes French-language teachers instinctively reach for their red pen, to subtract a *point-faute* from a student's total grade.

The notion of error is primordial in identifying a calque and separating it from other linguistic phenomena. And this error, this "point-fault," is directly related to not blurring the border between native and foreign elements. Michel Ballard, at the very end of the first volume of his detailed typology of translation problems, observations and actions, offers a short typology of errors as regards the contact of languages (*Versus* 1:263–266). These include *l'impropriété* ("impropriety"), *le faux sens* ("false meaning") and *le barbarisme* ("barbarism"). All three of these can be found in Bloomfield's "A sympathetic day." An example of *impropriété* can be found in the use of the words "achieve" and "deceive," and has to do with using a word with a common root in the wrong way. An example of *faux sens* is found in the title "A sympathetic day"; Ballard relates this to the example of false friends. The last, a *barbarisme*, has to do with the deformation of words, creating static in the form of language, for example, with the use of *-ing* in words like *brushing* and *dressing*.

The history of moral politics can be read in the use of the words "impropriety" and "barbarism," and even "false" insofar as it calls up fault, dissimulation, even abomination (one might think of false idols here). In the word "propriety" we find "propre," which in French means "own," as in one's own, in linguistic proximity to property. The link between translation and property relates the distinction between languages to the ownership of texts (and languages), and also drives imperialist practices and theories of translation, as we'll see more in the next chapter. Barbarism comes from *barbaros*, or "foreign" in Greek, modeled on a mockery of the sounds produced by foreign speakers, "*barbarous* being an imitation of babbling" (Hejinian 325). Interference is improper, barbaric, it goes against civilization itself, as a set of imperial technologies.

But in experimental translation, whose intention is to put into question translational norms, *bar***bar**e becomes an aubergine, a place for linguistic play and collage, and the relationship to error is entirely shifted. In the previous chapter, I theorized the way in which accent can be used as an instrument of linguistic oppression and exclusion, and how this very same instrument can be transformed into a principle of composition, for example in Katalin Molnár's *Quant à je*. Molnár's work is written through not only with her accent, as a way of posing a threat to the politics of standardized and standardizing French, but also with linguistic errors. Molnár also proposes a typology of three errors, distributed at sporadic intervals in her book.

type de faute	solution	remarque
fautes liées aux prépositions: manque, mauvaise, superflue	en cas de doute, en mettre plusieurs	et si pas de doute ?

Source: Molnár 43.

type de faute	solution	remarque
confusion entre les mots	chépa	kan jédédout, jepeuvérifié mé kan janépa ?

Source: Molnár 115.

type de faute	solution	remarque
mauvaise construction de phrase	se permettre une grande liberté tant que ça reste compréhensible éclater la phrase en plusieurs morceaux	cf. Rabelais cf. groupes rythmiques dans la parole (4–5 syllabes)[4]

Source: Molnár 163.

All of Molnár's errors are types of calque, although only the second one falls into Ballard's categories, and could serve as an umbrella for all of them: "confusion" between words; "confusion" is one possible translation

for Babel. In each of these examples, we see a resistance to the standardizing force of error, with the references to doubt and the strategies she uses,
or doesn't, not so much to "correct" her errors but to hijack them to deconstruct the terror of error, which (has) ruled language-learning classrooms
for centuries, although many teachers have begun to question the efficacy
of this oppressive atmosphere for language learning, whether the goal is to
eliminate errors or to welcome them (Bouhmid "Diversity"; Greaves and
Schultz). Error is appropriated in Molnár as an attack on linguistic conventions and authority in the classroom, which is the first place where national
ideologies are transmitted, and students made to submit. And in the errors
Molnár describes, we find solutions that could almost be Outranspian procedures: when in doubt, add more or break it up into smaller pieces, and of
course the use of homophonic writing again.

But to return to the idea of falseness, there is also the duty to equivalence, to likeness that is betrayed here, what Bellomo calls "the abomination of the mirror," which casts doubt upon the authenticity of origins,
and upon the order of things in representation. Bellomo gives an example,
taken from anthropologist Georges Didi-Huberman, of an aboriginal practice from South Australia whereby a shard of glass is placed in a footprint
to give a limp to its maker. In this example, the imprint coincides with its
origin: there is no longer any separation between the representation and
that which it represents. It is this separation, a moral and political separation, that is upset with calque.

Champs en fleurs
We all indulge in egosurfing from time to time: the embarrassing but
irresistible urge to Google our own names. Sometimes, if your name is
common enough, you might find intruders, eponymous doppelgang-
ers, doubles. "Doubles" is the name of de la Torre's poem that began
as an egosurfing session that gave rise to a series of avatars, or what I'd
like to consider as false friends: same words with different erring (in its
archaic sense of "roving") meanings. De la Torre's poem presents these
avatars in epistolary form, as Mercedes Correche searches for her biological mother, who disappeared in Argentina when Correche was two years
old, a woman engaged in "subversive activities" of whom Correche has

very little information apart from her name: Mónica de la Torre. The poem unfolds as a series of emails from Correche to all the Mónica de la Torres she finds on the internet. Along the way, she finds the regional student representative for Santa Clara, California; an officer at the Door Legal Services in New York; a tennis player; a stripper and performance artist; the manager of a hotel in Girona; a graduate student at A&M University in Texas; and a high school student. The result is a diffracted, algorithmically generated collage of Mónica de la Torres. The "original" Mónica de la Torre who generated the electronic, hopscotching montage is likewise double, both the mother of Mercedes Correche who (spoiler alert!) is never found, the object of her search, and the author herself, Mónica de la Torre.

Funnily enough, this multiple doubling and performative decentering of an original that is not to be found is doubled in the translation process, which, like the invention of the web of Mónica de la Torre, is nominative. The poem "Doubles," as though enacting its own title, was published twice. The first time (as fiction) on the Words Without Borders website in 2006, where the words "Translated from the Spanish by the author" appear directly under de la Torre's byline. The second, in its original English two years later, in 2008, in de la Torre's book of poems *Public Domain*. The original Spanish thus haunts the English original, both translation and original, both fiction and poem, fiction of a translation of a fictional original. The Spanish haunts the English, both there and not, like false names, false idols, a concrete expression of an "abomination of desolation."

I'd like to take this idea of the same name referring to different people and run with it, into a field of flowers, a *champ en fleur*, which is a calque on the name Bloomfield. Because there is another Bloomfield, besides Camille, who goes by the name of Leonard, Leonard Bloomfield. And it is to this Bloomfield that English-language translation studies owe their version, their translation of calque, as "loan-translation" (Meriläinen et al.), by way of Haugen, among others.

It can be very difficult to distinguish between an *emprunt* and a *calque*, and at least part of this has to do with the fact that in English the distinction between *emprunt* and *calque* is far less tidy than how it is found in VD, although perhaps this tidiness also is only surface deep. L. Bloomfield, Haugen and many subsequent scholars situate "loan-translation" as one subcategory within the broader spectrum of linguistic borrowings—which means that in English (and German) calque is not distinct from borrowing, but rather one example of it. And in comparison to the panoply of divisions and subdivisions that exist in most linguistic accounts of borrowings and calque (Bloomfield, Haugen, Gómez Capuz, Smith, Larizgoitia)—whether they consider these as two separate phenomena or not, VD's division of calque into *calque d'expression* and *calque de structure* seems a bit bare.

In VD, a *calque d'expression* ("lexical calque" in Sager and Hamel) is a word-for-word translation that respects the syntactic structure of the arrival language. VD give *"compliments de la saison"* as an example of a *calque d'expression* from the English "compliments of the season," which is not a great one because the syntactic structure is the same in both languages. I think a better example would be my own pet calque on "PowerPoint," which I translate as *"point de pouvoir"* when speaking French, which on a good day might get a laugh from French-translation geeks since *point de pouvoir* could also back-translate as "no power at all," but also because the common translation of "PowerPoint" in French uses *emprunt*: *"PowerPoint"* (with a French accent, of course).

A *calque de structure* ("structural calque" in Sager and Hamel), on the other hand, is the copying of a construction not native to the arrival language. VD give the example of *science-fiction* in French, which copies the compound noun structure of English. A non-calqued translation of science fiction might give something like *la fiction scientifique*. And given that modifiers usually find themselves after the noun in French, whether in a noun-adjective phrase or in a compound noun, *science-fiction* should give the meaning of "fictional science" rather than "scientific fiction." The example of *science-fiction* is also a pretty bad one though, since "science" and "fiction" are both cognates in French and English, and so there is really no way to tell whether *science-fiction* is a *calque* or an *emprunt* except by taking VD's word for it.

There are a few things missing from VD's typology (or division might be a better word, since VD give us only two categories of calque) that we find in other typologies—and also in the three types of errors described by Molnár. Besides the reflection on morphological elements, be they parts of words, grammar or syntax, the notion of "semantic calque" is missing. A "semantic calque" as it is used by scholars (Larizgoitia, Smith), or "semantic loan" in Haugen, substitutes a foreign meaning into the shape of the native equivalent. One example of this is the use of the French word *souris*, which is the translation for "mouse," but is also used for a computer mouse in French; or an *estrella* ("star") in Spanish to refer to a movie star. Larizgoitia talks about the "widening" of words in the arrival language as they gain new meanings.

Haugen separates semantic loans into three categories: analogue, homologue and homophone. An analogue loan is an *emprunt*, where word and meaning remain intact across the transfer to the arrival language. With a homologue loan, the resemblance is purely semantic, whereas in a homophone loan, the resemblance is purely phonetic. To give examples: an analogue loan could be the French *soufflé* as it is used in English to denote the egg-based dish. A homologue loan could be embodied in the above example of the *souris*, and a homophone loan in C. Bloomfield's use of the French word *baskets* to refer to sneakers. A basket is not a sneaker. But we can see how *baskets* might have slid, sneaked over to the meaning of sneaker, since you wear sneakers to play basketball.

This follows the temporality of loans in Haugen and in other linguistic studies. Loans (or calques) tell a story. In the examples of *soufflé, souris* and *baskets*, you can trace the borrowing with historic linearity. They tell stories of the influence of French cuisine, or of American techno-linguistic or sports globalization ("glowballization" in Rachel Galvin's translation of the Outranspo's *Acts de fundación*).[5] This kind of story is very important in L. Bloomfield's treatment of semantic shifts and loan-translation. History can tell us how words change, but words can also tell us how history has changed. In the first example Bloomfield gives for a loan-translation, he refers the reader to the term "conscience" as it is derived from the Greek συνείδηση [sun'ejde:sis], which joins a derivative of the Greek verb for "to know" with the preposition "with." This is then calqued into Latin with "a compound of *scientia* 'knowledge' and *con-* 'with'" (L. Bloomfield 456). Bloomfield traces this same process through several Germanic languages as well, to tell the story of Enlightenment beliefs from Greeks to Romans to the plethora of European languages.

But L. Bloomfield was a linguist. And when the loans and calques hit translation studies, something else happens. In translation studies, calques become not just the record of past exchanges but the potential for innovation or error, tapping into what L. Bloomfield refers to as the "queer marginal" (437) meanings of words in language exchange. In this version of calque, it is not only the story of the translation that gets rewritten but the story of the sign. In translation—and especially in experimental translation—the signifier is not the record of a diachronic story of a cultural exchange, but a motor of new meanings. It is this potential that experimental translation taps into to decenter words from their meanings and double down on the haunting proliferation of language contamination.

In C. Bloomfield, the polyphonics of potential meanings embodied in translations that cross rebelliously between morpheme, lexeme and sememe are broken down and collaged to create poetic reconstructions and layering, for example, in her "sympathetic day," which is not *sympathique* at all, but perhaps invites the reader to sympathize. To relate this back to the story of the two Bloomfields, two *champs en fleurs*, two fields of flowers, a name traced forward into correspondences with no prior meaning, referents get aligned that have nothing to do with each other except that they share the same name. And in this alliance, a story of calque gets told in its temporal unraveling. There is a rerouting of the direction in which words mean, a rupture in the way they mean, in the way a word takes to or represents or embodies a meaning. Instead of a record: a spell. Sign systems and theories of representation are also temporal, like translation studies, and tell a story of what leads to what, of what translates what, of arrival and departure, and also of what represents what (or who, whom), what reproduces what, and how. This is story of signs lining up and getting in line. Or, of signs in disorder, getting out of line. Impropriety. Barbarism. Error.

Creative calque

Samuel Trainor's work on "creative calque" begins with a critique of transparency in translation studies, with distinct attention to the materiality of the various and contradictory ways the metaphor has been deployed. In Benjamin, Trainor argues, transparency is foreignizing, a "true translation" should convey "syntax word for word" (Trainor "Transparency"), whereas in Venuti transparency is domesticating, "giving the appearance that it reflects [...] the essential meaning of the foreign text" (Venuti, cited in Trainor). Trainor also takes the reader through Georges Mounin's metaphor of *verres transparents* ("transparent glasses" or "transparent lenses") and *verres colorés* ("colored glasses" or "colored lenses"), where *verres transparents* give a domesticated text that reads as though written in the arrival languages, and *verres colorés* a foreignized text where the structure of the departure language creates a "pastiche"[6] in the arrival language. Trainor does not comment on this, but we once again see the idea of the foreign as "colored." Trainor wonders if the word "transparent" itself is not a false friend, since the metaphor for transparency can be used for a host of seemingly contradictory translation strategies.

Nonetheless, in all these cases, the view to the other side remains intact, as it does between clear and colored lenses, which are both transparent, by the way. Likewise, whether we are tracing an exact and faithful reproduction of a text over a pane of glass or taking a picture of one, the intention remains the same: to produce a clear, coherent, mimetic image that lines up with what is depicted. In other words, to produce a translation that can be taken as a substitution of an original, where signifiers and signifieds line up and get in line, and where sememes are translated with sememes, and lexemes with lexemes, where words and sentences in translation mean what they were intended to mean in the original, whatever the strategy taken. But reflection on a pane of glass or a lens can distort the view to the other side, and Trainor invites us to pay closer attention to the flaws in the glass, the places where translation becomes visible, "the reflections, distortions, magnifications, depths, dust, cracks and blemishes that render a pane of glass perceptible."

Solange Arber takes her reading of the metaphor of transparency and its contradictory meanings in translation studies back to its source, with Chateaubriand's description of his translation of Milton "*calqué à la vitre,*" "traced over glass."[7] The reference to the technical procedure of reproduction draws my attention back to the material dimension of calque as described by Bellomo—not only in terms of the way that translation practices are described, but also the way in which they are determined by contemporary technologies of reproduction. Chateaubriand uses the image of tracing over glass to describe the extent to which his translation enacts an exact reproduction of the original. It is interesting to note that Chateaubriand's translation appeared only three years before the invention of the daguerreotype—a process that would promise exact, technical reproductions of an original reality. In Arber, the metaphor of transparency evolves concomitantly, in interaction with the evolution of techniques of reproduction, moving from reproduction to refraction. This shift accompanies a heightened sensibility to the subjectivity of the translator as the person who views and reproduces the original, like a photographer. This story of transparency and reproduction shows the extent to which translation practice and the translator's positionality, ethics and discourse are conditioned by or along with the material, technical practices of the reproduction of images and documents, as can also be read throughout the work of Karen Littau.

Today the word *calque* has other significations, other uses in French, where it denotes the image layers in Photoshop, as Trainor notes in another article (*"Cinema Skopos"*). This articulation of calque gives us less a reproduction through proximity—or distance—and more of the assembly or montage of fragments, like in Avant-Garde art. This could also be compared to the shift in the word "window," which is a semantic calque on the French word *vitre*. Now the word "window" gives not only the clear pane of glass for looking through (or reflecting), but also the opaque illusion of depth with windows layered one over another on my screen as I type this: Word, Adobe, operating system windows and internet browser tabs stacked together in calqued layers.

Word windows are also the unit of word vectors, the set of words within which the frequency of co-occurrences, the values of tokens are calculated and then cross-referenced with each other to form deep, layered, multidimensional matrices. These matrices then provide the data for the algorithms that produce the NMT output. And likewise, all MT functions through montage, rather than proximity, tracing, pressing, rubbing or the direct or indirect imprint of light onto a metal or plastic surface.

MT is not mimetic. All language in neural networks is ready-made, collected from found language on the internet and other databases. To create a translation, an algorithmic translator selects and rejects units of meaning and collages them together like a Jean Arp poem. The human's role in the translational process has followed suit, with humans reading back through the collages, examining and suturing the gaps and fissures, or with computer-assisted translation (CAT) tools like TM (translation memory), terminology databases, etc., collaging fragments into a final piece.

This is shown perhaps nowhere better than in another work of experimental translation by C. Bloomfield, "Deep Dante," which translates line 142 of Canto V of Dante's *Inferno*: "E caddi, come corpo morte cade,"[8] by collaging together all the solutions offered by DeepL.

J
Et j
et je suis et je me
je me suis... je suis tombé tombai
       tomba

moi, je tombe, moi,
la chute, le corps

     devenu descendu enlevé chuté
     en train
        mort chuté
        ainsi tombé
        resté tombé
           en quelque sorte
           retombé en tombant,
              chu[9]

What results is a poetics of calque: the reproduction of a structure, where the distinction between "wrong" and "right" translation is suspended in favor of a polyphonics that gives us an array of possible meanings and possible combinations, decomposing the syntagm into its individual words and assembling them back together in a rhizome of potential combinations. The individual words are translated in their full homophony, drawing out the word as a sensitive lexical matrix like a spinning light around a diamond or spirits from a crystal. Meaning and value get multiplied and confused here as the multifarious value of a word (its total use across the full extent of its contexts) becomes the motor for its meaning(s) in translation.

Trainor ends his article on creative calque with a practice-based proposition for four creative calques that not only multiply the possible variants of a line spoken in French by James Joyce in Jacques Mercanton's memoir *Les heures de James Joyce*, but flay it open to "queer marginal" (L. Bloomfield 437) meanings found in Trainor's own intertextual creative-critical reading. Here is the original along with two translations in French cited by Trainor in his article.

Original: "N'importe, c'était terriblement risqué, ce livre. Une feuille trans-parente le sépare de la folie" ("Transparency" 5).

Alan Bass's translation: "In any event this book was terribly daring. A trans-parent sheet separates it from madness" (5).

Lloyd C. Park's translation: "Nonetheless, that book was a terrible risk. A transparent leaf separates it from madness" (7).

Below are Trainor's four creative calques.

1. "Une foyll transpaREnte le say-par de la folly" ("Transparency" 8).
2. "Anyway, it was frightfully risqué that book. A transparent figleaf sepa-rates it from sheer folly" (8).
3. "In any case that book was terribly audacious. A see-through folio, a tissue paper insert, separates it from sheer insanity" (9).
4. "In any case, that book was frightfully [f]risky./A see-through folio sep-arates it from [sheer] folly" (9).

In the first, in a very Molnárian spirit, Trainor gives us a transliteration of what the original French might have sounded like in Joyce's mouth, speaking French with an accent. The second is inlaid with intertextual commentary, as both "figleaf" and "folly" refer to moments in *Finnegans Wake*. The third underscores the materiality of the book, and in this "see-through folio, a tissue paper insert" separating the book from "insanity," we recognize the fabric of a calque, a tracing paper. The last is a "synoptic conclusion," a "synthetic metacalque," a palimpsest that overlays the previous two translations in a rhizomatic multitude. Rather than clear or colored glasses, I am reminded of the shifting lenses of a phoropter, the device used by eye doctors to try out the different degrees of correction needed for a patient to see clearly, and the varied clicks of vision affecting my reading of the letters on the eye chart coming in and out of focus. I am reminded of the blurred lines of English and Spanish stacked on top of one another in de la Torre's self-translated "Equivalencies/*Equivalencias.*" Of two Bloomfields shimmering and shaking in a queer parallax, coming in and out of line like a faulty stereoscope.

The strategy of "creative calque" as laid out in Trainor's article on transparency and modernist translation is part of his larger project of "contrapuntal" translation and his "synoptic hypothesis," which proposes that in the future, reading and composition will become increasingly interactive across the simultaneous multiplication of texts in various states of becoming. Trainor attributes this to "new technologies of publication and composition that will make it increasingly common for multiple versions of texts to be interactively read, modified and composed together" ("*Cinema Skopos*" 58). He gives the example of screenplay translation, which works across several media, where neither the original nor the translation is ever fully at rest, caught in-between shooting, editing, subtitling software, doubling technology and later post-production publications. He even gives the example of the metaphor of *calque* as "a conceptual device in digital image editing software" ("*Cinema Skopos*" 59). In Trainor's synoptic hypothesis, translation and composition are not oppositional techniques but overlaid and overlapping, not linear. Trainor's process of reflection is creative-critical, and he puts his synoptic hypothesis to work in his "Synoptic Translation Prototype for *Sir Gawain and the Green Knight*,"[10] where, as one scrolls over the phrase "*votre version ici*" ("your version here"), lines from the original appear under the cursor, while on the opposite side of the screen, six translations appear at once, three in French and three in modern-day English.

In Trainor's four examples of "creative calque," however, only one type of calque is actually used, and it happens to be the one that is *not* proposed in VD: semantic calque. This is the type of calque that translates the "queer marginal" meanings of a word's internal form, whether through analogue, homologue or homophone loan (calque), impropriety, false sense or barbarism. There is a great deal of proliferation, of translating synonyms of individual words to try to get at all these queer marginal meanings, for example, the (mis)translation of *feuille* by "figleaf" or the added play on "sheer" or the double translation of *feuille transparente* in the third creative calque by "a see-through folio, a tissue paper insert." This is because calque does proliferate meanings, open to a word's potential to multiply meanings, read and compose simultaneously, synoptically.

In the Outranspo, we have several different ways of describing this kind of creative-critical experiment:

- Limentranslation: translates using the extreme limit of a word's meaning. For example, the translation of *feuille* by "figleaf."
- Hommeauxtranslation: translates the homonyms or homophones of words in the source text. Here I give the example of "sheer" in Trainor's addition of the word to "sheer folly," although technically the homonym is found on the side of the arrival text, since "sheer" translates *transparente*, which does not have the sense of "unmitigated" as it does in English.
- Ekphrasotranslation: translates by replacing a word or expression with a description, as in Trainor's translation of *feuille transparente* with "a see-through folio, a tissue paper insert."
- Multitranslation: translates with multiple simultaneous options of the same word or sentence of the source text.
- Distranslation: simultaneously produces two possible translations of a single text and edits them side by side, which can be seen in the collage of different variants to be read all together in Trainor's calque.

While the Outranspo never actually uses the word "calque" in our classification of constraints, I would argue that the above procedures are all variations and expansions on semantic calque, and demonstrate the capacity that creative calque has to function as a kind of semantic, etymological or philological creative-critical research.

Translation in six steps

This procedure of calque and of experimental translation more generally is probably what explains experimental translation's love of language-learning materials, and for the language-learning process in general. Or, this love is a question of readership and practicality, and of linguistic situation. On some level I will always be approaching experimental translations that work with languages I don't speak as foreign-language learning, floating in the ephemerality of the irreducible strangeness of foreign-language signifiers. Good news, I like being there. And maybe there is something deeply poetic about language learning, and we should do more poetry with students in language-learning classrooms.

"Translation in Six Steps: Thai to English," the second-to-last in the series of poems that make up the book *Trespasses* (2006) by Padcha Tuntha-obas, calques passages from a Thai language-learning book for grade 1, provided by the Ministry of Education and the Thai Teachers Association (*Trespasses* 74). The first calque here is of text type, since the translation pastiches poetry over the pedagogical text, copying, but also displacing, like a cut-up of the text from its context. This is another sense in which calque is a form of Avant-Garde translation, reacting to MT as the Avant-Garde did to photography: beyond collage, it also works with found text, decontextualized from its original ends and signed as art. However, the desire is different, since, rather than a critique of the institution of poetry, it is a critique of the institution of language. Tuntha-obas's poem reads language *as* poetry, reads the script of language as a poetic text. This is another kind of displacement operated by calque.

The first of Tuntha-obas's "six steps" begins with the original passage in Thai script, transliterated into the Roman alphabet below. Next, the reader finds a syntactic translation, a word-for-word translation that respects the syntax of the original text, with English words interspersed between Thai ones on the right-hand side of the page, like so:

(ชูใจ) (scratch) (neck) (สีเทา) (gently) (gently)

(มานี) (laugh)

(สีเทา) (raise) (neck) (satisfied)

(โต) (approach) (มานี)

(มานี) (scratch) (head) (โต)

(โต) (raise) (neck) (satisfied)

(ชูใจ) (laugh)

(มานี) (satisfied)[1]

Fig. 6. Step two in Tuntha-obas's "six steps" (*Trespasses* 69).

This translation is accompanied by a footnote: "In elementary school, there lived these two friends, manii and choojai, and their friends, seetaow the cat and toe the dog. Their textbook-world translated into our world, their language arose into ours, Thai" (69). This footnote allows the reader to understand that they are being led into the poeticity of Thai, through a translation of a grade school reading textbook. It also allows the attentive reader to notice that what is not translated, what is left in Thai in-between the word-for-word translation in English, are the proper nouns of the children and the animals: manii, choojai, seetaow and toe.

As Tuntha-obas's translation progresses, we are taken through a slow conversion of Thai writing conventions into English ones, with the addition of each layer to both the Thai and the English syntactic translation in parentheses. The English-language reader who does not speak Thai (like me) learns that Thai does not have commas or full stops. Tuntha-obas kindly guides us in the footnotes again: "But we learn, in English, people pause (,) and stop (.). A friend asked how I know a sentence ends. Straightforwardly, I answered, 'It says all it wants to say' " (70). The final phrase, "It says all it wants to say," appears without the period in Tuntha-obas's poem, betraying punctuation conventions in English. At the same time, the reader notices periods appearing in the calqued translation of the passage from the language-learning manual, there where they weren't before. She carries out a similar operation with capital letters, which also do not exist in Thai.

And Tuntha-obas does not stop there. The translation proceeds in a fully grammatically extended translation (translating the arrival language using the grammar of the departure language) applying the same strategy of adding the English signs onto the Thai transliteration, as they are added to the English translation. Each time, the reader gets a helpful pedagogical guide in the footnote, first indicating the added conjugation markers (the *s* on the third person), and finally, the addition of prepositions and possessive adjectives. The reader is left with a Thai transliteration upset with noise and foreign-language grammatical poeticity (in bold in the book), along with a fully transparent (in Venuti's sense), fluid and readable text that obeys all the reading conventions of the English language:

Choojai kaow**s** kor of Seetaow, baow baow.
Seetaow choo**s its** kor, porjai.
Manii hua-ror**s**.
Toe mahar**s** Maanii [*sic*].
Maanii kaow**s** hua of Toe.
Toe choo**s its** khor, deejai.
Choojai hua-ror**s**.
Maanii *is* porjai.

> Choojai scratches Seetaow's neck quite gently.
> Seetaow purrs, satisfied.
> Manii laughs.
> Toe approaches Manii.
> Manii scratches its head.
> Toe raises his neck, happy.
> Choojai laughs.
> Manii is satisfied.

(74)

This aesthetics of progressive collage, of exhibiting each step in the process of a language becoming another, is also used in Tuntha-obas's chapbook *Composite Diplomacy*, but in reverse. The reader begins with a self-translated poem written simultaneously in Thai and English. As Siobhan Hodge remarks in a 2016 paper devoted to *Composite Diplomacy*, there is an initial tension between the fact that the original is written in an ancient form of Thai poetry called KHLOONG SII SUPHAAB, while the English is written in a free-verse mode with no rhymes. However, what is happening is that the free-verse English is actually calqued from the formal structure of the Thai poem.

The translation of *Composite Diplomacy*, much like "Translation in Six Steps," unfolds in four steps, which Hodge refers to as "evolving layers" (8). The first follows a similar logic to the "six steps" in *Trespasses* published the following year, with a syntactic translation of each word in Thai calqued into English in parentheses for each line of the poem. The second layer is a blurb explaining how the poem functions in Thai. In the third, the reader is given a series of transliterations of the Thai syllables splayed across the page with an accompanying poetic commentary beneath each one. And, in a final section, these syllables and English calques are diagrammed in a visual representation of the complex system of rhymes, tonal pronunciation and intonation marks in each line as they are found in the traditional Thai form. Below these diagrams, the reader finds precise prosodic, formal, grammatical and lexical delineations for each syllable.

But what is the interplay between syllable and word? Between morphological and lexical unit, between microtranslation and lexitranslation or syntactic translation? I've lost my bearings, I'm disconcerted, dispersed to the side of full access, which is another norm of translation challenged by Tuntha-obas: Slater's "navigability," Cronin's "ultimate translatability." And indeed, "in Tuntha-obas's collection, it is ironically the English language reader who is made increasingly more 'foreign' by the English-language translation process" (Hodge 15). For Hodge, this is related to Tuntha-obas's "anti-colonial tone" (2) and intention, "inviting other translators, as well as readers of poetry, to question historical and contemporary processes of translation and transmission" (2). In the

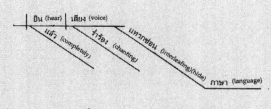

ยินแล้วเสียงร่ำร้อง   แทรกซ่อน   ภาษา

[Completely, (I) hear (a) chanting voice, interleafing that which speaks.]

Line 1

syllable 1: ยิน /yin/. t.p. 1st level; t.m: none. Verb. To hear. syllable 2: แล้ว /laew/. t.p. 4th level; t.m:2nd level. Adverb. Completely, Already, Readily. syllable 3: เสียง / sieng/. t.p: 5th level; t.m.: none. Noun. Voice. syllable 4: รำ /rum/. t.p: 3rd level; t.m: 1st level. Verb. To sing persistently. syllable 5: ร้อง /rong/. t.p: 4th level; t.m: 2nd level. Verb. To sing. (syllable 4 and 5, because of their alliteration and similar meaning, form one "double" word. รำร้อง /rumrong/ means to sing in chantry. syllable 6: แทรก /saack/. t.p: 3rd level; t.m: none. Verb. To interleaf. syllable 7: ซ่อน /sonne/. t.p: 3rd level; t.m: 1st level. Verb. To hide (syllable 6 and 7, again because of their alliteration and similar meaning, form one "double" word. แทรกซ่อน /sack-sonne/ means to hide by way of interleafing. syllable 8 and 9: ภาษา /pa-sar/. t.p: 1st level / 5th level; t.m: none / none. Noun. Language.

16

Fig. 7. Line one in Tuntha-obas's translation (*Composite Diplomacy* 16). Reprinted with permission of Tinfish Press.

context of this discussion on calque, we might wonder to what extent this has to do with the politics of specific languages in translation and relate this to a poetics of grammar, dictionaries and language-learning manuals that hijacks the standardizing, national or colonizing instrumentality of these materials.

Diction err

I want to turn now to another poet who takes the poeticity of a language as the script of its poetry calque, but in a very different context. Like Tuntha-obas's *Trespasses* and *Composite Diplomacy*, Nisha Ramayya's *States of the Body Produced by Love* interrupts reading conventions in English by taking the structures of language apart and rearranging them in a cut-up fashion. In this case, Ramayya situates herself on the side of the language learner (whereas Tuntha-Obas situates the reader in this position), as her writing follows in some sense the story of her study of the Sanskrit language. She takes this study as the material of her poetry, and relates this to the poeticity and specificity of the Sanskrit language.

I began the study of Sanskrit after a friend told me that this ancient language is poetry itself. Imagine the correct words breaking loose, line breaks arranging themselves in the burble. The terms of the promise are manifest: Sanskrit, *saṃskṛta*, well-formed, perfection of the gods, the beauty of artifice; hallowing conventions, preserving numbers, names of rivers and the rounded shapes of the aftersound. I am not alone in the *sanctum sanctorum*, nor free from intrusion. The nineteenth-century lexicographer Sir Monier Monier-Williams, author of a Sanskrit-English dictionary, guides me through the language like poetry; I crouch in definitions, dragging lamps. (Ramayya 18)

Monier-Williams's dictionary project was supported by the University of Oxford, with funds allotted by the will of Colonel Boden, "who stated in his will that 'the special object of his munificent bequest was to promote the translation of the Scriptures into Sanskrit, so as 'to enable his country-men to proceed in the conversion of the natives of India to the Christian religion'" (Ramayya 18). Ramayya's project is one of poetic questioning and resistance to the political and linguistic heritage of this colonial story, cutting up, dismembering, dividing her English with Sanskrit calques as a way of writing back. In doing so, she takes the poeticity of the Sanskrit language itself in its historical relationship to the English language, which also plays a part in her cut-up. The historical specificity of translation as conversion, as conquest, is also underpinned with an etymological specificity that runs through Ramayya's book like a pedal tone, as the homogeny and hegemony of the English language undoes itself in its material indebtedness to Sanskrit, as one of its language family roots. Ramayya undoes English through Sanskrit, also because English always already is undone by Sanskrit. However, her way of making poetry with the specificity of the Sanskrit language goes beyond its relationship to English, to its system of signification, which is totally different from systems of signification proper to European languages. This is not simply because its syntax, grammar, lexicon and prosody are different, but also because the semantic structure, the way these words mean, the way meaning inheres in language is different. This is what Ramayya means when she says that the language is poetry itself.

Ramayya quotes her Sanskrit teacher, "an Irish woman with her own pronunciation of the mantras": "It doesn't matter if you don't know what the words mean, they know you and speak you clearly" (21). This locating of signification in the words themselves rather than in a meaning that would be dissected and apart, abstracted from the word, extends to all literal features of the language, from alphabet to grammar. On pp. 22–23, Ramayya transliterates and then translates the Sanskrit alphabet for the reader, creating a poem entitled "Little Mothers." This title is derived from the fact that, in Sanskrit, the letters of the alphabet represent "the body of the goddess" (27). The consonants and vowels, and their placement in the mouth, represent a cosmogeny, an ontology and a metaphysics (although this translation into European categories of thought is not entirely apt): "Categories of letters are categories of existence" (28). The study of grammar is also a spiritual practice, and the universe is coded in microcosm into the structures of language: "The laws of this language reflect the laws of the universe, we might never come closer to truth. This language does things to me, this language that speaks you more than you know. This is putting you into practice. The linguistic and grammatical sequence parallels spiritual progression" (27). The Sanskrit language is fully material and fully performative, like a spell. Speaking and writing do not represent being, states or becoming, they *are* those things.

In her reading of Monier-Williams, Ramayya also asks, early on in the book, what she means: "My name is Sanskrit, I ask Monier-Williams what I mean" (19):

निशा **niśā**, f. night; a vision, dream; turmeric [Cf. *nak* & *nakti*; Zd. *nakht-uru, nakht-uru*; ... Lat. *nox*; Lith. *naktis*; Slav. *nošti*; Goth. *nahts*; Angl. Sax. *neaht, niht,* Engl. night, Germ. *Nacht*].

There are subtle elisions here, between naming and identity: "I ask Monier-Williams what I mean." First is the double entendre of asking this question, "what I mean," to Monier-Williams, the Oxford scholar appointed to help "enable his countrymen to proceed in the conversion of the natives of India to the Christian religion" (18). Ramayya's "what I mean" could then be read as a parody of sorts of the imperial impositions of naming on colonial lands and people. This double entendre is squared in the elision between what her name means and what she herself means, an elision that is possible within the poetics of the Sanskrit language, but not in English, where names are either familial, arbitrary or significant only in the very local context of the family.

In a sense, what Ramayya is doing here is translating her own first name as language. Amongst colonial languages, proper names are usually not translated (Ballard, *Versus* 2:106). However, names sit differently in different languages, and there are many languages where it is not at all uncommon for names to have meaning in language, beyond referring to the singular identity of the person they represent. In Sanskrit, names are chosen in accordance with strict astrological rules pertaining to the symbolic performativity of the alphabet described above in relation to lunar asterism, the month of birth, the family deity and the zodiac sign (Das).

Nicoline van Harskamp's project *My Name Is Language* gathers together a series of monologues from non-native speakers of English (the majority of English speakers globally) telling the stories of their names. In some cases, the stories have to do with naming practices, such as the Afghani practice of collecting names written on small papers and then choosing the name that appeared most commonly among the papers (42). Many of the monologues reflect on how colonial practices influence naming, for example, with the practice of women taking their husbands' names (53). There are administrative officials who reflect on policies of naming, like the fact that some countries, like Portugal, provide a list of acceptable names by law, 3,985 for girls and 3,496 for boys (61), whereas in other countries you can name your child anything you want: Rocket to the Moon (63), Batman (82) or Jite (88)—the last one being the fifth son of a woman who wanted a daughter, whose name means "enough" in Urhobo.

Jite goes on in his monologue to give some examples of Urhobo nicknames that "are like little poems, little narratives of their own," such as Onovughakpor ("who can predict what life can bring?"), Ighomuedafe ("money intoxicates the wealthy"), Ojakorotu ("everybody depends on everybody"), Udumebraye ("my presence gives them a heartache") and so on (88–90). For each name throughout the book, Van Harskamp provides a calque of all the names mentioned in the translation into English (even when the original monologue is in English), adding the mention "the one who" before each, so that Angela Merkel becomes "the one who is a messenger, who is a border guard" (68). Desmond Tutu becomes "the one who is from the south of Munster, who lives by the cliffs" (92). Shakira becomes "one who is full of grace," Rihanna "one who is basil," Britney "one who is from Brittany" (62).

In the performance of *My Name Is Language*, audience members are invited to sit in a bureaucratic environment, as though waiting for a visa or passport; they watch the monologues play on screens. These aesthetics of administration underscore the extent to which naming is political, a legacy of conquering state or colonial practices, or the way names get changed or mishandled in violent border crossings. Names get changed by officials who don't understand or don't care, or people may change their own names to hide their origins, or to separate themselves from a violent colonial heritage. Families can be separated by these name changes, or alliances challenged because of confusion in the transcription process from one alphabet to the other. Many of the stories told in the piece return to the practices of domination that can be inscribed in naming or renaming practices, and in the imposition of European, colonial naming practices, in a parallel way to the standardization and division of languages into monolingual, national entities:

We have 7,000 languages on the planet. Only 280 have been standardized and 70 of them dominate the world. All the other languages are in permanent transition. It's the same with names. Names can be stabilized and canonized like languages. The more complex the social structure, the more fixed the names. In an open urban networked society you need to have exact labels. The system needs to take your taxes, to punish you, to send you to the military, to monitor your data. If reference is all we still care about, we might as well be named with numbers.

(Serge, in Van Harskamp, *My Name Is Language* 50)

The intention behind Van Harskamp's collection of monologues and installation is to restore specificity to names and to naming by using the motor of calque to splay open names to their plurality of meanings. In Serge's quote, this joins with a politics of language specificity that is part of the global project of experimental translation: to give visibility to the points of conflict, which are also nodes of creation, in language difference.

PROCEDURES

2.1 Renaming

With a workshop guide sensitive to the delicate politics of naming, players are invited to translate their own names (this works well as an icebreaker with groups who do not know one another), or one another's names (for groups who know one another well), using Outranspian strategies such as

- antotranslation (translating by the opposite);
- microtranslation (breaking down a word into units and translating those units);
- endotranslation (translating by summary or generalization);
- ekphrasotranslation (translating with definitions or explanations);
- limentranslation (translating at the limit of words' meaning); and/or
- sonotranslation (sound translation).

2.2 Choose your own translation (syntactic translation) I

Using a collection of all the translations in a bilingual dictionary (such as wordreference.com) for each single word in a departure text, players are invited to trace their way back through the text by choosing one translation for each word—and not the one that corresponds to the original meaning—sticking to the order of the words in the departure text.

2.3 Les mots-gonds (hinge words)

Write a poem or other text using interlingual homophones—words that exist in more than one language and either mean the same thing (cognates) or don't (false friends)—as hinge words, repeating the word at the end and beginning of each line as players shift between languages.

2.4 Infinite sense translation (multihommeauxtranslation)

Find as many hommeauxtranslations (interlingual homophones), or simply translations, in as many languages as you can for one single word. Make a poem out of their translations.

See the supplementary *Handbook of Translation Procedures* for full, detailed instructions and creative results.

3

Literal Translation

vale solo lo que valen sus rocas   the obstacle to translation   el obstáculo a la traducción
is translation   es la traducción   and embodying that obstacle   y darle cuerpo a ese
obstáculo   is always a litoral wager   es siempre una apuesta litoral   veamos dónde
acabamos   let's see where we've ended up
                —Urayoán Noel, "Litoral Translation/Traducción Litoral," *Transversal*

Wokitokiteki.com is a website where poet Urayoán Noel regularly posts videos of himself walking in different environments while recording himself improvising self-translated poems into his smartphone. While the videos rove from city to city, the most regularly repeating sites are Randalls Island, NYC and Rio Piedras in Puerto Rico. This errancy follows the poet's sites of geographical belonging, but also the architecture of his self-translations, which alternate between English and Spanish from line to line in his poems. The above passage was transcribed from a wokitoki-teki stroll crossing the Bronx Kill from the South Bronx to Randalls Island, through a Puerto Rican area that is "rapidly gentrifying" (*Transversal* 28).

The poems also enact the theoretical knot of self-translation, which throws into chaos and confusion any binary that relies on a chronological or hierarchical order between original and translation, and their corollaries. One way it does this is by constantly changing the order of which language comes "first," as in the above translation, which alternates from English to Spanish, translating "the obstacle to translation" into "*el obstáculo a la traducción*" and "is translation" into "*es la traducción*" and so forth, until the end of this passage, where the order is switched, so that Spanish comes first: "*veamos dónde acabamos*" into "let's see where we've ended up" (29). This makes it impossible to track which text is the original and which is the translation.

But Noel also does not translate everything. Noel admits, "my translation are nonequivalent / mis traducciones son no equivalentes" (28).
Pebbles, rocks slip through the cracks, crags, as in the first segment of the
above passage, "*vale solo lo que valen sus rocas*," which corresponds to the
last segment of the previous section, which reads solely "is": "*por lo tanto
el barco de la traducción*   is." This is a kind of literal wager,[1] since what
"is" (and here "is" can also be heard as an equal sign), what is (not) translated, are the rocks, "the rock formations and the voice formations   *las
formaciones de roca y de voces*" (31). What are these untranslated rocks?
They are the "*extensiones   del roquedal americano*   extensions of our
hemispheric American cragginess.... that define our cities   que definen
nuestras ciudades" (31), the material of our landscapes, linguistic, geographical, digital, print and political. And there are some things Noel
chooses to translate, and others that he can't, for the very reason of their
materiality: the geopoetic imagery conjured in the word *roquedal*, or the
fact that in the English translation, Noel is obliged to add the word "hemispheric" to the singular Spanish *americano*, which, unlike in English, does
not just refer to the United States: the cragginess encountered in the translation or the untranslatability of "our" and "*nuestras.*"

This is what Noel refers to as the "litoral wager," which embodies the
obstacle to translation, which is translation. This "litoral" is nomadic, connected and crossing, situated in borderlands, both but also in-between
Noel's home places in Rio Piedras and Randalls Island. It is the shoreline,
a mobile boundary that is neither quite the sea nor the land, but the space
of negotiation between them—a space that is rising, overflowing, increasingly riddled with the material bodies of humans and animals, and of
pollution. It also marks the nebulous end of a nation-state's boundaries,
which is a literal metaphor for Puerto Rico, an "unincorporated territory,"[2]
both the United States and not the United States, where the political slo-
gan of the "American" revolution—"no taxation without representation"—
has yet to take effect. Noel is situated in the diaspora, in another litoral
zone: New York.

And "litoral" of course is also a pun, a homophonic play on "literal,"
which VD describe as a "word-for-word translation" (in Sager and Hamel)

that the translator can carry out without having to worry about anything other than linguistic servitudes. Literal translation is "a unique solution which is reversible and complete in itself" (VD/Sager and Hamel 34). But the meaning of "literal" (the word) is actually the opposite: various, meandering and incomplete. The word "literal" is also a pun in a way, because it is actually figurative, if we trace it along an archaeotranslation, looking at its semantic shifts, its slow, diachronic calques. Throughout the middle ages in Europe, "literal" referred to the letter, as in alphabetic letters, writing. In the Renaissance, however, through contact with the classical Greek figuring of metaphor as opposed to literality, it comes to mean its complete opposite (if you oppose sign and sense), referring to the natural *meaning* of words. Thus, literal is associated with the "proper," and is aligned with direct meaning, whereas the figurative or the metaphorical is aligned with the "turning" or "wresting" of these natural meanings toward an alien one, a foreign one, as Eric Cheyfitz posited in his 1991 *Poetics of Imperialism* (36). This is, in Aristotle, and in the later rhetorical texts and colonial practices that Cheyfitz analyses, aligned with a relationship of domination whereby the literal or the proper is consigned to the master (proper is also related to property), and the figurative to the foreigner, the barbarian and the slave.

This use of the word "literal" is actually at odds with the way the word "literal" is often used in French translation studies, and in particular in Antoine Berman, whom I will read through the work of Jonathan Baillehache. Literality and literal translation in Berman are associated with the letter, the *lettre*, and its "carnal, tangible, living reality on the level of the language" (Berman, *L'auberge* 76; quoted in Baillehache, *Désir* 83)[3] and includes rhetoric, because *la lettre* belongs both to the texts and the languages in translation, their specificities, as I described in the previous chapter. This is why Baillehache, following Berman, must distinguish between two types, or rather two phases of a literal translation, "translation of the letter" (*traduction-de-la-lettre*) and "work-on-the-letter" (*travail-sur-le lettre*) to differentiate between the letter of the original and the letter in the translation. This distinction is glossed in Cheyfitz, because Cheyfitz glosses language difference. Indeed, he aligns translation with the figurative (*metapherein* is and was a word for translation in Greek), and so there is no literal translation, because the literal is opposed to the figurative and thus to translation itself. By doing so, Cheyfitz actually repeats the erasure of translation that he reads in the colonial poetics he is critiquing, which he himself admits: "Lacking any direct knowledge of Native American languages I am forced in my description of kinship economies to use the process of translation that I am criticizing" (43).

Regardless, in Cheyfitz, literal translation is domesticating, whereas in Berman it is foreignizing. This foreignizing has an ethical intention (a *visée éthique*) insofar as translating by way of the sense, the natural meaning "hides a blind loyalty to the letter of one's own language"[4] (Baillehache, *Désir* 124). This *visée éthique* is located not in the appropriating of the sense—or the letter, for that matter—of the original, but rather in a desire to interrupt the logic of one's own language, to find "nonnormative zones, ways of speaking which, while remaining completely within the mother tongue, depart from the dominant norms of discourse"[5] (149). Baillehache reads these nonnormative zones as holes in the mother tongue, the "empty spaces in a loops of a fishing net" (85); a "translation-of-the-letter seeks in the language of the translation a heart made of holes" (86).[6] This is also the opposite of VD's approach to translation, which seeks to fill holes (as discussed in chapter 1), rather than to make them.

Here is where the notion of experimental translation, along with Baillehache's reading of Berman's literality, reaches a kind of limit, insofar as it is based off its oppositional relationship to norms: norms of translation in the case of experimental translation and norms of the mother tongue in Baillehache. Opposing norms presupposes them or at least sets them up in a specific time and place; the norms that I am critiquing through the lens of experimental translation are those established by MT, which were inherited from an ideology of the text as a record of property, authored, signed and inscribed into standardized languages—as unique, reversible and complete.

The title of Noel's poetry collection, *Transversal*, in which his "Litoral Translation" can be found, is also a kind of play on words, since we hear the verse of poetry and the trans of translation, but also a critique of the universal, as well as the "literal" meaning as a line that cuts across other lines. The epigraph at the beginning of the book tells us "transversal" is also a reference to Glissant's *Caribbean Discourse* translated by Michael Dash. The work of Glissant is a wonderful place to put into question the politics of challenging linguistic norms.

In the section devoted to *Langues et langages* in *Le discours antillais* (*Caribbean Discourse*, which I will read here in the French), Glissant gives us sixteen different versions of a warning printed on flags attached to the back of Martinican cars to dissuade cars behind from driving up too close to the car in front of them.

texte original : NE ROULEZ PAS TROP PRÈS
créolisation "probable" : PA ROULE TRO PRE

numéro d'ordre dans le texte	texte des créolisations pratiquées	nombre de cas
1	PAS ROULEZ TROP PRÈS !	10
2	PAS ROULEZ TROP PRE	1
3	PAS ROULE TROP PRÈS	1
4	ROULEZ PAS TROP PRÈS	2
5	PAS ROULE TROP PRE	2
6	PAS	1
	ROULEZ PRÈS	
	TROP	
7	ROULE(!)	2
	PAS TROP PRE	
8	ROULE PAS TROP PRE	1
9	OU TROP PRE	2
10	OU TRO PRE! TI PAPA	1
11	PA ROULE TROP PRE !	2
12	PAS OULE TROP PRE	1
13	SI OU ROULE TROP PRE SE PO	1
14	ROULEZ	1
15	ROULEZ PRÈS !	1
16	ROULEZ PAPA	1

Fig. 8. Glissant's table of variants (*Le discours antillais* 607).[14]

In Glissant's study, the creolizations make the French wiggle like a fish caught in the holes of a net. Now, is this a literal translation in the sense of Cheyfitz or in the sense of Baillehache? Does it appropriate the original and erase the poetics of the French? Or does it interrupt the norms and create holes in the net of its own arrival language? The answer of course is that it does both, but more importantly, neither. The French is far too present in the different articulations of the creolizations to say that it is erased; only the first example, "créolisation 'probable': PA ROULE TRO PRE" is in Creole—or rather, a "probable" Creole. This "probable" is why we cannot say that Glissant's observed variants are literal translations in the Berman/ Baillehache sense, because it is the norms of the departure text and language that are undone, rather than those of the arrival language. In fact, this undoing of norms is actually the norm of creolization. Creole already does—or at least did at the time Glissant was writing—what Baillehache's literal translation and my experimental translation seek to do by opposing norms that are the property of imperial languages. Once I leave these imperial languages and their attendant translation practices, these norms, and thus the articulation of my opposition to them, are undone.

Glissant's example is not an example of literal translation, but of litoral translation, "where standard English and standard Spanish (both languages of Empire) are disrupted and queered and where nonequivalence between languages is celebrated" (Noel, *Transversal* xiii). And while in Glissant's case the language of empire that is disrupted is French, there is a shared desire for a decolonial practice of poetics in translation that recognizes both the history of violence in colonial practices of translation and also the potential for resistance.

Technical resistance

This desire of litoral translation to resist politics of linguistic oppression is also related to technology. Noel's wokitokiteki project is litoral also because it is "lit oral" (*Transversal* 41). What you read is a transcription of an improvised oral composition. For Glissant, the oral is also an agent of resistance and disruption into the standardized norms of imperial languages, which privilege written literary traditions over oral ones, which

Glissant calls *oraliture*. The written is also where standardization happens, such as in the debate surrounding the standardization of Creole orthography; likewise, writing practices are historically reserved for the elite, or at the very least transmitted by an elite. Of course, for Glissant, the answer is not to return to a folklorist oral tradition but rather to move into new writing forms interrupted by oral traditions. To quote Glissant in Dash's translation:

In such a circumstance, the limitations of any attempt to standardize Creole are obvious. It is of no consequence whether you choose to write *Man acheté en hameçon* or *Man acheté en lanmson*, or *Mā āste ā amson*: the method of transcription that you will have used, no matter how distinct from a French transcription, will not prevent the weakened form of this language from already existing in your expression. We must begin by going back to the poetics of the language: the mechanism it uses to avoid the potential danger of linguistic compromise. It is based on this poetics and the consequent exercise of creativity that little by little the future forms of writing in Creole will emerge. That is the job of the storyteller, of the performer within the language. (Glissant/Dash 193)

The circumstance that Glissant is referring to here is the transformation of a phrase in "functional" Creole (191), used by Martinican fishermen: *Man gin-yin an zin*: "I bought a fishhook." For Glissant, the autonomy of a language (not its purity) is related to the autonomy of the circumstances of material, economic, ecological, agricultural and litoral production. The fisherman who uses this phrase catches his fish "in creole" and is thus "master of his technology, capable of transforming it, finding someone to transmit it to" (Glissant/Dash 192). He goes on to describe what happens to this phrase as it is uttered in superstores and specialty fishing shops: *Man acheté an amson*. Why? Because the language of superstores in Martinique is French, and thus the fisherman must adapt his tongue to the imperial standard of French in the same way that his fishing materials are standardized, mass produced, imported to be consumed: "The language of prestige has both established its values in the wider community and imposed itself on the practical world of the fisherman. It has imposed a written form, integrating its linguistic structure in a form of expression that then ceases to be expressive" (Glissant/Dash 192). In the French that corresponds to

Dash's translation, for "it has imposed a written form," Glissant writes: "*elle l'a littéralisé*" (*Le discours antillais* 609). Writing is like fishing: the literal is a kind of technology, and literalizing technologies of writing, transmission and standardization are likened to litoral technologies, those used to fish. How does this play out in Noel's "litoral translation"?

Noel is not just speaking when he records his wokitokiteki litoral translations, he is walking and recording into a smartphone. This is a kind of litoral translation of the figure of the flaneur into the digital age:

Baudelaire's flaneur fluttered in and out of the noise and bustle of the modern city, but in the digital age there is no flutter: we are all connected in profound and ugly and banal ways, and the flaneur is now a techie (TEKI) in a meaningful way but also simply as a composite of crappy apps (TEKI as in TECATO, Puerto Rican slang for a junkie but also something crappy or low quality). We are global overshare junkies yet we are lo-tech-tribal, much like the smartphones (digital WOKITOKIs) we carry. We are also at war (walkie-talkies rose to prominence in and after World War II): with ourselves, our cities and our bodies, as they are occupied, avatared, displaced, data-mined, profiled, surveilled, and, yes, bludgeoned in remorseless daylight." (Noel, from his website)[7]

Noel's poetics are therefore situated not just in the place where he is literally walking and composing, but also in the changing or changed technology of the literal itself, where the letter is not an affair of text and language but of code and voltage, data and algorithm, in the dynamic layers of the flickering signifier. And in fact, the ambiguity in the word "literal"— hesitating between meaning and letter—encapsulates an obsession with dividing the sign that has run through centuries of European thought and its fallout that takes up the question of signification. This division sets off a chain reaction of binary nuclei—signifier and signified, speech and writing, native and foreign, original and translation—that get exploded in the algorithmic age, where there is no signifier and no signified but data, tokens and algorithms transforming language into complex mathematical operations that the human understands through code and the machine through pulses.

It is worthwhile, therefore, in the discussion of how technology is changing the politics and poetics of translation, to compare Noel's processes of litoral translation to the history and contemporaneity of MT. The mass-produced, standardizing impulse of universalist ideologies that Glissant refers to as a literalizing process can also be found in MT, throughout its various incarnations. At each step of the way, Noel's litoral translation can be read as a questioning, a hijacking of these processes, to resist but also to try to understand fully their mode of operations.

When Warren Weaver first set out to build a machine translator to counter the problem of polylingualism, he sought to discover a universal code that would erase these sticky untranslatables between languages. He referred to his project as a "Tower of Anti-Babel" (cited in Slater). And thus he produced the quote cited in the introduction: "When I look at an article in Russian, I say 'This is really written in English, but it has been coded in some strange symbols. I will now proceed to decode" (Weaver 18). In this vision, as Slater has shown, translation is figured in militaristic terms: "not only is enemy language the language spoken by a group deemed an enemy, [but] even further, language itself is attributed subversive, enemy traits in its 'resisting' decryption, defying grammatical law, and hiding its intuitive patterns in plain view." We can see echoes here of Cheyfitz's reading of translation in imperialist poetics: "Postwar machine translation proceeded from the view that linguistic traits of incommensurability, ambiguity, figurality, idiom, and opacity were so much noise occluding the simplicity and power language could otherwise embody" (Slater). And indeed, Slater traces the genealogy of Weaver's code paradigm to the logic of enlightenment transparency—a logic that is also critiqued quite profoundly in Glissant. There is a desire in this search for a universal code not only to erase the "other" (of machine English in Warren's case) but to destroy them. As Noel remarks, we are at war, and his wokitokiteki invokes the walkie-talkie, a communication device introduced during the same war that spawned the first machine translators. However, this war is also being fought on different fields now, within our own bodies and the technologies that occupy, avatar, displace, data mine, profile, surveil and bludgeon with remorseless daylight.

In the 1990s, with the development of SMT, stochastic algorithms using aligned bilingual corpora were trained to predict the most likely translation of a segment. This alignment process was multiplied by individual language models that sorted out the language awkwardness arising from the fact that languages do not line up with each other. Stochastic translation using bilingual corpora is standardizing because algorithms that measure probability are inherently norm leaning, or tend to lean the data into norms. That is what a stochastic algorithm does: it determines the likelihood that a string of linguistic material will be translated in a certain way. It then proceeds to translate in the most likely way, which, because of this translation, becomes even more likely. There is an inherent, general path toward linguistic standardization as the machine learns and grows. Claire Larsonneur poses the question of this standardization not only in terms of linguistic norms but also of meaning itself: "Lack of diversity, standardization and control of language are iterative processes, so this trend may be massive. Finally, from a wider perspective, AI powered language production raises the issue of authority, not in terms of copyright but as the gateway to meaning" (9). For Slater, this is a problem inherent to what she calls transcription, the reduction of language to mathematical operations, where "translation and transcription become synonymous through the combined power of many, recently emerged apparatuses for quantifying language."

In NMT, instead of algorithms that line up language to language, there are algorithms that encode languages, and the equivalences are made in the encoding and decoding process. A set of numbers ascribed to a token in its vectorized state in one language aligns itself with a set of numbers ascribed to a token in its vectorized state in another: this is the form the process of transcription takes in NMT. Driving this, perhaps, is Warren Weaver's "Tower of Anti-Babel" being built higher and higher, data brick by data brick, because NMT presumes that once a language is encoded, it can be put into equations where two languages can be made numerically equal (or close enough) to one another. It presumes that the neural nets, massive imaginary spaces where words are plotted according to how they occur in relation to others, can be made to align, like vision in parallax, from language to language. But, does this mean that words and strings of words naturally have equivalent vectorized values? That if you entangle the words in just the right way, languages meet up in their embedding in these massive imaginary matrices? If "happiness" = .0456... in one corpus and context, does "*bonheur*" also equal .0456... in another? If "self" equals .12946..., does "*mismo*" also equal .12946...? If "*otro*" equals .327610..., does "*разное*" also equal .327610...? Does that mean that linguistic difference has officially been eradicated in the mathematical magic of word vectors?

No, or at least not all on its own. The machine must be trained. And it is through this training process that the values are brought slowly closer together, translation by translation, transcription by transcription, until "happiness" becomes equal to *bonheur*—in the right context, and not always. In NMT, the neural network used for one language is encoded and then decoded into the other and fed back through a process of comparison to existing translation corpora to measure how close the machine has come, and teaches it to reduce the difference, or the "loss" between the two. Massive bilingual corpora of both human- and machine-authored translations are used to bring the neural networks of the two languages closer and closer together, to make them more numerically equivalent, more universal and standardized. This opens the door to a great deal of shifting and uncertainty—something much closer to what might be expected from human translation. If you enter a text to be translated into DeepL at 10 a.m., and enter the same text in at 4 p.m., you could conceivably get two different results. Sometimes I like to read this as the machine learning to doubt, to hesitate.

While there are AI researchers that seek to embrace this uncertainty and doubt and fold it into the machine's modes of operations, Warren Weaver's dream for a Ur-code continues to haunt the industry of MT, where the goal is to reduce language difference to be as small as possible and to create sets of universally equivalent numbers that can encode and decode to produce accurate, faithfully translated texts in the blink of an eye. These translations seek to be literal in both senses of the term—faithful to both letter and meaning. And in NMT, this dream, which is not a new one, comes to a kind of fruition as the distinction between signifier and signified is replaced by mathematical values that seek to eliminate discrepancy and loss so that all meanings of literal are reduced to one. Letter and meaning, literal and figurative, meet in the number, their division undivided in the transcription where they have been processed so they can be extracted, mined for their data value to be submitted to algorithms whose malleability relies on the fixity that allows language to be calculable and thus grow and multiply in a general drive toward quantification for means of commodification. MT aims to offer a superstore of languages, where anything and everything is accessible at any time of the day or night, provided it fits into the capitalist imperial framework, mass-produced and delocalized, like the Martinican fisherman's fishhook.

One of the major motivations of this reification of languages is to reduce the weighty cost of human translation. And this is another thing that happens in the age of algorithmic production: the collapsing of the wage economy into an economy where everything is subject to value extraction. Carina Brand in her work on extraction and data mining in capitalist dystopia describes the way in which the "*extractive impulse* is written into algorithms that control all digital platforms and the software we use, from Spotify to Uber; the apps, devices and software that 'make life easier' are designed to extract value from our everyday actions, making us increasingly cyborg or constant capital" (104). This has the effect of "transforming social processes into quantifiable norms and outcomes through increasing biopower" (112).

But again, if the extractive transcription process of algorithmic capitalism is total, it is not entirely fixed. Algorithms are always shifting and the machine always learning as it sucks in data, and this data is calculated in relation to other data, both human and machine produced, which humans then use to produce their translations. Humans live inside the machine, just as the machines live in us.

This logic of occupation becomes a logic of hijacking in Noel's litoral translation, living within while always learning and undoing. Noel does this in a variety of ways, and first of all through his various processes of transcription and remediation, moving between multiplying media technologies in such a way that they move in the opposite direction of the one described above by Larsonneur and Slater, exploding out, multiplying and proliferating rather than reducing down to univocal codes, from voice to phone to video to text to internet to print. But his remediations also extend a heritage of orality interrupting the fluency of written forms in colonial languages belonging to the archipelagic tradition into which Noel inscribes himself. "Créole orality, even when its aesthetic expression is interrupted, holds a system of counterculture, a counter-culture; it carries the testimony of ordinary genius applied to resistance"[8] (Bernabé, Chamoiseau and Confiant 33-34). Bernabé, Chamoiseau and Confiant, in their *Eloge de la Créolité*, where they also cite Glissant, are not calling for a return to oral forms, but a drawing from the memory of these oral forms mixed together with the written—performed in the transcription process in Noel—that will give rise to a new literature of resistance.

Noel connects this remediation to embodiment: "And what if we added that translation is embodiment?" (*Transversal* 34) And this is another way that Noel hijacks the occupation of data-mined spaces, through the inscription of the specificity of his body in situ. This is three-fold, occupying digital space with intimacy, historical specificity and collective movement. It begins with the hijacking of the screen of his smartphone, a space under surveillance, where he shares the intimate, unique experience of his face and body, walking through the streets of the place where he is physically anchored but also displaced, in dias-pora. This intimacy is directly connected to history, both his own and of the place(s) where he walks. The beginning of "Litoral Translation/ Traducción Litoral" immediately situates him crossing the Bruckner Expressway: "a way to express   una manera de expresar   the leg-acy of Robert Moses   el legado de Robert Moses   en mi voz vasta y devastada   in my vast and devastated voice   de colonizador y colonizado   equal parts colonizer and colonized" (*Transversal* 28). The legacy of Robert Moses, who engineered forced displacements of poor and so-called minority communities, and built low bridges across expressways—such as the one Noel crosses in his video—to restrict bus access to recreational areas like parks, beaches and pools.

Noel's political positions, while complex, are clear. And this is the other way that he uses voice and embodiment to hijack smartphone space, by invoking the modalities of collective action, as Samuel Ginsberg ana-lyzes in his reading of "babel o city (el gran concurso)" in Noel's *Hi-Density Politics*: "More than just a recording device, the phone also symbolizes the communities and connections that technology can foster, transforming an individual voice into a collective one. While the hyperdigitalization of culture threatens to amplify the invisibility of marginalized subjects, that same technology helps create a sonic archive of countersounds that resist dominant soundscapes" (Ginsberg 145).

While I prefer not to speak in terms of "marginalized subjects" as I feel it groups too many diverse situations and identities into one basket and opposes them to another monolithic but in fact marginal (insofar as it represents an elite minority) voice, I do agree with the sentiment of occupying to reclaim space. Occupying to reclaim is an action that in its intention and its modalities brings together political struggles in solidarity. Rather than speaking for marginal voices, I read Noel's litoral poetics as joining in both the sentiment and the modalities, the practices and poetics of this struggle, in particular in digital spaces. This is not a polite, abstract form of resistance that in the end does not leave the page. This is real, embodied, engaged, litoral and literal resistance.

And Noel, as always, brings this back to languages:

but I'm more interested in   poetics that unsettle discrete languages   poéticas que desestabilizan los lenguajes discretos   devolviéndonos al cuerpo   returning us to the body   think of Anzaldúa   pensemos en Anzaldúa   fighting off the guards   sacándose de encima a los centinelas   her only weapon   su única arma   la agudeza   the wit   that lets her undo   que le permite deshacer juridical borders   fronteras jurídicas   logical borders   fronteras lógicas the borders that legitimize   las fronteras que legitiman   la violencia contra esos otros cuerpos   the violence against those other bodies   which are most bodies   que son la mayoria de los cuerpos   all bodies really   todos los cuerpos de hecho. (*Transversal* 34)

The remediation of litoral translation is not limited to a binary. And by binary I hear (at least) two things: the division of letter and meaning embodied in the ambiguity of the word "literal," and the binary codes that set off the material reaction that brings us to the technologies that occupy, divide and code for languages as discrete entities. But, this division of languages that the machine codes for is not hardwired, it is programmed by a legacy of imperial languages distinguished by nation-state borders, which is also, as Noel points out, a very literal history of violence against bodies.

And so the machine carries on—because humans program it to do so—the history of political violence that lives and is reproduced in the structures that divide languages. This also means that code-switching or mixing languages is a tremendously fecund site for experimenting at the borderlands. Any bi- or multilingual speaker can attest to the frustration of trying to navigate between spellchecker and word-prediction programs incapable of thinking beyond discrete language-scapes. And this is yet another arm of Noel's litoral translation that hijacks and occupies the machine, turning its own logic against itself (as it frequently does all on its own): using the interfaces in ways they were not intended to be used, and in particular with regards to language.

Meaning's undermining

In his *Hi-Density Politics*, Noel includes a series of thirteen poems, "trill set," that are "(mis)translations" (*Hi-Density* 6) of César Vallejo's *Trilce* read in Spanish into English-language voice recognition software, and then arranged to imitate the shape and form of the original on the page. This piece can be read off the page and also performed, as the poet tells us in his acknowledgments, either alongside the original or with Clayton Eshelman's translation. I hope you will read here the converging of the other figures of VD's "direct translation," as I have sought to hijack them in the previous chapters, as a material play of the sound and graphic of the letter in an *emprunt*, and also of the disruption of meaning in the unit of the word in *calque*. And indeed, Noel's work carries on translational work on Vallejo's *Trilce* as a site for experimentation of this kind in James Wagner's homophonic (or "auralgraphic" as he calls them) translations by the same name (*Trilce* 2006). Reading Noel's "trill set" alongside the original also gives a strange, slipped up sonotranslation with sounds aligning and splicing with meaning, hijacked for new meaning, lining up and getting out of line and slipping at the touch points of cognates and false friends between English and Spanish, full of improprieties, false meanings and barbarisms.

Mónica de la Torre, who also references Anzaldúa, and for whom borders are an important site of poetic invention and reflection as well (as in her translation using words of Anglo-Saxon origin analyzed in chapter 1), uses similar hijacking techniques in *Repetition Nineteen*. She does this in several ways, taking us through an adventure of human and machine interference that also tells the story of the temporality of the machine's poetics, which have radically evolved since 2012 (ten years before I am writing this). This is where de la Torre starts her first departure from the "original self-translation" (already a complicated site of origin) in "T4: Early Google Translate version from 2012," which she comments on in the third part of the book, devoted to readings of her translations. She cites Jorge Luis Borges and David Bellos at cross-purposes:

> Enter Google Translate, the most neutral of readers, perhaps the best possible one since it has no preconceived knowledge of what it translates or of the context of an utterance, and in producing **literal** [my emphasis] translation makes not only, as Borges would put it, "for uncouthness and oddity," but also for strangeness and beauty." It avoids reading *into* a text and does not differentiate between, say, a poem, a legal document, or spam. It takes words at face value, since as David Bellos explains, "it doesn't deal with meaning at all. Instead of a linguistic expression that requires decoding, Google Translate (GT) takes it as something that has probably been said before. It uses vast computing power to scour the Internet in the blink of an eye looking for an expression in some text that exists alongside its paired translation." (*Repetition* 81)

For VD as well, literal translation, or in fact all three of the first "direct translation" procedures, is the purview of the machine. And toward the end of their definition for literal translation, they actually reference Locke and Booth's 1955 *Machine Translation of Languages*, where Weaver's article cited above appears, although they ascribe the pertinence of MT to science and technology documentation only and consign its potential to "the existence of parallel passages in SL and TL texts, corresponding to parallel thought processes" (VD/Sager and Hamel 34). Like Weaver, they do not allow for the possibility of the machine translation of literary texts, where, presumably, thought processes would change as the text transforms to join its new language. As an aside, if you look at any translation of a technical manual, as I do with my first-year master's class in translation, the thought processes—along with the culture and norms of technology—vary radically from one language to another, almost as though speakers' thoughts about technology changed to suit the technology itself (or the inverse—the order is not what counts).

VD don't, however, seem to concur with Bellos's rejoinder cited in de la Torre above that "it doesn't deal with meaning at all." In fact, it is only because of corresponding meanings or thought processes (although perhaps those are not the same as meaning) that parallel passages can be made to line up. In fact, at the end of this section on literal translation in the third part of their introduction, VD lament that there is no "conceptual dictionary with bilingual signifiers" (35)—this is Sager and Hamel's explicitation of VD's original French: "*dictionnaire de signifés*" (*Stylistique comparée* 49)—and claim that if such a dictionary existed, "translators would only need to look up the appropriate translation under the entry corresponding to the situation identified by the SL message" (VD/Sager and Hamel 35). But, VD are Saussurians, and "the positioning of a word within an utterance has an effect on its meaning" (35). This is slightly stronger in the original, where "*le sens d'un mot étant fonction de place qu'il occupe dans l'énoncé*" (*Stylistique comparée* 50)—the meaning of a word is a function of where it is located in the utterance (my translation). This is, actually, precisely how meaning is determined in word vectors and neural networks: as a function of where it is located in an utterance. And so there is a way in which what machines translate is exactly that: meaning. That is how programmers refer to the vector values of a word: as its meaning. And if you look closer, it is the letter that machines often have a hard time translating, which, reading Berman through Baillehache again, differs from text to text and from translator to translator, and is what serves to *undo* norms (whereas the machine is trained to reaffirm them). And the list that Baillehache offers for some of the places Berman locates the letter can read as a list of places the machine bugs out: "in the syntax (inversions, enjambments, displacements), in the lexicon (neologisms, archaisms, use of unexpected or concrete meanings), and in the sonority (assonances, alliterations, meter)"[9] (*Désir* 84-85).

This complements an inherent paradox that is at the core of de la Torre's experiments and also of the meaning of the word "literal," for if we put Bellos's quote next to Borges's (both cited by de la Torre), what makes the machine a potentially fecund site for the translation of poetry is not the fact that it does not translate meaning but rather the fact that it does. That is precisely what it translates: the meaning. It is the letter that it leaves intact (that it cannot translate), in its materiality—at least in Bellos's description, where the machine is recuperating material and aligning that recuperated material to make equivalencies that change the meaning, that translate it. And this in turn is what accounts for the "strangeness and beauty" of the result.

Bellos misses this because he doesn't take into account the fact of the intervening "translation" in MT into code—and also, of course, because MT, as well as the access of the popular imaginary to its inner workings have changed radically since 2011, when his book came out. Now, although bilingual corpora are indispensable in the training of NMT, as discussed above, it is not exactly what gets translated. And even in 2011, when SMT was drawing from bilingual corpora, a process of decoding was still fundamental to the machine translation process, which is how Bellos defines a human process of translation that would oppose itself to the machine: "Instead of a linguistic expression that requires decoding, Google Translate (GT) takes [meaning] as something that has probably been said before" (134). While it is true that the machine presumes that the meaning it is looking for has probably occurred in a previous linguistic utterance, don't humans do that as well? How could we understand each other if meanings were not iterative at least from one human being to another? I won't come to any definitive conclusion on *that* question, but regardless of whether you believe humans understand each other's linguistic utterances or not, the decoding that Bellos opposes to the machine is actually the literal definition of meaning as it is processed by the machine. In fact, in some sense, read in that way, the machine actually has a great deal more faith in meaning than Bellos. Perhaps Bellos's extensive work studying and translating the Oulipo has led him to give greater weight to the automatics of MT than it in fact deserves?

Whatever the configuration of algorithms processing the data coming in, meaning is material for the machine. Bellos imports the opposition of the literal between letter and meaning into a system that does not code for it but that codes rather for numerical values ascribed to the material situation of signifiers, the likelihood that they will be found to line up or be in the vicinity of others. With the strategy of bilingual corpora that Bellos is referencing (SMT), this has to do with the likelihood of correspondences, whereas in NMT it is the likelihood of syntagmatic location, which corresponds to paradigmatic similarity within a given corpora. This too shows the extent to which machine translation has changed since 2012, when machine translation "did not differentiate between, say, a poem, a legal document, and spam." And in some sense, it is kind of unfortunate that machine translators are starting to take into account text type (this is already a common option for privately contracted machine translators), since this reduces its potential to make concrete poetry out of any text that it stumbles upon, by operating, paradoxically, a literal translation in the Berman/Baillehache sense, as a translation of the specific language into the "strangeness and beauty" of a plastic, poetic text.

In de la Torre, correspondence is also material, as she relies on the misspeaking and mishearing of phonemes by foreign speakers, and the use of the voice recognition in Google Translate (voice recognition is where NMT got its start, by the way). In all of these experiments, the difficulty of disentangling matter from meaning emerges as a common function of both human and machine: "the mind's inability to succumb to utter incomprehension" (*Repetition* 87). This is used as a way of subverting translational norms, to lean into matter to create erroneous meanings, which places de la Torre in opposition to the machine, which not only translates meaning, but seeks to do so well, without error (and it does not succeed).

T9 introduces a third language, translating from Spanish to Japanese to English, with occasional contributions from Merriam-Webster. In T9, "Your turn," de la Torre writes in the corresponding commentary that the poem "is not a concrete poem, but it aspires to Gutai" (100). Gutai is the Japanese translation of concrete, although de la Torre gives us the other dictionary definitions for the word, "*tangible, material, dense, firm, physical, solid, strong, compressed, hard* and *compact*," as well as the English "*specific, particular, existing* and *actual*." She also takes us through its etymological origins, the Latin *concrescere*, "to grow together," and traces the word to its first grammatical use, for "words that expressed a quality viewed as being united with the thing it describes" (100). This grammatical use of the word "concrete" brings us back to the machine, where the distinction between words and things gets collapsed into data processing, and where meaning is concrete. But of course, de la Torre's reference to Gutai is primarily a reference to the Japanese Avant-Garde movement, and in the purposeful accidents of meaning made by the machine, one might read Yoshihara Jirō's dictum from the "Gutai Art Manifesto," quoted in de la Torre's commentary: " 'When matter remains intact and exposes its characteristics, it starts telling a story and even cries out. To make the fullest use of matter is to make use of spirit." De la Torre's translation of her "original" from Spanish into Japanese and back into English aspires to this use of matter: "Its matter, issued forth by the ghost in the machine, is left unaltered" (100).

Another translation of Gutai is "embodiment,"[10] and de la Torre's translations, be they mechanical, human or cyborg, are situated in the corporeal situation of the translator—much as Noel's wokitokitekis always begin with Noel's voice and body in a specific time and place. This is the thrust of de la Torre's experiments with embodied voices—voices belonging to different bodies with different tongues—as they get reincarnated into the machine in voice recognition and translation software. In the commentary section, this also takes the form of de la Torre telling the story of her translations—for example the story of where she and Jane Fine were the day they made T5, a "version of the poem produced by a person with partial knowledge of Spanish upon hearing the original" (30): in a rapidly gentrifying Williamsburg, New York, where "the Mexican bakery where they sold quinceañera cakes has already closed, after their rent was jacked up to $12,000" (84), soon to be replaced by a trendy, expensive steakhouse. Or in the following translation, T6, "Composite of Google Translate app versions back and forth from Spanish to English using voice-recognition function, 2018" (31), which she compares to Alfred Stieglitz's *Equivalents* series, looking for figural resemblances in photographs of clouds. The singular perception of the viewer of clouds animates matter in such a way as to undermine the homogenizing impulse of the technology used for reproduction—the camera or Google Translate. De la Torre finishes this section of her commentary with a short passage, in a singular Spanish, describing the difficulty of interpreting the meaning behind clouds.

And yet, interpreting, giving meaning, is precisely what she does, in the paradox of matter precipitating inevitably into meaning. For the commentary to T15, de la Torre asks the machine what the poem means in what I presume is a transcript of Siri's responses to the live reading of "Llamaradas Are Blow Jobs," the "Unedited version produced by the Google Translate app upon a non-Spanish speaker's oral delivery of the original. Courtesy of Bruce Pearson" (71): "Go ahead, I'm listening. I don't understand what you mean by 'Camaradas are blow jobs.' How about a web search for it? Here's what I found: Madonna Promises Blow Jobs for Hilary Clinton Voters" (108). And so on. Here, it is the machine that provides interpretation.

T16 is the "Unedited version produced by the iPhone's autocorrect function upon trying to text the poem via SMS" (43). We read from the poem that her phone is trying to cope with Spanish while it is ill-equipped to do so. The machine bugs out as she does this, producing a polyglottal Dada mash-up entitled "Equivocation." Hunting for English in Spanish matter, it finds barbarism and impropriety, but also other languages. Here is the first stanza compared to its original:

T16 "Equivocation"

> UNO. Um solemnly, Ina llama dada.
> Um Sorbonne de café antes de que super smart.
> Um boho denture de um sfumato.

Original

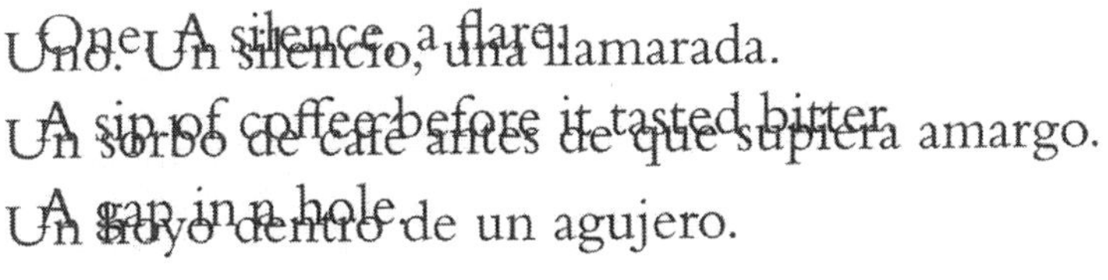

> UNO. Un silencio, una llamarada.
> Un sorbo de café antes de que supiera amargo.
> Un rayo dentro de un agujero.

Fig. 9. "Equivalencies/Equivalencias" (*Repetition* 27). Reprinted with permission of Nightboat Books.

The first UNO I read as the international card game. The poem in T16 then proceeds to stutter, searching for meaning in proper names and animals and art movements, in French, Spanish, English and Italian codeswitching. De la Torre's own commentary confirms this reading: "The ghost

in the machine is fond of radical code-switching" (110). She then proceeds in the commentary to give a stereoscopic exegesis of the poetics in
a kind of third text of the translation, a reading of a meaning produced
in-between the two versions that exists in neither of the two texts on their
own. She makes a list of "the ghost's astute swerves," bilingually, beginning
with "Ina llama dada," which can be read in English as the introduction of
an absurdist animal character, (Ina, the dada llama) or "Ina... and a given
flame," back-translating from Spanish, "llama dada." She continues on,
reading the switch from "libros" to "libido" later in the poem as pertaining
to the erotics of the book, of "nombre" into "bomb" as "underscoring the
violence of naming," and so forth.

In taking this final step of the "literal" translation of the machine into
a "literal" interpretation of the "nonsense" produced by the machine, she
collapses the borders reaffirmed by histories of the literal. The ambiguity
in the heart of the word "literal," belonging both to letter and meaning,
becomes the motor for new meaning in a move that appropriates and
hijacks the machine. The ambiguity can also, as we have seen, be traced to
histories dividing foreign from native, whether that division is articulated
as an opening of arrival language to foreign structures, or figured as an
alienation of the foreign through the affirmation of literal, natural meaning. The machine has of course inherited a strict division of languages,
which is the legacy of imperialism and of the nation-state. And so de la
Torre both adapts and adopts the machine logic of collapsing matter and
meaning, while intervening and occupying by pushing the machine to a
heterolingualism that it is not programmed to process.

From e-stranger to estranger

I have presented the different technologies for machine translation in a
teleological narrative, from rule based to bilingual corpora to neural networks. This is in part because this is the narrative that the technologies
themselves tell, in particular the social structures that carry them, the busi-
nesses, but also the scholarship and popular discourse surrounding these
technologies. The reality of course is much more patchwork than that, and
the way a language gets translated depends greatly on the status of the

language on a global scale. Standardization is also related to the status of a language, its place with regard to national borders and in the history of linguistic imperialism, and in particular to the dominance of English transnational flows of data and capital. The big languages of global imperialism are translated using neural networks and rely on massive quantities of data garnered from transnational digital flows. Smaller, regional, nonnational or minority languages have to contend with a kind of technological bricolage, and especially if neither of the languages being translated are colonial languages. If you want to translate, for example, Galician to Malayalam on Google Translate, you have to—or at least had to, up until recently[11]—pass through a third language like English, translating from Galician to English and from English to Malayalam. And while NMT advances are making this less and less the case, the NMT technology used to catch these languages in common neural nets will always be able to be traced back to models built around imperial languages, and in particular English. And even if minority languages don't have to pass through English to reach another minority language, the native language of code and the internet is English, as Rita Raley has shown ("Global English"). Likewise, while Google Translate is ever expanding to suck smaller and smaller languages in, many regional or nonnational languages do not appear on machine translators at all, which sets them up as privileged but also precarious sites of resistance.

But to continue on the cyborg codependency narrative that I have been following throughout this chapter, it is not just machine code that gets subsumed, englobed into English-language hegemony. People do too. In 2014, Annie Abrahams, a digital performance and language artist was on residency at CONA, the Institute for Contemporary Arts Processing in Ljubljana in Slovenia. While Abrahams speaks a number of languages, including French, English, Dutch and a bit of German, she does not speak Slovenian. In her book issued from this residency and continuing on her blog *(E)stranger*, she comments on the difficulty of getting people to speak Slovenian with her, citing an audience member who spoke up after the performance to state that they had to pretend not to be able to speak English or German to get Slovenians to speak Slovenian with them (Abrahams 51). The same is true, according to Abrahams, in her native Dutch, and she also references a project carried out by Martine Neddam, a French artist living in Holland, who organized workshops training Dutch speakers to learn and tolerate what she calls "Broken Dutch" (32). Abrahams also recounts her own experience of being advised to always start professional conversations in France in English: "Your French needs to be really good, otherwise it will be assumed you are stupid. It took me ten years to get over that stage, and still then some people said I was 'sauvage'" (26). This sauvagery is precisely what Abrahams sees in the figure of the *estranger*: "invisible, exotic, unidentifiable, rude, hybrid, blurry, deformed, subversive, incomprehensible, complex, pliable, lonely, abject" (64). One of Annie's experiments carried out during her residency, *ENCOUNTER*, involved her and Slovenian dancer and choreographer Maja Delak engaging in a five-hour meeting without resorting to English. Abrahams and Delak had met only twice for brief periods preceding the performance and share no other language (40). There is also a critique of linguistic mastery and an embracing of error as resistance to that legacy of mastery and linguistic domination in Abrahams's work.

Of course, the politics of French, Dutch and Slovenian are quite different, and the reasons for resorting to English vary in accordance to the political histories and currencies of each. Being advised to speak or write English in a French context has more to do with the continuing French complex of cultural superiority that motivated their colonial enterprises in the first place, and continues to inform their international policies, be they political, social, economic, cultural, linguistic or otherwise. In Slovenian, it is rather because Slovenians are enjoined to master English because of the minority position of their own language in the global hierarchy of languages and presume that foreigners do not speak their language because of this positioning. Even within Slovenia, it is only one of three national languages, alongside Italian and Hungarian.

When it comes to linguistic politics and diversity, machines and humans are relatively in sync—particularly when it comes to the obligatory passage to or through English. It is at the site of this hitch—or glitch—in the chain-link between human and machine languages within global linguistic asymmetries that Annie Abrahams carries out many of her experiments with language and digital technologies. Another of her experiments, performed and subsequently transcribed during her residency at CONA, is called *Kaj misliš s tem? / What do you mean?* During the performance,

Annie Abrahams, along with Martina Rusham, Jana Wilcoxen and Chantal van Mourik, carried on a live conversation on a shared text pad, where each participant typed in their own mother tongue—Dutch, German, French and English. The conversation is translated into Slovenian line by line by Google Translate and then copied into the Proteus text-to-speech (TTS) interface to be read aloud. Abrahams comments on the strangeness of the fact that, at that time, the Proteus TTS interface only contained programming for male voices, and so the texts written by the women in their mother tongues were not only being transformed by the two machine interfaces but were also changing gender. A recording was made of this machine-mediated voice, and Milena Gros, not present at the performance, transcribed what she could understand of the recording into Slovenian. In a final remediation, Igor Stromajer translated this transcription into English, which you can read on Abrahams's *(E)stranger* blog.[12]

Beginning with Stromajer's final translation from Gros's transcription of the title of the original piece *Kaj misliš s tem? / What do you mean?* into "You have to accept (a FEW times). New Language.," the reader is witness to both the "uncouthness and oddity" but also the "strangeness and beauty" of machine-translated texts from this time (2014). And Abrahams is situated in a tradition, growing longer by the minute, of artists, performers and poets carrying out language experiments using machine translators, beginning with (as far as I can tell), Scott MacLeod's *Tales of the OOtd War* from 1999,[13] which weaves together multiple source texts, all somehow related to war, and translated back and forth between languages using "online translation engines"—MacLeod does not say which, and this perhaps points to the increased agency of machines in culture since the turn of the millennium. His goal as well is quite the opposite from Abrahams's and that of the texts discussed in this chapter from de la Torre and Noel:

By similarly devaluing the appropriated texts' specificity of situation and voice by grinding them through the millstone of inadequate (and automated) translation, I hope to arrive at lean and sinewy, yet multi-faceted and hallucinatory texts that might refer to historical baggage without actually having to carry it. For me, everything is to some degree an act of translation, and "bad" translation is as much an opportunity as it is an obstacle. "Bad" translation, like war, can be a powerful agent of change. (MacLeod 123)

Here again we see the idea that machine translation is somehow "neutral," which I associate with the glossing of translation itself that I read in Cheyfitz. The idea that "everything is to some degree an act of translation" in fact mines the act of translation of its specificity, and therefore of its political engagement. This is the opposite of what MacLeod wants to do, which is rather to carry out a commentary on the way that war is a product of cultures' "inability or unwillingness to communicate through less violent symbolic forms." (123)

Baiden Pailthorpe's 2011 *Eighty-Four Doors: Google Translate vs George Orwell's 1984*, part of his *Lingua Franca* exhibition, specifically cites Google Translate in the title as he passes each paragraph from the novel through every language available on Google Translate at the time—fifty-eight—returning to English each time as a pivot between each translation. Rita Raley reads this not as a devaluation or appropriation of the "specific situation and voice" of the original but rather as "[asking] us to come to terms with, to process... the machinic dimension of the symbolic" ("Algorithmic Translation" 133). In a process allegorical to how photography or film changed the way people see, or how the printing press changed the way texts and knowledge are circulated and languages standardized, MT is changing the way humans are processing language, "from the grammatical to statistical calculation" ("Algorithmic Translation" 132), and contemporary experiments with machine translation are inclined to articulate not against but with the culture, politics and aesthetics of "human" language.

In other words, as the technology changes, so do the cyborg poetics of the artists working in this media. Bloomfield's "Deep Dante" is an excellent example of this, since, with the progress of DeepL, it is less and less possible to obtain results with adequate "uncouthness and oddity" by simply plugging a text into a machine translator—especially if you are working with imperial European languages. But another thing that all of these artists share is the desire to interrogate the machine, to inhabit and occupy its mechanisms, in a move that brings together a desire to understand and a desire to hijack and disturb. This is the Avant-Garde tendency of experimental translation, which situates it in line with a through narrative of the Avant-Garde as responding to material and technological changes. MT, like Glissant's fishing equipment, as discussed above, has a returning tendency (could we speak of a desire or a need?) to fix language in post-national norms, both through its collection of data and through the performative reifying of these norm-seeking algorithms that produce translations and learn from the bilingual corpora fed into them as well as from the translators who use them.

When a translator plugs a text into DeepL, each word in the resulting text hides a secret potential, a drop-down menu containing all (or many) of the possible translations gathered from the databases and by various data-mining algorithms. At the top of the list appears the most frequent choice based on the calculations of the neural nets. As you scroll down through the list, the choices become less and less probable, more and more unusual, odd and uncouth. Bloomfield's "Deep Dante" harnesses the potential for strangeness and beauty in the odd and uncouth in her arranging of the different potentials on the page in her translation, in a move that extends and updates the strangeness and beauty that Google Translate has slowly, progressively been losing over time.

There is also a way in which Bloomfield's "Deep Dante" experiment is in dialogue not only with Dante, and with readers of her translation, but also with DeepL itself, since DeepL is learning from her choices—all of them. In a way, as Bloomfield selects all the choices, from the most to the least probable, she is leveling out the algorithm that sorts these choices and codes for the best one—that is to say, the one that best calculates the norm. She is unlearning the machine, teaching it to lean into "Linguistic Remix. Shit translation. Beautiful errors," as Pailthorpe tweeted in his *Lingua Franca* project. This is first of all establishing a line of compassionate communication with the machine, because Bloomfield is teaching it to embrace a poetics that is all its own on some level, accepting that our languages are "no longer properly ours" (Raley, "Algorithmic Translation" 133)—and maybe never were. However, there is also a militant strategy here, an occupying and hijacking of the machine not only against the fixing of linguistic norms and the standardizing of languages, which increase the discrepancies in the hierarchy of languages, but also very materially for the human translator who might be worried about what these changes will mean for their job.

PROCEDURES

3.1 Choose your own translation II

A variation on "Choose your own translation I," this procedure copies down all of the menu options for each of the words of a text translated by DeepL onto a spreadsheet. Players are invited to work their way back through the options, selecting one word option from each column to recreate a translation without having seen the original. A wonderful variation on this is to use multiple items, as in Bloomfield's "Deep Dante."

3.2 Lutz to speech

A guide prepares the procedure by selecting a source text and running it through several languages on a machine translator. After printing the results, the guide cuts up each individual word from the machine translations and arranges them into separate envelopes to distribute to the players. Players then rearrange the words in the envelopes to make new poems that they can back-translate using the photo option on a translation app, or by speaking it aloud into the voice recognition translator function.

3.3 Blind faith translation in six steps

Beginning with a source text, players carry out first a "blind faith" translation, translating using no external resources whatsoever beyond their own knowledge, body and intuition. After this, they rewrite their translation with the aid of dictionaries, online resources, etc. They then carry out a word-for-word translation inspired by these resources, or plug the original text into a machine translator. A fourth step creates a translation that combines elements from the first three steps. This result is then back-translated into the original language. Finally, players can write about their process in a reflective composition.

See the supplementary *Handbook of Translation Procedures* for full, detailed instructions and creative results.

4

Transpose

Chingshi:

About north me hears is learned-up everything new langis
I heard in north, they learn made-up language everything new.

Si-gis letter being issue in some center automation, single-for-single being-living
A central automation issues 6 letters that are unique to each living individual

With that only need at them this one name.
And they need only this name.

Bato:

Ce last name never?
No last name?

Ce number never?
No number?

Nicoline van Harskamp's short film *PDGN* proposes a future English based on the fact that most speakers of English don't consider English to be their first language (Van Harskamp, *My Name Is Language* 8). There is a slow kind of translation happening within the English language, gradually transposing its features into a hybrid, nonstandardized new language, which Van Harskamp fast-forwards to create the script for the film, quoted in the epigraph above. In the film, women work on a construction site, building a new environment for themselves in a post-apocalyptic, but also post-capitalist and post-patriarchal society. Like Glissant's fishing pole, their language mirrors the material construction of their community, in this case, building a hodgepodge bricolage from repurposed elements and structures: "A proposition for a future language implies a proposition for a future world" (Van Harskamp, *My Name Is Language* 10).

The script for Van Harskamp's *PDGN* was built from years of artistic research recording, transcribing and creating performances and installations in collaboration with other non-native English speakers, speaking what she calls "Englishes" (8). This research was carried out both through her *Englishes* video series studying the history and future of English[1] as a non-native language and through her *My Name Is Language* project discussed in chapter 2. From these interactions, and always in conversation with collaborators,[2] Van Harskamp began to keep a list of linguistic divergences that "turned out to lend themselves as algorithms with which to modify a script in English" (9). With the algorithms, Van Harskamp composes, decomposes and recomposes English to use in the writing of the film. She calls these algorithms "distorters" in order to stress the aural and also subjective nature of PDGN, which she refers to not as a new language but as an "individual analogue tool." The procedure is only partly automated by "PDGN software," meaning that it is also partially artisanal. This tension between algorithm as a structural, procedural set of rules applied to language and the personal, organic application or undergoing of process, of code as language and language as code, is the place where I want to begin my hijacking of the procedure of transposition.

A data bank of these distorters can be found in *My Name Is Language*, some of which can be deciphered in the passage that begins this chapter. For example, in the first sentence, "<u>move</u> propositions [*sic*] to beginning or end of sentence" (165) as well as "<u>randomize</u> use of subjective and objective case" (152) and "randomize past and present verb tenses" (163). In the second, one finds "<u>omit</u> third-person singular verb ending '-s'" (160) and "<u>replace</u> indefinite article 'a' with 'one' or 'some'" (159). In the last two lines, there is "<u>add</u> 'ce' to beginning of sentence to indicate question" (166), and so on.

But not all shifts are specified in the list of distorters, and "distortions" also exist that are not listed as such, in the form of non-native "errors" (you can see this above in the confusion between "preposition" and "proposition"). However, these "errors" are part and parcel of van Harskamp's project—they are the very motor of invention of PDGN. And in fact, the idea of error, as I have been critiquing it all along, dissipates into the organic flow of language invention to such an extent that I am inclined to wonder, with Avishek Gonguly, in his reflection piece included in Van Harskamp's book: "What if we let go of the idea of distortion entirely when it comes to imagining future Englishes?"

Van Harskamp's PDGN is not a new language system, but it was inspired by one: Láaden. Láaden is a language invented by Suzette Haden Elgin, introduced to the world by way of a trilogy of feminist science fiction novels published in the 1980s. Like PDGN, it has an expressly feminist vision, aiming to solve for the feminist critique of male-centered language that occludes female perspective. To do so, it proposes a syntax, grammar and well-stocked lexicon that asks the question: What would a language look like if it was constructed in order to account for a female-centered reality? This includes a more complete and detailed set of morphological markers to describe feminine biological realities like menstruation, pregnancy and menopause—for example, *osháana* is "to menstruate"; *ásháana*, "to menstruate joyfully"; *husháana*, "to menstruate painfully"; and so on—included in the first language-learning lesson. It also includes markers that code for emotion, intention and relationship in language. Of course, one might critique this as an essentializing vision of femininity that reinforces gender binaries and excludes lesbian vocabulary (Okrent 248). Nevertheless, it is in an important source of inspiration for PDGN, and demonstrates an area where experimental translation overlaps with language invention: in its critique of technologies and power structures coded into language, and in its performative interrogation in the form of a decoding and recoding of linguistic structure.

Láaden—like Klingon, Dothraki, Esperanto and many other invented languages—is what is referred to as an *a posteriori* invented language, meaning that it was built from the lexical, grammatical and phonetic structures of existing languages, mixed together to form a new one. Elgin was also a linguist and a specialist of the Navajo language, which heavily impacted her creation of Láaden. It is also influenced by Nüshu, a Chinese phonetic script from the Hunan province that was developed and used exclusively by women. And so, like PDGN, it is a product of linguistic hybridity and mixing, a kind of deep layer translation coded into the foundations of the new language's syntactical, grammatical and lexical structures.

Charles Ogden and I. A. Richards's Basic English also shares a common point of departure with Van Harskamp's PDGN, in the rewriting of English to be spoken by the non-native speaker. By paring the English language down to 850 words and creating a system of simplified, regularized grammar rules, Ogden hoped to make English easier to use and learn so that it could serve as an international auxiliary language. While Ogden had Utopian intentions, one must not overlook the politics of English-language domination inherent in this idea. In 2106, Ogden's Basic English becomes the language of an authoritarian government in H. G. Wells's *The Shape of Things to Come*. Similar languages such as Jean-Paul Nerrière's Globish have international trade in mind, hoping to facilitate the movement of capital across borders.[3] Nicoline van Harskamp's PDGN has the opposite intention: rather than standardizing and universalizing English, she wants to deregulate it, messing with its rules in a way that is impossible to totalize, introducing chaos, opacity, distortion, multiplicity and foreignness to upset its hegemony. That's the aesthetics of experimental translation.

Weaver actually cites Ogden and Richards's Basic English in his 1955 article, likening it to machine translation, which "involves a presumably tremendous amount of work in the logical structure of languages before one could be ready for any kind of mechanization. This must be very closely related to what Ogden and Richards have already done for English—and perhaps for French and Chinese" (cited in Raley, "Global English" 295). If we situate Weaver's tower of Anti-Babel within the history of European invented languages, we can see that it is a continuation of a tradition of linguistic and philosophical inquiry that sought to unearth the hidden, universal code from beneath the mess of human sounds and scriptings. As T. Poibeau writes in *Babel 2.0*, "if a universal language existed, it would eliminate the problem of translation" (31).[4]

Arika Okrent begins her tale of invented languages in the seventeenth century in Europe, at the moment when mathematical notation had evolved from using words or syntactical abbreviations to a set of standard, universal symbols. This set off a revolution in thinking about how to create a universal language: "After all, by learning a few basic numbers and a system for putting them together, we can count to infinity. Couldn't the same be done for language?" (30). In her *In the Land of Invented Languages*, Okrent tells the story of Sir Thomas Urquhart of Comarty, whose Logopandecteision (1653) sought to build an "arithmetic of letters by which every single thing in the universe could be given a unique name that, through simple computation, showed you its exact and true definition" (27), and of Cave Beck, who assigned numbers to concepts in his Universal Character (1657). John Wilkins, whom Okrent treats at length, developed a massive arborescent taxonomy to classify notions into sections and subsections, where each notion would be represented by a syllable in his Philosophical Language (1668). These invented languages and others, called *a priori* invented languages, rely on concepts and structures from which to build a language system that would capture the purity of abstraction in language. Looking back at these universal language projects from the Enlightenment, the picture emerges of not only a common goal but a common methodology apparent in MT: to replace the messiness of linguistic meaning with the clarity of calculation. MT can be read as a continuation and a response to this history.

Leibniz's *characteristica universalis* developed a calculus of meaning in parallel to his invention of the binary calculus, whereby a set of primitives—notions that, like prime numbers, could not be reduced to a combination of elements. The logic of Leibniz's *characteristica universalis* is uncannily similar to that of word vectors. In Leibniz's *characteristica*, if you multiply or divide a combination by its elements, you end up with a numerical result. Umberto Eco, translated by James Fentress, gives the example of the definition of a man as a rational animal, where animal = 2 and rational = 3. Man could thus be expressed through the number 6. As a counterexample, he gives a monkey, represented by the number 10. However, 10 can be divided by 2 (animal) but not by 3 (rational), therefore monkeys are not men (Eco/Fentress 274–275). This is precisely the way that word vectors work, except that word vectors are even simpler: instead of multiplication and division, they use addition and subtraction, as in the example of "king – man + woman = queen."

Eco theorizes Leibniz's attempt not as a way of getting at the primitive elements of thought, but rather as a way of developing a procedure, a calculus, that would be purely rational, and yield true results, regardless of the input. This is exemplified in the transformation of Leibniz's *characteristica* into a binary calculus, based on his erroneous initiation to the *I Ching* (Eco/Fentress 284–287), from which Leibniz derived his system of binary codes inspired by the patterns of yin and yang represented by the broken or solid lines.

Those binary digits 1 and 0 are totally blind symbols which (through a syntactical manipulation) permit discoveries even before the strings into which they are formed are assigned meanings. In this way, Leibniz's thought not only anticipates by a century and a half Boole's mathematical logic, but also anticipates the true and native tongue spoken by a computer.... This is the language in which the computer can truly "think" without "knowing" what its own thoughts mean, receiving instructions and re-elaborating them in purely binary terms. (286)

For Eco, Leibniz's calculus is marked by a shift away from philosophical languages that sought to uncover the hidden essences of the universe and toward a system that sought this pure calculation in its ordering, its arrangement and procedure: "Syntax, which he called *habitudo* or propositional structure, was more important than semantics" (284). In other words, Leibniz was looking for truth in pure calculation, in the infinite possibilities offered by permutation and combination of the relationships between elements. Slater has drawn for us a line connecting the project of MT to Enlightenment logic. But Eco takes this back even farther, and reminds us that Leibniz was inspired by Raymond Lull's *Ars Combinatoria*, a mystical project sprung from the more magical thinking of the Medieval period in Europe. In some sense, then, MT not only carries on or carries out the dream of the philosophical and mathematical languages of the Enlightenment, but connects them with the strange magic from whence they came. NLP programmers are often heard referring to the "magic" of word vectors. How does this magic of combination, the potential for the calculability of truth in the permuting of syntax, play out in experimental translation? This is the question I will try to explore through the material metaphor of transposition.

Transposing transposition

Transposition is the turning point in VD's typology between "direct" translation strategies and "oblique" ones, and refers to translating parts of speech by other parts of speech, such as in the figure of the *chassé-croisé*, the transposition between verbal and prepositional phrases: "Blériot flew [v.] across the Channel"/ "*Blériot traversa la Manche en [prep.] avion [n.]*." To pick up where VD's rejoinder on automatic translation left off, oblique translation is what the machine cannot do. It is where the human steps in, and proves the necessity of the human translator. As the turning point from direct to oblique, transposition in VD lies at the fringes of the human, where the human meddles in whatever it is not. It is both mechanical and organic, mathematical and zoological. But of course most of today's machine translators carry out shifts between grammatical categories without batting an eye.

VD's description of transposition relies upon the functions of grammatical categories (things like gender, number, modality, aspect, etc.) and parts of speech (verb, noun, adjective, etc.) or what they call *espèces*: species (hence zoological), which Sager and Hamel translate as "word class." Here, I see the shadow of the arborescent structure used by Wilkins's philosophical language, which later became the base of Linnaeus's taxonomies of the natural world (Okrent 71). But also, in the idea of grammatical function, the function of calculus, the deep structure of mathematical thinking in language.

But actually, the term "transposition" as it is used in VD comes neither from biology nor mathematics, but from music, in the sense of the transposition from one musical key to another, which actually does the opposite of rearranging elements but rather picks them up and sets them down in another place without changing anything else. But if the term in VD seems contradictory, arbitrary and obtuse, it is probably because it is divorced from its original context. The metaphor originates from Charles Bally, whose use is much more diffuse and refers to any shift in grammatical function (not just limited to the play between word species as in VD) that maintains the "functional equivalent" (*équivalence fonctionnelle*) of a message. Bally's choice of the word comes from his idea that grammar is musical. For Bally, linguistic functions and procedures are inextricably tied to those of song, such as "intensity, melody and intonation, duration, silences, rests, and in general anything belonging to the nature of rhythm (for example, repetition)"[5] (42). To effect a grammatical or syntactical shift in language is to change its tonality, its sound. As Anna Gibbs writes, in a fictocritical meditation on mimesis in language: "We may have learned to sing before we learned to speak, by imitating birds" (7).

Locating grammar in music makes it not only organic but also notational and procedural, which is what will connect it with another use of the word transposition: as encoding process. Craig Dworkin's contribution to the 2003 volume of *Chain* substitutes each letter from an excerpt from an essay by Christian Wolff with its corresponding musical notation for letters A to G, with all other letters being represented by rests. The result is an eerie, minimalist composition of Cage-like indeterminacy. Dworkin's transposition treats musical notation as a code for letter distribution.

A code differs from a cipher insofar as a code substitutes symbols (usually letters or numbers) for a set of original or corresponding elements. Ciphers, however, are purely procedural, content to rearrange the elements in a message and substitute nothing. Transposition ciphers, in particular, consist of transcribing all the letters from a given text into a set of columns or rows, permuting the order of those columns or rows and then retranscribing the letters in their new order. Here is an example of a columnar transposition using the word "transpose":

3 1 2
TRA
NSP
OSE

Results: RSS APE TNO

There are a multitude of other ways to carry out a transposition cipher, using rows instead of columns, distributing the letters on diagonals, indicating a path for decoding like a spiral, adding in blank spaces between the letters, adding in the letters from a keyword to be deducted from the final result, etc. But like Leibniz's *characteristica universalis*[6]—or MT and

NMT—the original is deduced procedurally, through an instruction or set of instructions. One might call that an algorithm.

What emerges from this idea of transposition as a cipher? Let us not forget the coincidences of history here, between VD's *Stylistique* (1958) and Weaver's article on MT (1955), of whose experiments VD were well aware. Weaver's machine was a product of wartime logic, much like another landmark in the engineering of automation, the Turing machine. For anyone who has read Neal Stephenson's *Cryptonomicon*, you know that Turing's idea was inspired by organ stops, which control the rank (timbre) of notes on an organ. Okrent reminds us of the proximity, both historically and intellectually, of the development of musical notation and mathematical notation in Enlightenment Europe. This short story of the crosspollination between music and language, both leaning into the creation of a set of signals on the level of a metadiscourse that would represent—or generate— systematicity, connects once again "the postwar paradigm of code" to the "logic of enlightenment transparency" (Slater). There is thus an ideology deeply rooted in this impulse to systematicity that figures the foreign language, the language to be decrypted, as enemy. Seeing the "foreign" (text, language, people) as an enemy to be conquered or destroyed, this impulse to systematicity also shows itself to be grounded in the protection of national boundaries, much in the same way as the standardization of language functions as a vector of national reification, and also of colonization, which was one of the more unfortunate products of Enlightenment thinking.

In this drive toward standardization, then, one finds the desire to bring grammar closer to code, to systematize it in a deep structure that would transcend language differences, what Slater referred to as transcription, the reduction of language to numerical values. But transposition is a cipher, not a code: no numerical values are ascribed. Rather, the letters are submitted to an overarching superstructure, a procedure, that permutates the original material. There is an aesthetics of combinatorial automation, and of the matrix, that can also be seen in some of the poetic experiments in dialogue with the structuralist turn in linguistics, which was likewise fundamental for the first rule-based experiments in machine translation, for example in Dada and Oulipo. This might be likened to the aesthetics and epistemic virtues of scientific modernity in experimental writing as analyzed by Cecire. The same idea can be carried over into experimental translation that seeks to lean into this idea of grammar as a code and code as grammar. This influence does not go one way. Not only does technology influence art, but art influences or foretells technology, and many of these experiments actually prefigure technological developments. But before I get to that, I want to dig a little more deeply into what it means to see code as language and language as code in the age of algorithmic production, and also in the translational age.

Translating PDGN

One potential avenue for delving into the puzzle of language as code and code as language is to see what happens when code gets translated. Recently, there have been programmers and programming communities who have resisted the tendency toward English-language domination in programming as a heritage of colonial capitalism. One of these is Yorlang, a programming language based in the Yoruba language and written by Nigerian programmer Anuoluwapo Karounwi. Another is Jon Corbett's Cree# Language, which not only uses Cree words and syntactical structures, but also links this to the cultural uses of the Cree language, for example, with the use of the "smudge" command. The smudge command in Corbett's language clears the buffer, and resets the machine in an analogous fashion to ceremonial cleansing rituals practiced by the Cree. Outi Laiti's case study on an Indigenous (although she problematizes this word) approach to computer programming in comprehensive schools in Ohcejohka in Lapland provides a good theoretical framework for issues relating to writing code that resists English-language dominance.

But would calling this "translation" in some sense reassert English-language dominance, because it would presuppose that these programming languages were being translated from English, as a kind of base code? It is perhaps more politically potent to think of these programming languages as new writings, with their own structures, poetics and performativity, their own way of linking language, machine and world. In this sense, even if I wouldn't want to call these projects translation, I might call them experimental translation. But I would rather not call them anything, and let them call themselves what they would like to be called, in their own languages.

In programming languages, the line between language and code is not always easy to parse. This is first of all because of the sticky question of whether code itself is a language. A complicated question from the get-go since there are an ever-expanding and difficult-to-delineate number of programming languages and coding languages, and also because code is what the humans use to communicate with the machine. In this sense, it might be likened to a pidgin—or better, maybe, a PDGN.[7] What the machine "understands," on the other hand—what Eco refers to as the "native tongue" of the computer—is a series of binary pulses of voltages, which makes me think of the native tongue of the Ilish, a language family spoken by alien creatures called ils, who communicate through electric shocks.[8] If you think, like I do, following George Kennedy, that rhetoric is a form of energy, and by that logic that animals, even if they don't have language (which they might), have rhetoric, perhaps a comparison could be made between the native language of the computer and animal communication (again, both mathematical and zoological). But I'll save that for another time. In any event, I would hesitate to liken code or its voltages to something like a transcendental signified: digital signification is always flickering (Hayles).

It is not always easy or possible to tell where code ends and language begins (or where language ends and code begins). This is nowhere more evident than in the translating of electronic literature that codes for structures in the departure language where the translator is faced with a kind of dance between translating the content and translating the structure in a way that goes beyond the traditional sense in which all translators carry out this dance. The project Trope Tank started in 2007 by Nick Montfort at MIT takes on this kind of question as well as other questions related to the intersection of digital media and language, and is the context of many of the experiments I will discuss here.

Take, for example, Nick Montfort's translation into English of Andrés Viedma Peláez's "Olvido Mortel"—which was already in a sense a translation, insofar as it adapts Graham Nelson's Inform 6—a platform for interactive fiction,[9] into its Spanish-language version, InformATE. To do so, it must use a Spanish parser as well as Spanish keywords in the programming language in the place of Nelson's original English, because, as Montfort and Fedorova remark in their Trope Tank report, the commands given in an interactive fiction program must be in the language of its user. Code and human language overlap. When Montfort converts the code of "Olvido Mortel" back into the original English Inform-6, he leaves some of this code in its "original" Spanish: "The variable names, however, were left in Spanish. Strings of Spanish were commented out and the new English strings were added beneath them. In this translation there was no attempt to 'clean up' the original code" (Montfort and Fedorova 9)—although the authors of the report go on to lament this. But in most experiments translating code, it is English that appears in fragmented, linguistic debris. For example, Amílcar Romero's "Poem 21"[10] is written in Spanish in a BASIC program where many of the keyword instructions remain in English ("poke," "for," "print"). If you wanted to translate these into Spanish, you would also have to translate or recreate the assembler language that is underneath the code. When Nick Montfort translates the poem into English, this discrepancy disappears.

But the complications of the code and language overlap go even beyond that. It is not only because of the way language and code mix together in different interfaces, different programming languages and the fact that this proliferates along porting and remediation, but because when code meets natural language, each side reveals the other's hidden seams: the untranslatabilities of texts and languages that emerge and create problems when they get articulated in code, and also the way language is written into that code. And like any natural language, this gets messy.

Different translators of electronic literature have approached this in different ways. Some, like Andrew Campana, have opted for literal translations of the content, such as in his translation of Shinonome Nodoka's 2021 Javascript program that automatically generated parodies of contemporary Japanese poetry. The results give calqued translations that displace the untranslatable parody of the Japanese conventions into a poetics of foreignness reminiscent of Berman's overliteralizing strategies ("vegetable/the vegetable is troubled/it is troubled because it is a vegetable," to give one random example). Campana carries out an experiment that operates with this same dynamic in a bilingual piece that literally translates a series of phrases that could all be pronounced "seika no kôshô" in Japanese. The varying phrases ("The Artisan of Vacation Requests/The Authentication of Essence/The Loud Chanting of One's Parents' Home," etc.) permute and recombine, and the reader, whether they are reading it in English or Japanese, hears the same commonality, "seika no kôshô," like a deep pedal tone, overlapping yet diverging from the script they are reading.

Others, attempting to translate e-lit that is generated on the level of the formal structures of the language such as grammar, collocation, prosodic features or alphabet, choose to translate the underlying linguistic features that produce the final text. In these cases, the final text may be radically divergent, almost original, and the translation is faithful only to the generating principle. This is the case for the transliterations into Cyrillic (by Nick Montfort and Natalia Fedorova) and Greek (by Christos Dimitrakakis and Thodoros Chiotis) of "Concrete Perl" (Perl is a programming language), designed by Montfort, which generates concrete poetry based on a set of thirty-two characters in automatic recombinations (Montfort and Fedorova). In this case, it is not the text of the output that is translated, but the input material: Cyrillic or Greek alphabets rather than Roman. This, regardless of the experimental nature of both original and translation, as a translation remains wholly faithful to the original, which was not intended to make "sense." To translate its "sense" would then be, to a certain extent, nonsense.

Aleksandra Małecka and Piotr Marecki's translation of Michael Rudolf's Polish Perl program that generates poetry using context-free grammar, in a similar but more complex way, must use the arrival languages' grammatical systems as input, rather than the text that is produced by the original. It is quite interesting to note that Małecka and Marecki's translation was published in the same year that NMT exploded, since it works in a similar way: rather than translating departure text into arrival text, departure and arrival language meet in the translation of their own respective deep structures, neural nets in the case of NMT and context-free grammars in the case of Małecka and Marecki's translation. And, it is worthwhile to note that before NMT hit the scene, researchers like Michel

Galley and Chris Manning were attempting to develop MT on the level not of context-free grammar but of dependency grammar, but by way of a translation happening at the grammatical level of a text nevertheless.

And, in fact, attempting to translate e-lit of this nature, one that generates text automatically from formal linguistic structures, reveals linguistic code in a systematic way. In their contribution to the 2014 publication following the conference on *Translating E-Literature* held in June 2012 at Université Paris 8 Vincennes Saint-Denis,[11] Montfort and Fedorova give as a case study, among other examples (including the translation of Concrete Perl cited above), the translation of a poetry generator called "The Two" that rearranges syntagms to create a series of stanzas telling an aleatoric story. Each of these stanzas begins with a subject—such as the babysitter, the shopper, the driver, the student, etc.—a verb and another character to whom the first character relates. The second line of each stanza picks up with anaphora, a pronoun relating back to either the first character or the second—the reader does not necessarily know, and is perhaps invited to derive this through inference and circumstance, and the ambiguity is perhaps then deliberate. To give one example among the exponential proliferations derived from the individual elements:

> The student knocks on the teacher's door.
> He berates her.
> Each one learns something.

English is well-known for its ambiguous pronoun references and the hilarious miscommunications that can ensue. It is, in fact, one of the most notorious puzzles for programmers of MT that continues to turn back erroneous results (Douglas Hofstadter, for example, gives this as proof in a 2018 article entitled "The Shallowness of Google Translate" that machine translation can never replace humans). Who is the "he" and who is the "she" in this sentence? Montfort left this deliberately ambiguous: "The reader is left to resolve this reference."

When translating into French, Spanish or Russian, this system of reference encounters a number of difficulties, in particular with regard to the translation of grammatical gender. In French or Spanish, many professions or identities are gendered, but so are the determiners (*le/la* or *el/la*) and the pronouns (*il/elle* or *él/ella*). This is the case for the translation of the above sentence, which DeepL returns as "*L'étudiant frappe à la porte du professeur. Il la réprimande. Chacun apprend quelque chose.*" Not only is there no longer any ambiguity about who is reprimanding whom, which reinforces both gender and institutional conventions of expected power relations between humans in different roles, but the student is misgendered in the second sentence composed of pronouns (the masculine *l'étudiant* by the feminine *la*). The French translator resolved this issue by using only professions that do not take gender markings that also start with a vowel, so that the *l'* can be used in the place of *le* or *la*, for example, *l'économiste* or *l'entrepreneur*. In Spanish, problematic pronouns were replaced with *la persona* where possible. In Russian, these gender markers are stylistic markers, as gendering a profession in the masculine makes it sound more official or formal, whereas gendering it in the feminine often makes it sound more familiar or colloquial.

It is interesting to linger here for a moment to appreciate the way in which these translations demonstrate how it is not only technology that must contend with obsolescence, but also linguistic conventions. MT is sexist, and DeepL naturally automatically returned a masculine form of "student," *l'étudiant*, when I plugged the above text into its online platform. This is entirely unnecessary, as French, Spanish and Russian now all have forms of inclusive writing (even if they are contested), in the form of word endings (such as *étudiant.e* in the French), in the form of gender-neutral pronouns (*iel* or *el* in French, *elle* in Spanish, *kotorye* in Russian), etc. (Kirey-Sitnikova). In 2022, this would be the obvious way to get around the gendering issue in the case of the translation of "The Two," but it was considerably less obvious in 2012 (and it is likely that the translation itself was done even before that).

For automatically generated texts that work with story or narrative, the discrepancies in the grammatical code, as they meet the code for the automatically generated text, can also appear on the level of textual cohesion. Montfort and Fedorova make reference to the problem of anaphora, the translation of personal pronouns in the case of their translation of Montfort's "Through the Park" that permutes the sentences of a story such that, in each telling, nine of the twenty-five lines are omitted, creating new stories with each running of the program through randomly generated ambiguity, ellipses and erasure. When the story is translated into Russian, the translator must be careful not to introduce anaphora of this kind as the gendered pronouns would not cohere with the person they were referencing.

Montfort and Fedorova are careful not to include any of these pronouns either in the original or in the translation. In their discussion, their approach on translation is revealed to be surprisingly conventional: "The issue of reference does not present a problem for an attentive, precise translator. The sentences would probably be translated in a usable way by such a translator if they were simply presented without any additional instruction. However, it is true that a less careful translator who decided to work more loosely and introduce pronouns and reference would encounter difficulties" (7).

Here, both translation strategies and procedures are presented in terms of the classic translational binary of source and target oriented. And this underscores a common thread in all of the translations presented in Montfort and Fedorova's report, and indeed for other projects proposed by the Trope Tank, like the *Renderings* publication on Curamag.com, as well as in the articles published following the 2012 conference on *Translating E-Literature*. Namely, that although they deploy many experimental techniques because of the experimental nature of the text being translated, the translation is not in itself experimental; in fact it coheres absolutely to that most sacred of all translational norms: fidelity. Montfort and Fedorova are quite clear on this in their writings describing their translation process. But to take a quote from Robinson on translating experimental novels that I think applies here: "Why, after all, should the novelist be experimental and the translator traditional? Why should the novelist be wildly creative and the translator humbly supportive?" (*Experimental Translator* 78).

There are, however, e-lit translations that take translation to be the very mode of their compositions, and as such come much closer to what I have been trying to elaborate as a collection of experimental translation practices, rather than normative translations of experimental writing or coding practices. They do this by making translation the impetus of their composition, while at the same time also proposing a text and project of translation that departs from translational norms. It is not exactly the case that these translations oppose fidelity, but they certainly interrogate it, consciously, testing the limits of what it means to be faithful to an untranslatable text.

With this intention, Jonathan Baillehache's translation of Russian *zaum* poetry invites transposition into its translation practice.[12] He describes his procedures in his article for the *Translating E-Literature* publication, as well as in another publication that I will treat a little further on, *Translating Constrained Literature*. The fact that Baillehache speaks of the same project in these two different contexts is revealing. To understand why, I will give some context about *zaum* poetry and how Baillehache went about translating it. *Zaum* poetry in many ways is an analogue forerunner of Montfort's "Concrete Perl" discussed above—and indeed, Baillehache draws on Montfort for inspiration in his translations. *Zaum* poetry combines letters, phonemes and morphemes, in a more or less aleatoric fashion, to produce text that looks like words in Russian, but isn't quite. The linguistic material thus gives way to a constantly flickering interpretation, hovering between sense and nonsense, depending on the subjective experience of meaning housed in the random form generated by the text.

For Baillehache, the materiality of *zaum* poetry "raises the question of the difference between media transposition and proper translation" ("Remediation"). The nonsense words generated by the random rearranging of letters in *zaum* poetry also suspend the letter itself, in-between an alphabetical unit, capable of creating a word and thus meaning if put together in just the right way with other letters, and a letter as a visual, graphic sign. *Zaum* poetry is as much a visual, typographical art as it is concrete poetry. Baillehache thus undertakes to translate *zaum* poetry through remediation, across three different digital contexts, each giving its own potential for a creative-critical practice of experimental translation.

In Adobe, this is first of all a question of whether to treat the letters as typescript or as graphics. After reflection, Baillehache goes first for the graphic, cutting and pasting the original Cyrillic letters in Adobe, tweaking them when necessary to make them look like Roman-alphabet characters, performing "amputations" or removing "a leg or an arm from a Cyrillic letter in order to sew it back onto another and create a Roman character." This is combined with another form of experimental transposition with regard to spelling, since the traditional Roman-alphabet transpositions of Cyrillic would have given the arrival text an "exotic" feel that would have impeded the process of interpretive flickering and hallucination of meaning that happens with the text in the original ("Remediation"). In this translation using Adobe, Baillehache reworks the traditional fabric of transposing letters between languages in two ways, stemming from the dual nature of the characters of *zaum* poetry, between graphic and linguistic sign.

Multiplicity, translation in serial, is another hallmark of experimental translation. And in Baillehache's translations into Javascript and HTML, the play between "media transposition and proper translation" spins out even more. In Javascript and HTML, Baillehache is once again translating both the text and the media it is expressed in. In HTML, in order to translate *zaum*-poetry puppet shows, he creates an evolving translation that reveals itself in layers as the reader traverses the text, clicking from one stanza to another as in the stages or levels of a video game. To translate— or transpose—the performance aspect of *zaum*, he "used a soundscape of old computer blips and the sound of a wired internet connection from the 90s and hooked those sounds to the display of text generated by the user's interaction with the interface." This is combined with a visual aesthetic of digital nostalgia using the glowing green-on-black interface of early computer technology. Baillehache refers to this work as a "transposition" of the original aesthetic: "the imagination of retro-computing in contemporary cyber-punk fiction seemed to be an interesting **transposition** of Russian primitivism" (my bold).

For the Javascript transpositions/translations, Baillehache was inspired by both Nick Montfort's automatic generators of the kinds mentioned above (Baillehache cites Montfort's naming of Baillehache's program as a "*zaum* generator") and by John Cayley's *Translation*. Cayley's seminal work of e-lit presents the reader with a mash-up of two texts (Benjamin's "On Language as Such and on the Language of Man" with intrusions from Proust's *In Search of Lost Time*) in three languages: English, French and German. The three languages and six texts are submitted to algorithms that program for the text to appear and disappear across three varying states: floating, sinking and rising.

This is part of Cayley's project of playing with the notion of poet as engineer, and the way that "literary outlawry" (*Grammalepsy* 17) can be carried out in a digital context, which, for Cayley is not at all in radical rupture with non-digital experimental language practices, but rather in continuation but also in co-simultaneous dialogue with them. This idea of the poet as an experimental engineer joins in with the meaning I am hoping to give to the word "transposition" in the context of experimental translation: as a creative-critical way of tampering with the normative structures of language in the culturally charged space between languages on the level of syntax, grammar and code, and how these structures carry meaning, or not.

It is therefore notable that one of Cayley's earliest forays into this kind of experimentation happened with the desire to translate the non-linear structures of Chinese poetry, in his work *Wine Flying: Non-linear Explorations of a Classical Chinese Quatrain*:

Mutli- and non-linear poetics is a recurring theme in my work for other, more contingent reasons and is one of the concerns which originally inspired my move into machine modulated writing. As a trained sinologist who did research on parallelism in Chinese prose and poetry I was well aware of non-linear rhetorical techniques in writing. The computer's programmable screen offers the possibility of representing such tropes directly, and the development of writing for new hypertextual media should also lead to the development and better understanding of non-linear poetry generally. (*Grammalepsy* 17)

Cayley is primordially interested in what happens when overt attention is turned to language technics, the materiality of text in both its analogue and electronic guises. Turning the attention of a text to the materials and procedures of its own composition has the possibility to make visible and thus interrupt and disturb readerly expectations and conventions. One way to do this is through translation, precisely because it is where the materiality of the language and the materiality of text come up against each other as the relationship between language and text must be undone and redone in the process. Translation for Cayley thus becomes a model with which to expose the technics of writing and reading.

In Cayley's move between the classical form of the Chinese quatrain and programmable media, translation is taken as the impetus, the model of algorithmic processes, in both the electronic and the analogue sense. In the essay cited above, Cayley compares his translation of Qian Qi to attempts he made to create random text generators, but also how he was inspired by a letter from a friend written in an acrostic coded into the twenty-six letters of the alphabet. It is writing under constraint that prompts his idea to put programmable media to the service of the translation of the quatrains. His encounter with the formal structures of classical poetry written in a foreign language and culture therefore play a similar role in his creative process to that of his encounter with contemporary texts written under constraint in his own language of composition. That is because he is looking for and at ways to use what he calls "process" to bring the technics of language into high relief—the materiality and technology of their medium, whether it be print or digital, but also in terms of the formal constraints, the algorithms of language itself.

Interestingly enough, in an article for the *Amodern* issue *Translation-Machination*, Cayley uses the term "algorithm" to refer not only to a set of rules to be followed by the computer, but in a much larger sense to the procedure that undergirds or generates texts, whether this be in the constraint-based writing of the Oulipo or in the formal constraints used in classical poetry, such as the Chinese quatrain referred to above: " 'algorithm' might be understood as a regular procedure without any need for the constituents of this procedure"; "writing in programmable media" merely "literalizes process as algorithm" ("Translation of Process"). Let's not forget that the word "algorithm," like writing with formal constraint, existed long before computers.[13] Cayley goes on to rename his notion of algorithm as "explicit process" as a springboard to discuss examples of the "translation of process" that I explore a little later on. This use of the word "algorithm" supports Van Harskamp's use of it as an "individual analogue tool" and allows us to see the way math and experimental translation influence one another beyond a shared interest in programmable media, to the place where language and math collide, and sometimes explode, in translation.

Translation of process

In many of the examples cited above, electronic programming emerges as a kind of constraint on the departure text and also provokes the creation of new constraints. This can take the form of parallel constraints for the arrival language, as in the case of Małecka and Marecki's transposition of two different systems of context-free grammar. It can also take the form of grammatical constraints that must be invented and applied to compensate for the lacunae produced by the automatic parameters not working out in one language as they did in another. This happens almost as a kind of performative allegory of the way e-lit must be rewritten and recoded to contend with technological upheavals, to contend with the progressive drive toward obsolescence that requires old programs to be rewritten or retranscribed into new interfaces, new programming languages, new software.

This is part of what John Cayley refers to as "the translation of process," but again, it is not reserved for e-lit. Rather, it is a transposition of a "compositional engagement with technics that reconfigures or reforms the linguistic artifact in such a way as to enable readings that are significantly or affectively distinct" ("Translation of Process"). Part of what Cayley is doing when he refers to the translation of process is situating e-lit in a longer context of writing that plays off conceptual constraints and procedures. These writings, both digital and paper based, take up the question of the technics of writing—technics in the sense of the materiality of language and the technology that houses, supports and mediates it, but also generates it, and the relationship between those two materialities. It is not without cause, then, that his contribution to the *Amodern* special issue devoted to *Translation-Machination* focuses on the translation of texts under constraint.

There is a way in which translating texts under constraint confronts the same issues encountered in the translation of e-lit. Both of them reveal the structures and procedures that were being used to disrupt the reading expectations. This also brings out structures in the language in a very similar way to what I describe above, where e-lit pieces had to translate the alphabetical, grammatical, prosodical or other system fully in order to translate the generating structure. Cayley cites Carol Richards's translations of John Cage's mesostics, which have to rearrange the structure of the vertical name coded into the horizontal lines of poetry into another language, where the letters do not fall in the same place. In this example, we see the fascination with code and the rearranging of structure that motivates a lot of writing under constraint. In Urayoán Noel's acrostic self-translations, he encodes the DNA sequence of SARS-CoV-2 (*Transversal* 102).[14]

Cayley also cites Gilbert Adair's translation of Georges Perec's *La Disparition*, which is written under the Oulipian constraint known as the lipogram, a text written without a particular letter or group of letters. In the case of *La Disparition*, it is the *e* that is absent from the novel. The confrontation of constraint and language difference in the translation of process sets off a chain reaction of untranslatable structures, just as it did in the translation of e-lit. Cayley references the fact that, in Adair's translation, losing the letter *e* also means that you lose the past tense in English. And so, Adair's translation is transposed into the present tense. Other translations of *La Disparition* that Cayley does not cite take the translation of constraint even further, such as in the case of the collective Spanish translation, where the *a* was removed,[15] or the Russian translation by Valéri Kislov, where the letter *o* was removed. In these two examples, the most common letter in those languages was swapped out for the *e*, the most common letter in French, in order to preserve the constraint. In Shuichiro Shiotsuka's translation, this is further complicated by the fact that Japanese has three different writing systems, one of which is not phonetic, since Japanese also uses Chinese characters. Shiotsuka thus took recourse to back-translations of transcriptions of Japanese into Roman-alphabet letters, but also—since he did not find this constraint as restricting as the original—added to this the removal of the vowel sound (Shiotsuka 3). This is further complicated by the frequent reference and plays on the shape of the letter in the novel, and the fact that the original is divided into twenty-six chapters following the twenty-six letters of the alphabet. In Russian, this becomes thirty-three chapters, and in Japanese, thirty-nine, except that nine of these letters must be eliminated because of the constraint, resulting in thirty-three chapters. Shiotsuka uses the verb *transposer* several times when referring to the processes he engineers to translate Perec's constraint (1–3).

What we are witnessing here is the translation of process, whereby the translator must play the role of engineer, reengineering the constraint and thus not only translating but transposing the original. Nevertheless, as Cayley points out in the case of Richards's translation of Cage and Adair's translation of Perec, these translations are seeking on some level to do justice, in the most traditional sense, to the source text. But isn't the translational *visée*, desire or intention, at the end of the day, entirely normative? The brilliant and highly ingenious translations of Perec are the work of very clever translators, doing their job well. Can we call that experimental translation?

Some texts written under constraint resist this kind of compromise and compensation whereby the translator can navigate in-between form and content, preserving the constraint and, at least to some extent, the meaning of the original, as a good, well-behaved and faithful translator should do. These texts become completely impossible to translate "literally," and in a certain sense, a literal translation becomes a disobedient one, since it is no longer faithful to the original. This displaces the line of what is a just translation and what isn't, or at least sets it into a suspended state of the kind where experimental translation is working. As Camille Bloomfield and Hermes Saleda write in their contribution to the *MLN* volume devoted to *Translating Constrained Literature* cited above: "The translation of constrained texts often give rise to inventions which turn the figure of the translator into a figure of an author of texts liable to create a system of their own, relatively independent of the original, and to reformulate the traditionally vertical relationship between source and target text, in favor of a horizontal relationship rife with fruitful exchanges between the two texts" (966).[16]

One of the ways Bloomfield and Saleda refer to this work of invention is by way of transposition, *"la nécessité de transposer la contrainte"* (980), as do other contributors to this volume (Schilling 842). Baillehache uses it in the title of his contribution to the volume, "Traduire la littérature à contraintes: Traduction ou transposition?," which turns around the difference between transposition and translation, and the way he deploys both in his experimental translation of *zaum* poetry. This points to the fact that the way that constraint works within languages is a shift that displaces this kind of translational work from translation proper, locating it in the realm of experimental translation. It is no coincidence that the conference on *Translating Constrained Literature* that gave rise to the publication was also the event of the creation of the Outranspo, and that seven of the fourteen contributors to the volume are current Outranspians.

One of these Outranspians is Chris Clarke, who, in his contribution to the volume refers to the translation of constraint as a "*de/recoding*," "a process of reverse engineering, which is followed by the act of translation itself, and finally by a reinstitution or reactivation of the constraint within the source language" ("Impact" 882). You can witness this process of reverse engineering in his own translations of texts written under constraint. For example, in his translation of two S+7 texts for the anniversary edition of Queneau's *Exercises de Style*, Clarke used a dictionary as close as possible to the original one that Queneau would have used, found each load-bearing lexical item (so not determiners, prepositions, etc.), and counted back down seven words to find the original word to reconstitute the text. Once he had the original "floating base text," as he calls it, he reproduces the constraint in English. One of the examples given by Clarke involves Queneau's experiments using a basic, restricted lexicon from *Le Français Elementaire*, which Clarke associates—you guessed it—with Ogden's *Basic English*. The desire to deconstruct the constraints of an invented pidgin reappear here through the application of external constraints—what Cayley call a translation of process.

The fascination with the phantom of a basic code or structure underlying the messiness of language is precisely the material one plays with when one gets into the land of constraint. The figure of transposition that I have been treating in this chapter is all about systems, playing or inventing with the metareflective codes that have been invented to measure and classify language—or inventing new ones. In one of Clarke's ongoing projects, he is attempting to translate a nineteenth-century masterpiece by doomsday prophet and poet Jacob-Abraham Soubira, who composed a series of quatrains and cinquains each of which adds up to 666 according to a system whereby each letter of a word carries the weight of its corresponding placement in the alphabet (A = 1, B = 2 and so on). Clarke's translation attempts to follow the constraint to both letter and number, producing quatrains and cinquains adding up to the same sum in English.

Still other translations of texts under constraint translate the constraint itself. Karen Van Dyck's translation of Yiannis Efthymiades *9/11 or Falling Man* transposes a numerical constraint in order to reproduce a prosodic feature. The twenty-seven poems of Efthymiades's original are

written in twenty-seven lines of twenty-seven syllables, meant to symbol-
ize the twenty-seven falls from the World Trade Center on 9/11. The poems
are written in an "eerie conversational formality" (Collins 322) impossible
to reproduce in the sentence structures of English. In order to enable her
to recapture the song of grammar, Van Dyck passes through math, translating the twenty-seven poems of twenty-seven lines of twenty-seven syllables into twenty-seven twenty-syllable lines with a natural break in speech
between syllable 9 and syllable 11. This transposition of the constraint
itself goes beyond a reproduction of a constraint in a new language. And
this is indeed where Cayley winds up in his piece for *Amodern*, with Pascal
Poyet's translation of Lisa Robertson's *Cinema of the Present*. Robertson's
original is interwoven with an alphabetical constraint, with italicized lines
reordered according to the first letter, alternating with the plain, uncon-
strained text. This gives rise to a third text, by Poyet, a creative "index"
accompanying his translation into French that culls three words at a time
for Robertson's text. "Present: An Index" as an epilogue thus reads as a
series of twenty-six tercets, each composed of three words in English starting with the same letter. As Cayley remarks, Poyet translates Robertson's
doubling of plain and constrained text into a trio structure, reflecting the
interlocution of the translator's voice in the original.

Clarke's, Van Dyck's and Poyet's translations are all indicative of a
fetish for numbers and mathematics that one finds with many poets and
translators working under constraint. In Pablo Martín Ruiz's contribution
to the volume on *Translating Constrained Literature*, he elaborates at least
two ways that translation and mathematics might be brought into parallax.
One of these is the dream of a universal language as it is shared between
translation studies and math: that there is a code in-between or beyond
(which might be the same[17]) that transcends. Martín Ruiz cites Walter
Benjamin's *reine Sprache*, but we might also think of things like the search
for translation universals, Mona Baker's "third code" or, indeed, MT. MT
looks for or finds the location of ultimate equivalence, transcending language difference, in calculus. Babel, anti-babel.

Martín Ruiz also brings translation into the mathematical equation
through the notion of function. In math, a function is an equation that
solves for the relationship between two variables. The result of a function

is not a fixed entity, it is points on a graph that vary depending on how each variable plays off the other. Martín Ruiz sees in this an allegory for translation that he uses, in his playful, whimsical way, as a formula for "potential translation," the Outranspo variant of Oulipo's *littérature potentielle*: "Whereas usual translation would consider a limited number of possible outputs as permissible, potential translation could open those possibilities to any predefined relation between the two sets that we can, in principle imagine" (Martín Ruiz 927). To demonstrate this, Martín Ruiz offers us a list of speculative potential translations for Jacques Roubaud's sonnet "La Vie":

```
000000 0000 01
011010 111 001
101011 101 001
110011 0011 01

000101 0001 01
010101 011 001
010111 001 001
010101 0001 01

01 01 01 0010 11
01 01 01 01 01 11
001 001 010 101

000 1 0 1 001 00 0
0 0 0 0 0 110 0 0 0 101
0 0 0 0 01 0 0 0 0 0 0
```

Martín Ruiz proposes a number of potential translations for Roubaud's poem, including lexical substitutions or transductions, such as translating 0 as "death" or 1 as "love" (or the inverse), or as black and white, red and blue, etc. But this is translation after all, and he also proposes translating each line by a different natural language, or even into unknown languages. This translation toward the unknown can be derived from the function of the translation: "We can postulate or imagine a possible language for the original and proceed from there. All we need is to define a function, a relation between the two sets: the elements in the poem and the elements in the output" (929). He proposes translating the formal elements such as rhyme, meter or the disposition of the different elements in patterns throughout the poem. And, he suggests, we do not need to stop there: these translations can be retranslated (translated from the translation), retrotranslated (translated from the translation back into the language of the original), antitranslated (translated against a previous translation)... giving way to the combinatory and permuting, but also procedural character of potential writing and translation. It is from Martín Ruiz's invitation that the classification of Outranspian constraints and procedures were born. And this, of all the examples I have studied in this chapter, is the only one that, in my view, actually seeks to translate the computer's native tongue.

(Dis)solving

Martín Ruiz's vision of potential translation is grounded in something like the potential energy of a text (although he does not use this term), in the idea that a text can be infinitely translated, and that the relationships between these translations introduce a permuting, exponential dimension to texts. This proliferating quality is inexhaustible, to the point where all texts can be read as translations of all others. This is mimed in writing under constraint, which Martín Ruiz postulates as a kind of translation, if only because one might deduce, from a text written under constraint, an original where that constraint was undone—not unlike Chris Clarke's reverse engineering. For Rachel Galvin in the *Translating Constrained Literature* volume, "to translate is always to write under constraints. Translation is a constraint compounded since texts must be crafted in response to two sets of conditions" ("Reasons" 855). And this takes us back to Cayley's notion of process, the translation of process and translation as a model for process, and for writing under constraint.

For Cayley, this is also because the translation of process reveals the constraint, upheaves its layers. I mention earlier on that there is a way in which writing under constraint both responds to and foretells the regimes and relations of digital signification. Indeed, this is the guiding argument of this book, that experimental translation interrogates, mimes, resists, composes, decomposes, codes, decodes the innerworkings of the algorithmic production of language in translation. Computer language(s) are stratified, flickering and responding across interconnecting layers: this is how deep learning functions, across layers responding dynamically, in variable function to one another.

Experimental translation can be a transposition of itself, its own inner workings, its own constraints, housing a practice-based metareflection of its own grammar, as the laws governing linguistic arrangement. This is the case of Craig Dworkin's *Parse*, which translates Edwin A. Abbott's *How to Parse: An Attempt to Apply the Principle of Scholarship to English Grammar*.[18] Dworkin's transposition might be read as falling outside my overstrict parameters of what should be considered experimental translation in the true sense, since it is homolinguistic, translating a book written in English into English. However, although Abbott's book is in English, and is about English grammar, it is also in many ways about Latin, since its mission is to apply the laws of Latin grammar to English, as Dworkin tells us in the short postface. Thus Dworkin's translation is actually in Latin, written in the structure of Latin grammar, in spite of the words being in English. Because of this, it falls into the Outranspian category of the "grammatically extended translation" or a translation that follows the grammar of a third language. Dworkin's *Parse* is a potential translation because it doesn't just work between two sets but defines the elements of at least one of the two sets, and so can vary and deregulate the function of translation.

When I describe Dworkin's book to people, I often get a kind of blustery "but you can't possibly *read* a book like that" reaction, which is also the predicted and perhaps desired reaction of a lot of conceptual writing. However, not only does Dworkin's theoretical work provide ample guidebooks and road maps for how to read unreadable or illegible work,[19] but Dworkin's system, in a metacommentary on the system of grammar itself, breaks down in aporia throughout the text. These aporia increase and decrease across the span of the book, perhaps miming the lyric, rhetorical experience of Dworkin himself, his frustration, fatigue and fascination with the arduous task he has imposed on himself. A good example can be found about two-thirds of the way through the book: .

Locative Preposition noun genitive preposition plural adjective and plural noun all suggesting that the proliferating number of exceptions is beginning to cause the clear statement of categorical rules to slip in reality from the author's rhetorical grasp indefinite article Noun deigning auxiliary infinitive and participle put in a passive verbal phrase to suggest that the exceptions to the rule might be attributed to the vagaries of perversely exercised free will in the face of otherwise rational and divinely sanctioned laws adverb definite article Noun comma adverb em dash. (197)

Dworkin's translation of Abbott's system is not systematic. This is also Dworkin's reading of Abbott's grammar, which strives against all odds to be so. Dworkin's lyrical moments happen when the grammar breaks apart, or when his own contact with the text breaks apart, through rhetorical energy, moved by random lines of pathos in the examples or by his own frustration at the rigidity, stupidity, sexism, etc., in Abbott's grammar, or in a reflection on the domination inherent in Abbott's system and approach. These aporia take the form of both Dworkin's own voice inserted into the text, reading the original, and his own translation of it, or the form of non-translations, particularly of the examples, which are not systematically translated. Further on, the reader finds: "on account of a desire for brevity, for the phrase 'he would have loved her if she had been' masculine singular third person genitive case..." (*Parse* 231).

This transposes an example given in a section entitled "How to Explain Irregularities" in Abbott's book, which reads in the original as follow:

(1) "'He loved her *as* his own daughter,' *i.e.*, 'as (he would have loved her, if she had been) his own daughter.' (Brevity)." (Abbott 130)

In performative metareflection, Dworkin abbreviates the example, decontextualizing and recontextualizing a movement of pathos in the reader, or at least in this reader. As I noted in chapter 2, experimental translation often finds itself fascinated with language manuals, grammars and language-learning textbooks, with the uncanny, out of place "uncouthness or beauty" in the content of lines of language meant to be read only for their structure. Writing under constraint does not just see form, structure or material in the place of meaning, but it also reads meaning into structure where it is not intended to be.

You can also add a third language to the mix, translating between two languages with the grammar of the third. An example of this is Clarke's "Tlönslation," which uses the structure of the speculative language of the Tlönians, culled from Borges's short story "Tlön, Uqbar, Orbis Tertius" as a constraint on his translation of the poem "La Caverne" by Robert Desnos into English. As Clarke explains in the introduction to his translation, the Tlön language contains no nouns, "since for the Tlönians, nothing exists outside of perception (meaning there are no 'objects,' but only what human senses perceive)." In the first two lines of Clarke's translation, this gives:

Original: Voici dans les rochers l'accès du corridor
Il descend, dans la nuit, au cœur de la planète
Gloss: Here in the rocks the opening of the corridor
He descends, in the night, to the heart of the planet.

Tlönslation: Here in craggy petrous-gray, open and permissive to the long, narrow and passagelike /
Descending, in dark, sleepy and somber-starless to the most central, vascular and cardinal of the spherical, earthen and gravitational-bound /

Here, what we have is a translation from one given set to another, in the way of a usual translation (French to English), but interrupted by a third set in the form of a structure, or a structural constraint, creating disruptions in the plotted line of the function.

As with all of the seven procedures I have been hijacking throughout, the line between experimental translation and the translation of experimental and untranslatable texts is often overstepped. With transposition, this can often happen in the creation of a new language in translation—often by mixing languages together, in a gesture reminiscent of the creation of a posteriori languages like Láaden, Klingon or Esperanto. A notable example of this can be found in Samuel Millogo and Amadou Bissiri's translation of Ken Saro-Wiwa's Sozaboy. Sozaboy is written in what the author calls "Rotten English," a literary language unique to the author that hijacks colonial English by drawing on Nigerian pidgin and mixing it together with other interruptions and registers. To translate it, Millogo and Bissiri invent an "imaginary language"[20] shot through with influence from FPA (Français populaire d'Abidjan).

Another example is Erín Moure's "Frenglish" that she invents to translate Wilson Bueno's *Paraguayan Sea* written in Portunhal, a Spanish-Portuguese mixture from the border of Brazil, Argentina and Paraguay. Moure's Frenglish doesn't just mix French and English words, it contaminates their structures: "I can trumpet it avec ma bouche wide open, even if no one's paying attention to me: it wasn't moi who killéd le vieux guy."[21]

This contamination is not an easy math of 1+1 = 2 but a complex relay of multiplication that creates a third or nth code in the translation of Bueno's language-mixing process. This is one of the ways that Moure enacts a translation of process, and in so doing makes visible the algorithms of language, which in Moure are not only conceptual but lyrical—like a formal constraint. This lyricism is to be found in the model of translation as process and in the record, the archive of modulations in Moure's own personal translation experience.

PROCEDURES

4.1 Grammatically extended neotranslation

With a guide who has selected a line of text, players invent their own distortions based on rules inspired by linguistic systems other than that of the original, or by making them up. Using a board or projection, the players apply the rules along with the guide to form their own collective *a posteriori* invented language.

4.2 N-gram translation

This procedure is based on one of the early models for word vectors called N-grams, whereby the tokens in a word window are placed on the x and y axes of a grid and assigned a number that corresponds to the number of times each word appears next to another one in the cells where the x and y axes meet, respectively for each word pairing. Using a word window for the same set of words in at least two languages, players find combinations of words for which the numerical values ascribed to word proximity found in the cells add up to equal sums.

4.3 Translating (into) acrostics or anagrams

Using an already existing one or inventing their own, players are invited to translate or create bilingually a set of two mirroring anagrams, acrostics or mesostics. The difficulty varies greatly according to language pairs!

See the supplementary *Handbook of Translation Procedures* for full, detailed instructions and creative results.

5

Modulated

"The body that reads and responds to light and from which language emerges, is the body of translation. When light hits the mouth in that resplandor of reading, time reverses, to the time of first writing, unoriginal, but a point of origin, it emits another time, text, into the mouth and body of the reader."

—Erín Moure, "Paradox"

One day, poet and translator Elisa Sampedrín was standing in a hallway in Bucharest. On a shelf, she found a book by Nichita Stănescu with a warn, pale cover. Inside, she found a full sensory experience, a parallel dimension of cattle, a field, rain, a man hammering on a stone. She knew she had to read it, but she knew no Romanian. So she stole the book, slipped it into her coat pocket and later translated it. The fact that she knew no Romanian was no impediment, as Erín Moure explains, speaking of Sampedrín's translations, "when you translate from a language you don't know, you make fewer mistakes." Or as Oana Avasilichioaei, the "real" translator of Nichita Stănescu's work,[1] tells Moure with regard to Sampedrín's translations, "they're all wrong, but they're accurate."[2]

Or is that just a fiction? A tale invented, stolen or translated from someone else? Is Elisa Sampedrín even real? What does it mean to be real in language, to read, write or translate from a located, embodied subject position within lexicon, grammar, syntax and message? To read, write or translate from a certain point of view?

Modulation, in Sager and Hamel's translation of VD, is a "variation of the form of the message, obtained by a change in the point of view" (29). The original adds the idea of *éclairage*, of lighting, which can also be translated as perspective. For Moure, Sampedrín or Avasilichioaei,[3] "the stimulation of the tongue by the word is electro-tactile, and I am sure it activates the visual cortex, not just the language centres. Thus altering space itself, for space is a relation with the body" (Moure, *O Resplandor* 97). The "screen of my language" (4), Sampedrín writes, blue light, modifies circadian rhythms in the body, and thus modifies time, like the paradox of translation, which situates a text written "then," "now": "the detention or reversal of time by merging past with present (earlier text with later)" (Moure, "Paradox" 11). The figure and procedure of modulation thus asks the question of the affective, embodied locality of the translator in time and space, of who translates, and of where that who sits in language, from where it reads, writes and translates in lexicon and message.

Modulation, according to VD, is also where the human begins to fully intervene in the translation process, where translation is least mechanical, where the machine is least likely to take over (even if NMT today carries out many of the species of modulation detailed by VD). We saw this already in the passage from direct to oblique translation with the procedure of transposition, where it is no longer possible to substitute "parallel thought processes" (VD/Sager and Hamel 34) in a one-to-one fashion. With transposition, it is the structure of grammar that must supplement the failure of languages to line up. With modulation, it is the thought processes themselves. "In principle we could say that, generally, modulation articulates the contrast between two languages faced with the same situation but two different modes of thinking, by exposing this divergence in expression form" (247).

This joins with VD's thinking on the *génie* of the French and English languages respectively: that languages are not only divergent on the level of their words or structures, but that they are expressive of a particular national character, a way of thinking. They quote J. G. Weightman at the start of the third section on "message": "I often feel that anthropologists, by making a careful comparison between the languages of Dover and Calais, could long ago have discovered truths that they only brought to light recently by going all the way to the South Sea Islands" (Weightman, cited in VD/Sager and Hamel 157).

Human nature, as expressive of inherent anthropological—geographical and national in this account—differences, can be found in the divergences of language and the thought processes they represent. English, they argue throughout the book, is a more concrete language, focused on material reality, while French is concerned with the machinations of abstract thought: "Generally it can be said that French words function at a higher degree of abstraction than the corresponding English words. They tend to be less cluttered with the details of reality" (VD/Sager and Hamel 52).

This idea that national languages are expressive of different "modes of thinking" interlays their whole argument and classification system for the different species (*espèces*) of modulation that they treat in two sections of the book, first in the section on lexicon and later in the section on message. In the modulation between an abstract expression and a concrete one, the French will opt for the more abstract (what VD refer to as *mots images*), and the English, the more concrete (*mots signes*). They give the example of the translation of "*le dernier étage*" (literally: "the last floor") and "the top floor," or "*un filme en exclusivité*" and "a first-run movie" (89). Likewise, in the modulation between passive and active voice, English prefers the passive voice, "which is part of the nature of the language," "an attitude towards reality" (140) in which the English are focused on objective reality, and are "reluctant to express a definitive opinion or judgment," while the French "insist on interpreting."

The different species vary wildly and cover such diverse procedures as translating cause and effect, means and results, part and whole, one part for another, intervals and limits, sense modulation, geographic modulations, change of symbol, negative and positive, active and passive voice, space and time, as well as "fixed modulation in the message," which is actually equivalence, which I'll treat in the next chapter. In fact, with my students, I often refer to the procedure of modulation as the grab bag (or on bad days, the garbage can) of translation procedures that VD couldn't manage to find a home for elsewhere.

The original version of this chapter consisted of a close reading of Erín Moure's *Secession/Insecession*, her translation and echolation of Chus Pato's *Secesión*, using all the different species of modulation. In *Secession/Insecession*, Moure's echolation (*Insecession*) sits on the page opposite her faithful translation (*Secession*) and reads as a record, an archive of her translation process, but also of a modulation of her subject position. She echolates author for translator, writing for translation, but also time and space, lifelines and geographies, echolating Pato's subject position with her own. This is a creative-critical reading, in Grass's sense, of Pato's original text. Pato's *Secesión*, written in Galician, is about a lot of things, but one of those things is the division that happens in the *I* when it encounters poetic language, and the way identity sits with relation to the language that pronounces it and that language's relationship to nation. Pato's reading necessarily cannot line up with VD's (that a language is expressive of its national character), because her language—Galician—is nonnational, or rather, it has a totally different relationship to nation: a nation that exists out of time, a nation to be created, in opposition to the nation and language that tried to snuff it out.

In the end, the project of comparing Moure's translations and echolations to VD's modulations got too long and unwieldy for this book, but you can read it in a collected volume titled *The Translation Memoir*, edited by Delphine Grass and myself. You can also find these different species popping up in the procedures at the end of the chapter.

But let's get back to Elisa Sampedrín, who also makes an appearance in *Secession/Insecession*.

The time-traveling thief

It is Sampedrín herself who reveals in *O Resplandor*, a book whose cover says it is authored by Erín Moure (whoever that is), that the story of the original Romanian version pilfered from the hallway in Bucharest is made-up, or at least did not happen in the order originally implied. "How did I first encounter Stănescu? The story of the book in the București hallway it's true never happened. Or it happened much later. Or it happened years before, to someone else, who told it to me that evening, last spring" (7). This admission appears in one of the *crónicas* that intersperse *O Resplandor*. These *crónicas* are signed alternatingly by E.S. (Elisa Sampedrín) and E.M. (Erín Moure), with occasional interruptions in the form of quotations taken from conversations, notebooks, letters and postcards written by O. (Oana Avasilichioaei).

The *crónicas* are haunted by a kind of paranoid jealousy on the part of E.M., who is tantalized by a series of photos, postcards and documentary proofs that suggest that E.S. and O. knew each other and were in contact with one another, even though O. claims this is not the case. At the end of the book, E.S. reveals that she and O. had been at the same party, but never met. This story of missed encounters—or of encounters kept secret—is written in tandem with another story of looping and crisscrossed messages: that of the translation itself. In "Crónica Three," E.M. relates the story of O. finding a photo of E.S. taken in Bucharest in Stănescu's book in the library, from when she went there to work on her translations. However, it is only because of her encounter with O.'s translation that Sampedrín decided to go to Bucharest in the first place: "Elisa had gone to Bucureşti to find Stănescu, as a result of reading O.'s translations of his poems in a bookstore on Bank Street in Ottawa" (*O Resplandor* 30-31). How could a photo of E.S. be not only taken but slipped into the very book she would translate years later, in a city she would visit only after reading a published translation by O. that had not yet been completed? Who is the author of this translation? Which translation, which arrival and departure comes first? This creates a time-travel paradox wherein there can be no original point for this translation. The crossing lines of this paradox are further multiplied when E.S. admits that she wrote the first version of her translations from Stănescu's Romanian (a language she does not speak) in "Galego" (Galician), before translating into English, which E.M. refers to as "the language of no one" (17).

But who is Elisa Sampedrín? Is she a time traveler? A ghost? A construct? A heteronym? A thief? Or is she simply Moure, one dimension of her subjectivity, her interior, her observer, or her proxy? *O Resplandor* is not the first time readers of Moure meet Elisa Sampedrín. She appears first in *Little Theatres*, which came out after *O Citadán*, a work of collaged polyphony and citation intended as a meditation on the construction of the subject as assemblage and intertextuality. The writing of *O Citadán* opened Moure to a host of legal problems as there is no fair-use policy in Canada for the use of citations (and there are many in *O Citadán*). And so Sampedrín was invented to steal for Moure.

But she was also there for Moure when she could not write, after her mother died. As Moure writes in *Insecession*: "ES was the expedient

I adopted after the death of my mother in order to keep writing, thus in *O Resplandor*, ES translates from Romanian which she does not know; this is her way of writing. ES has no interior, she has a kind of stuffing that keeps her upright but no 'inner forum' or place where ethical action can be formulated" (160).

Moure actually crosses paths with Sampedrín, later, in Moure's book *The Unmemntioable:* first in Bucharest, at a café table, and then on the terrace of a Persian restaurant. From there, Moure and Sampedrín play a game of cat and mouse told sometimes from Moure's perspective and sometimes from Sampedrín's, echoing Moure's detective work in *O Resplandor*, hopscotching across the pages of the book, between the books, in a story of missed encounters, notes, books, postcards, letters to Chus Pato, translation drafts, photographs and one moleskin notebook that changes hands in a supernatural, time-traveling fashion, with the notebook disappearing only to reappear with its contents erased, or with notes and messages that confuse ownership: Whose notebook is it? Sampedrín's or Moure's? Who stole it from whom?

Many of VD's species of modulation consist in modulating the subject's point of view in the sentence or on the sentence, changing the position from which they view whatever is being expressed. For example, in "reversal of terms" with the translation of "Don't call up the stairs" and *"N'appelle pas du bas de l'escalier"* (literally: "don't call from the bottom of the stairs"), where the point of speaking literally modulates from the top to the bottom of a staircase (although the meaning stays the same, as always in VD). A comparison could be made here with the "geographic modulation" mentioned earlier, which, for VD is like the translation of "India ink" for *encre de Chine* (literally: "ink of China"), but which, in experimental translation, can be pushed as far as modulating the physical, geographical and national position of the authorial subject with that of the translator's (Moure modulating Pato's Galicia with Calgary, for example). But this can also happen with time, in a disruption of the space-time continuum that translation enacts, as well as in the temporal linearity that tells the story of a subject's identity, or their ipseity, their coincidence with their own self, the thought processes that are expressive of their national character.

A play of heteronyms

Elisa Sampedrín is not Moure's first foray into heteronymic play. One of Moure's early works, *Sheep's Vigil of a Fervent Person*, is signed Eirin Moure, with the added *i* in homage to Pessoa's heteronym, Alberto Caeiro.[4] It was in this "translation" as she calls it that she first begins experimenting with geographic modulation and other kinds of modulations that rewrite author as translator, translating the figure of Pessoa/Caeiro as herself, or one of her "selves." Even her own name, Erín Moure, could be considered a kind of heteronym as, after *Sheep's Vigil*, she changed the spelling from Erin Mouré,[5] moving the accent from the *é* to the *í*, striking a resonance with the verb "moor," or rather, "unmoor," as Shannon MacGuire remarks in her discussion of the poetics and politics of Moure's name changes, citing the preface to *O Cidadán*: "Can the name be reinvested or infested, fenestrated... set in motion again? Unmoored? Her semblance?"

For Douglas Robinson, "there is something profoundly subversive about [the translator as heteronym]—and yet in almost every way it is only a slight exaggeration and expansion of the translator's traditional role" (*Experimental Translator* 115). Indeed, couldn't the translator be considered, or consider themself, a heteronym of the author, or even, as Robinson argues in *The Experimental Translator*, of their own self, recreated "heteronymously *as* the source author writing in the target language" (117)?

Robinson probes, tests the limits of the subversive potential of this exaggeration in two works of experimental translation. The first of these is his transcreation of Volter Kilpi's (or Lemuel Gulliver's) *Gulliver's Voyage to Phantomimia*, a fan fiction and editorial experiment where Robinson both translates and completes an unfinished novel by Kilpi. His transcreation also includes a host of supplementary material (an editor's forward, a reader's report, a publisher's postscript, etc.) featuring characters at the liminal zone between reality and fiction, including Julius Nyrkki, a pernicious literary scholar, and Ezra Pound, who appears as a hallucination in the account of the editor heteronym named "Douglas Robinson" of the bizarre circumstances that led him to discover the original manuscript—not Kilpi's translation, but the original Swift (or would it be Gulliver's?) manuscript—in the Beinecke Rare Book Library at Yale. Robinson manifests these twists of authorship through paratextual phenomena, playing with the fiction of his own translation through heteronymic, heterotextual expression, as translator, editor, critic, creator: "One aim of experimental translation as I've practiced it is to create a *confusing* liminal space where the target reader finds it hard to get her or his bearings among conflicting heteronymous impostures" (*Experimental Translator* 167).

This confusion is taken even further in the copious footnotes that appear through the book, many of which reference Kilpi's translation or translation errors and therefore would imply that what appears *is* actually Kilpi's translation, rather than the original Swift manuscript. The novel, as it is published by Zeta books, also includes a (real) translation of Kilpi's own "translator's introduction." The manuscript exists therefore in a paradox where it is both original English and translation from Finnish. It is also paradoxically authored by Gulliver, Swift, Kilpi and Robinson, as Kilpi's novel itself began by carrying forward Swift's original found-manuscript trope in *Gulliver*, claiming that his version was a translation from English of a manuscript that appeared on his desk "stoutly trussed in up in ancient-looking sailing twine and caked with dust" (Kilpi 43)—presumably the same "twine" (19) that binds the manuscript Robinson finds in the Beinecke. Robinson's transcreation is thus also a *re*translation, back into English, of a manuscript that never existed, written not by Kilpi but by Swift/Gulliver himself. This is not only a paradox of authorship, but a time-traveling paradox, as many of the footnotes point out anachronisms in the "original," although perhaps this could be explained by the time traveling of the manuscript itself, "'lost' for almost two centuries, then 'found' by the Vorticism group in around 1913 or 1914, then 'lost' again, then 'found' by Volter Kilpi on his desk at work in around 1937 or 1938, then 'lost' again for eight decades, and then 'found' again by me" (33–34). This time traveling is also a metafictional traveling, as time traveling characters from the Vorticism group that appear in the novel participate in Robinson's hallucination in the editor's forward. The numerous anachronisms pointed out by the editor in the footnotes likewise give the text an unstable chronology.

I won't delve any deeper into the complex time-traveling twists and turns of Robinson's/Kilpi's fictional translation (or translational fiction) in *Gulliver's Voyage to Phantomimia*, nor will I attempt to give a comprehensive account of the practice of pseudotranslation, or translations of texts that don't exist. Briefly: the most famous example of pseudotranslation is undoubtedly Cervantes's *Don Quixote*, which purports to be originally written in Arabic by Cide Hemete Benengeli—what the reader reads is a found translation, translated into Castilian by an unnamed translator whom Cervantes refers to only as "the Morisco" or "Little Moor" (not Moure...). The *Quixote* example sits outside the bounds of the timeframe I have been setting up for experimental translation. And indeed, it does not oppose norms in the same way that the experimental translations I have been treating do, since translation at the time was not so much a sign of suspicion but rather "a gauge of authenticity" (Watier).[6] This practice of pseudotranslation as a way to elevate the value and seeming legitimacy of a text continued up through the nineteenth century.[7]

It is indeed the suspicion of translation—the idea that translation betrays its original—that allows pseudotranslation in the contemporary era to be set up not to prove a text's authenticity but precisely the opposite: to call attention to the hoax that is translation (although this does not necessarily mean debunking it), and to give the "translator" license to play and to stray, often under the auspices of heteronyms that liberate them from the unmanageable expectations placed on translators in our contemporary climate (to be both ultimately faithful and yet ultimately readable, and perfectly productive).

And this is precisely what Robinson does in his pseudotranslation *The Last Days of Maiju Lassila*, "written" by J. I. Vatanen, one of the heteronyms deployed by Finnish writer Algot Untola (another of which is Maiju Lassila). On some level, since the words "a pseudotranslation by Douglas Robinson" appear on the cover, there should be no doubt as to the "origin" of this text. And yet, Robinson goes to great lengths to invent a plausible if perpetually self-contradictory story about the "real" origin of the text, as a manuscript at the National Library of Finland. He introduces, once again, extratextual personae such as Väinö Stenberg, the head manuscript librarian at the National Library of Finland (also another heteronym used by Untola), and Julius Nyrkki—the same Nyrkki who tries to debunk the authenticity of the *Gulliver* manuscript. And last but far from least are the various Douglas Robinson heteronyms: "Douglas Robinson translator,"

"Douglas Robinson editor," "Douglas Robinson author"... —why would one presume they are all the "same" person? Instead, Robinson asks the reader to consider heteronyms as divergent selves as play, and also as a play, a theater of textual roles, where author, translator, editor and reader do impersonations of one another.

These personae all appear in paratextual phenomena: commentary, letters, preface, postface, footnotes and references to external sources. "Annotations are the experimental translator's secret weapon" (Robinson, *Experimental Translator* 110). And indeed, paratext is where the translator lives, where their subjectivity is positioned, *para-* meaning beside or against the text, in texts that are precisely *not* the text.

Paratextual phenomena

Footnotes are not generally well regarded by translators. As Pym writes: "Translators' notes have deservedly become unfashionable. First-year university students of translation tend to strew them all over the place, explaining every half-shaded detail, insulting the implied receiver's intelligence with massive overtranslation, and perhaps reflecting initial frustration at suppression of the translator's discursive position" (*Text Transfer* 90).

This place where first-year students of translation work out their anxieties over their discursive position as translators is exactly where modulation as experimental translation happens. It is where the translator de-locates and relocates and plays with their place of speaking (there are perhaps many ways experimental translators try to imitate first-year translators—calque, for example!). And indeed, Robinson's experiments are a cornucopia of footnote play (all the puns intended). Translators, editors and even source authors get in on the action, and it is perhaps the place that is most rife with Robinson's sleights of hands, leading the reader into the fiction of his pseudo- and transcreations and out again. In the preface to *The Last Days of Maiju Laissila*, the editor (or "editor") intervenes almost immediately in a footnote to a passage in the main text where Robinson comments on the different Douglas Robinson heteronyms that authored, translated and edited *Gulliver's Voyage to Phantomimia* to write: "This seems a bit self-aggrandizing for a translator's preface; could we at least bump this paragraph down to a footnote, or even possibly cut it altogether? [Ed.]." The translator responds: "That reminds me: is 'Douglas Robinson' the translator of this book not also a heteronym of 'Douglas Robinson' the pseudotranslator? [Tr.]" (*Maiju Lassila* vi). On pages 125–126, the translator gets into a veritable pissing match with the author themself—or *ta*self, to use Robinson's pronoun scheme in the book, which ostensibly translates the non-gendered Finnish pronouns of the non-binary characters. Their debate concerns the use of the term "hedge fund" (in Finnish, *hedgerahasto*), one of the many anachronisms that cast aspersions on the origin story of the manuscript. The pissing match ends: "I've got this fund that I sit on. Why don't you kiss it. [Au] / Oh, real mature [Tr.]."

But footnotes—and paratexts more generally—are not only a place to wreak cheeky, heteronymic havoc. It is also the place where the translator is situated, where the translator lives, as Grass comments in her writing on performative translations, referencing Theo Hermans: "What we call translation as opposed to an original work is in part reliant on the paratextual framing of translations which sign or declare translations to be translations" (Grass 46). For Pym as well, the performative "translated by" that appears on the cover sets up the translation as precisely *not* the discourse of the translator and thus, "I am translating is necessarily false" (*Text Transfer* 55). Pym's analysis also reads the translator's positionality as an alternating play of pronouns and of direct and indirect speech, which sets up the translator as precisely, again, *not* the person who is speaking.

But what happens when the translator does speak? This is the question the Grass asks when she reads autotheoretical experiments in translator writing. Grass identifies a veritable boom of what she (and I with her) calls "translation memoirs," which write out the translator's roving subject position in the process of translation, "in a way which both explores and questions the rules of engagement of translation" (20). For Grass, not only is this a form of creative-critical research, but it is also a deeply *embodied* practice:

The reworlding of the text through the medium of another time, place, language and relation that is the work of translation is therefore also, when translated into autotheoretical form, a work of re-embodiment and a material re-inscription of the spectral work of translation. As an authorial remainder of the translated text, the autotheoretical translation memoir thus can be seen to act as a reinvestment of the text into material realities normally pushed to the paratextual peripheries of the book as an institution, when it is not altogether invisible. The translation memoir as autotheory is thus a re-embodiment of the text, but also, as we have seen, of translation practice as a field of research and method of becoming. (40)

Moure joins the other translators that Grass references who use an embodied reworlding of their own translator subjectivities to unearth the hidden performative gestures that make a translation a translation, like the paratextual elements, like the implication that the author is not the translator, like the paradoxical inscriptions of original and translation in time and space, and the modulation between them. It is in this sense that the translators Grass analyses (Gepner, Grunenwald, Briggs, Siddiqi, Meur, etc.) could all be considered experimental translators, enunciating a reflection on the process of translation as modulation, as a shift in perspective, lighting, embodiment. Embodiment is also a red thread through Robinson's critical work, effectively and affectively echoed in his creative work discussed above.

Autotheoretical experiments in translation can also take the form paratextual play. In the final section of her book, Grass refers to this as a "transtopian literary space capable of queering geographies of belonging" (Grass 108), a place where source text, language and culture can be thickened, in Anthony Appiah's sense, as a "translation that seeks, with its annotations and accompanying glosses, to locate the text in a rich cultural and linguistic context" (cited in Grass 113). Grass compares Nabokov's supposedly literalist translation of *Eugene Onegin* and its volumes of footnotes "reaching up like skyscrapers" to the creative-critical translation experiments of Anne Carson, Christina MacSweeney and Chantal Wright. In Nabokov, Grass argues, the use of footnotes is an attempt to totalize the work as a scientifically knowable entity, to foreclose the becoming of its potential, to "perform and reinforce the immanence of individual works and languages along nationalist and patriarchal notions of authorship and reproduction." Carson, MacSweeney and Wright, on the other hand, use their original texts to "turn the space between cultures into a place of dwelling and thinking, opening our mental maps to historical and political counter-geographies of existing linguistic and cultural status quos" (115).

They all do this by leaning into the paratext as a space to write out translational subjectivity and positionality. In Wright's translation of Yoko Tawada's *Portrait of a Tongue*, similarly to Moure's *Secession/Insecession*, the reader gets Wright's faithful translation of Tawada on one side of the page, and on the other, Wright's creative-critical commentary, interpreting, giving thickness to the original, and also telling the story of her own translation process, along with personal anecdotes from her life that echo the telling in the original, but also read it through its translational tough spots for readers to experience in their full force and beauty. It is thus simultaneously translation, commentary and life writing, a record and archive of the translator's subjective experience of and while translating: a modulation of perspective, in a *para*text, a text along one side of the page.

Carson's *Nox* works from a single poem, "Catullus 101," and is an elegy of paratext. Published unbound in a box format, it is structured with poetic dictionary entries reminiscent of Ramayya's paleoekphrasotranslations discussed in chapter 2, untangling the definitional and etymological roots in each individual word in the original Latin poem to write lyrical entries in an imaginary dictionary. It is accompanied by records, scraps, notes, letters and photographs from an archive of her brother's life and her and her family's relationship to him, and reads as a meditation on mourning on her brother's death, just like the original Catullus poem.

This is not the first time we have seen reference to translation as mourning. Elisa Sampedrín was the medium Moure used in order to continue writing after the death of her mother. Translation again is what "destroys time" (*O Resplandor* 6) in Sampedrín's words, what takes us out of time and confounds then and now, makes another time speak through the body, the mouth of the translator: a paradox. This time-traveling paradox is also another paradox of modulation, that of the somatic position of the translator, as embodied but also embodying another's writing, in two locations at once. In Robinson's *Last Days of Maiju Lassila* (and in Saramago's *Ricardo Reis*, which Robinson is riffing off of), the heteronyms of Algot Untola linger on after his death, as embodied ghosts, both in and out of time.

One of the reasons "I am translating is necessarily false" is because when an interpreter speaks or a translator writes the phrase "I am frightened" (Pym, *Text Transfer* 56), there should be no confusion as to the fact that the translation is not referring to the translator's own affective state. Modulation, as I have been hijacking it, is the place where the fixity of these discursive positions, the subjectivity of the translator as relegated to performative paratexts is called into question, shifted, allowed to bleed over into the text as a record of the translation process in its full embodiment. Like the "reversal of terms" species of modulation in VD, the translation is in two (or more) locations at once, both at the bottom and the top of the staircase—I am reminded of Bhabha's "hither and thither of the stairwell, the temporal movement and passage that it allows, prevents identities at either end of it from settling into primordial polarities" (4).

It is also the place where translator emotions can be written out and expressed. This is what Carson does in her translation of Catullus's poem mourning his brother: she writes her own mourning into the translation. Interestingly enough, Catullus also does this, in poem #65, where he writes about how difficult it was for him to translate the Callimachus poem that appears as poem #66, because of the death of his brother. In his experimental translations of Catullus, Brandon Brown writes of Catullus's grief:

> I find it interesting that Catullus, who remains associated with the anachronistic but persistent mode of the lyric, constructs a practice almost always including appropriation. Translation, and certainly as Catullus himself practices it, is an artwork of appropriation. And yet much of contemporary translation as much as contemporary works of appropriation purport to cancel the somatic vehicle for lyrical material.
>
> That is, the conventional picture of translation, in which the translator is invisible, which excludes her body from the scene of translation, does not suggest a space in which the translator's desire—or grief—can find any entry into the imporous mimetic activity they understand as "translation." (93)

Brown's response to this is to, in turn, insert his own body into the scene of translation, not only in the form of his own mourning for a lost friend who translates this poem by Catullus, but throughout his translations. In his serial translation of Catullus's most famous couplet, *Odi et amo. Quare id faciam, fortasse requiris / Nescio, sed fieri sentio et excrucior,*[8]

Brown provides a long poetic exegesis of the Latin word *excrucior*, as the situation of the translator, as torn apart. Brown's nine-page translation explodes out into a multitude of serial translations, a record of Brown's and others' translation choices and hesitations, punctuated by the word "Dunno." Along with this is the archive of the reflection process, the ins and outs and whys and why-nots of each translation choice, along with intertextual, literary and interpretative commentary of both personal and scholarly nature, and also creative departures, playing off of symbols, imagery and sound.

The translator's body is thus torn into the body of the text, its explosion of variants, a record of the translator's reflections and doubts. I recognize here too, the first-year translation student's initial frustration at suppression of the translator's discursive position. And for me, the play of text, paratext, and commentary, and the insertion of the translators affective, somatic body in their physical and temporal location in culture betrays a deep anxiety over the place of the speaking (writing, reading, hearing, translating) subject.

When Brown takes on the challenge of translating Catullus, part of what he is translating is the translational situation of the original. Indeed, Catullus was a translator too. But, as I've mentioned many times now, translational norms are not fixed, and the norms during Catullus's times are actually much closer to what one might now call experimental translation than they are to the translational norms of our times. Omissions and additions, interpolations, rearrangements are all permitted procedures in Catullus's translations. Likewise, not all of Catullus's translations are signed with the original author's name, making the line between original and translation totally fluid to the point of dismantling that binary (could one speak of heteronymic play here?). Indeed, readers and translators of Catullus will never know for sure how much of Catullus's work is "original" and how much is a "translation" and to what extent.

In other words, Brown does not so much translate what Catullus says (although he does that too) as do what Catallus did. It's a time-traveling translation in the sense of going back and adopting poetic and translational norms and postures that are now anachronistic. Brown includes omissions, additions, rearrangements and interpolations that comment on the process of translation from his own discursive—but also somatic and affective—position as translator.

Translation as I understand it involves a preceding writing, a proceeding writing—in between is the body that translates. The preceding writing is absorbed by the body of the translator in the act of reading. And when the translator writes something down which proceeds from the act of reading the preceding writing, that is called "translation." However, far from idealizing repetition, this translation model wishes to privilege the *delay* between preceding and proceeding marks. To acknowledge the *fact of detour*. To suggest that things *go haywire*. Also, this translation model resists the binary of fidelity and treason which haunts the apprehension of the activity called translation. Instead, among other actions, the translator can *choose to not*. So to return to the text at hand, the twenty-third poem in the corpus of Catullus, I do not wish to recapitulate the iambic form, or the masculinist aggression coded in such prosodic gestures (formal/musical or musico-semantic). Not even if someone "takes away the napkin" or "likes to move (his) penis" or "supposed me to be immodest on account of my verses" or "wishes to anally penetrate the objects of my affection" or "has an anus dry as a little salt cellar." (Brown 38)

The imbrication of translation as commentary is not new; in both Pound and de Campos, translation and criticism were seen as closely aligned if not concomitant activities. What is new (or rather, radically not new, and so new again) is the way that Brown inserts his commentary, in the form of his speaking translator's body in its specific discursive locality, into the body of the text.

In this long extract from Brown's translation of poem 23 of Catullus, he tells us what he is not translating and why. Brown's "choose to not" is preceded by a somewhat lengthy (for the form) discussion on a shift in the word "iambic," whereby at the time of Catullus's writing, it did not refer to a poetic meter but to the content of a poem of invective verse, "content associated with blame." The iambic form was used as a way of shaming people who did things the poet didn't like. In Brown, there is a pretty clear moralizing reason for not wanting to translate Catullus's iambics, in spite of the fact that he then goes on to list some of the invectives Catullus uses. Clearly, Catullus's bald-faced insulting rhetoric against his friends offends Brown's Midwestern United States sense of moral decorum, where calling your friends "Dad of appetites" (42) or "Who has no piggybank" (43) "mini-wretched" (44) or "mud" (44), etc., is just not nice (Brown is very nice). Catullus's invectives are also aggressively masculine and misogynist, other positions that offend the moral sense of the readership that Brown is situated within and is himself a part of.

What we have here is a geographic modulation and a time-traveling modulation that happens in the "delay" and the "fact of detour," the place where "things go haywire" in translation. Brown inserts a lyric appropriation, through the entry of his own body into the scene of translation, into the poem he is translating, both omitting and adding. Again, what Brown is translating is the textual and poetic position of the original, rather than the form or content of the words themselves (although he does this too). Brown is translating from the United States of America, one of the most appropriative imperial powers the world has ever known—an imperial power modeled on the translational context of Catullus himself, in ancient Rome. But Catullus did not only appropriate, he also rebelled against traditional formal poetic constraints of the time, hijacking Greek forms and writing in an irreverent devil-may-care rhetoric that is part of what has made him appealing to experimental and Avant-Garde poets in the first place.[9]

This is a question that authors almost never ask themselves, but that translators must always ask themselves. It makes so much sense on some level, then, that this type of creative-critical experiment would come from translators, from translators writing about their experience, their lives. It is also a question for the sense-making potential of translation in the age of algorithmic production: If machines can translate, does that mean they also speak and mean? And if machines speak and mean, what does that mean for the human's affective, somatic relationship to meaning? Brown's play is also technological, as in his paratextual translations of Catullus's poems number 69, 98, 95, 70, 70, 107 and 73, which email a blind-faith translation from his Hotmail to his Gmail account and transcribe the ads programmed by the bots alongside the body of the email (187).

But if this anxiety is technological, it is also cultural, political and linguistic, seated at the knot, the *secession* between the subject and their national belonging and the way it is articulated in language. It is an anxiety of whose voice is getting heard, of who is translating whom and who is speaking for whom, from what location on the staircase.

In 2002, the poet Paul Hoover came out with some poems that he presented as translations from Latin American authors (with no originals). In her book *Talk Shows*, de la Torre performs back-translations of these pseudotranslations that she carries out through editorial intervention. Scouring through real Latin American poetry, she collected and curated lines from original poems that most closely resembled Hoover's pseudotranslations. From these collages she reconstructed poems in the original voices of Latin American poets, repairing the politics of appropriation in Hoover's original gesture, before translating her reconstructed poems back into English. Who is author, who is translator and who is editor?

PROCEDURES

5.1 Translate like Elisa Sampedrín

Relying on Outranspian constraints such as sonotranslation, limentranslation, hommeauxtranslation, ekphrasotranslation, etc., as well as gut instinct and the free-form imagination of translucinación, players translate a text written in a language they don't speak. Ideally this is carried out with a text that has an existing "faithful" translation by a translator with real knowledge of the language of the original.

5.2 Alter-ego translation

Translate the figure of an author in a text into the figure of a translator. Tangentially, translate writing into translating. This can also be carried out between translator figures. For added fun, try translating text type.

5.3 Geographic modulation

Translate the time and/or place of an original.

5.4 Archimboldo translation (à la Eliana Vicari)

Translate the lexical or figural field of a text, such as a motif or an extended allegory, into an alternative or set of alternatives.

5.5 Interspecies modulation—a work in progress

In fact, all of VD's species of modulations are already procedures for experimental translation, and can be used as a creative, research or teaching tool for reflecting upon and learning them by inviting players to choose and (over)apply one of the many species in a case where the original does not technically require it.

See the supplementary *Handbook of Translation Procedures* for full, detailed instructions and creative results.

6

Equivalencias

"I still owe 48 words, 47+1 so the book will be Canadian +1."
—Moure *Secession/Insecession*

This first line from the last poem of Moure's *Secession/Insecession* makes reference to the funding policy of the Canada Council, an organization that covers much of the financing of works of literature, especially unsellable books of poetry in Canada. The Canada Council does not fund the translation of literature by writers from outside of Canada, which means that it is nearly impossible to get funding to translate foreign literature into Canadian French or English. Moure, in order to receive funding for her translation of Pato's *Secesión*, had to write (translate) a book that was one word more Canadian than it was Galician. Her modulation was thus also a question of equivalence in the numerical sense, of how many words to how many words, and how many words it takes to make a work a translation and how many it takes to make it original.

This begins with the word "equivalence" itself, which is not the title of this chapter, nor is it the word that VD use. VD's word is *équivalence*, with the accent (both spoken and written), and is actually the last species of modulation in their typology. *Équivalence* is the translation of situation, or as VD have it in Sager and Hamel's translation, "fixed modulation of the message," such as the translation of "fireboat" and *"bateau-pompe,"* or the translation of idiomatic expressions.[1] Sager and Hamel translate this as "equivalence," which is indeed one way to translate *équivalence*, and maybe even the best way. But are equivalence and *équivalence* really equivalent?

Mary Snell-Hornby poses the same question as relates to the German translation of equivalence, *Äquivalenz*, which, funnily enough is not the first translation DeepL gives of the English word "equivalence" into German. The first word is *Gleichwertigkeit*, which means something like "equal value" and in German refers to qualitative equivalence, whereas *Äquivalenz* refers to quantitative equivalence. For Snell-Hornby, *Gleichwertigkeit* came to be equated with *Äquivalenz* in translation studies shortly after the notion of *Äquivalenz* first came into vogue "during the euphoria that hailed machine translation in the 1950s" (Snell-Hornby 17), when it became apparent that human translations did not express themselves through "one-to-one correspondence" (17). Challenging this correspondence corresponds to a first critique of equivalence in language as mathematical quantity. This is a notion I have been investigating throughout this book, beginning with the value a letter takes in a global economy of decolonial debt where translators also happen to be paid by the sign, word or page, but also in terms of what happens to language when it is transposed into numerical values in MT.

The mathematical sense of *Äquivalenz* is, almost performatively, where it joins with the English meaning, where there is a kind of mathematical equivalence between the words of the kind 1 = 1. But the English meaning exceeds the meaning of *Äquivalenz*. Snell-Hornby refers to the *OED* for the softer side of the definition of equivalence in English, referring to words "of a similar significance," that mean "virtually the same thing" (17). For Snell-Hornby, this ambivalence and nonequivalence in the words themselves in translation is a significant example of the fact that equivalence in translation is but an illusion, and that this illusion of a perfect symmetry between languages is also one that elides human difference.

For Snell-Hornby, this illusion is also embodied in the fact that "to my knowledge no translation theorist has ever doubted that *Äquivalenz* and *equivalence* are perfectly symmetrical renderings of a common interlingual *tertium comparationis*" (16–17) and that this illusion of equivalence exists even within one single language and especially in translation theory. Snell-Hornby goes on to delimit fifty-eight different notions and uses of equivalence in translation studies (Pym, *Text Transfer* 37). Here again, you can see the tendency of equivalence toward abundance. On the surface, this may seem like a paradox: isn't equivalence what reduces different elements to the same—*the tertium comparationis*, "a piece of reality or thought (a referent, a function, a message) that stands outside all languages and to which two languages can refer" (Pym, *Exploring* 17)? In VD, this is certainly the case as *équivalence* refers to finding equivalent expressions in two languages for the same external referent—presupposing therefore that such external referents not only exist but can be immutable, and are not themselves subject to procedures of shifting modulation and equivalence.

I think most translators *would* ask themselves whether equivalence and *équivalence* or *Äquivalenz* or *equivalencias* or 等效性 or эквивалентность or التكافؤ or any of the other thousands of words that might be equivalent to *équivalent* are actually equivalent, or rather, more apropos, whether this is the right translation for a given word in context. In any case, I would like to imagine that Sager and Hamel, who do translate VD's *équivalence* as "equivalence," did do so.

Pym, in his revisiting of VD's procedures, does not translate *équivalence* as "equivalence" but rather as "correspondence" (*Translation Solutions* 24). He does this not necessarily because equivalence is a bad translation of *équivalence* but because using the word "equivalence" to describe this translation procedure (Pym uses the word "solution" rather than "procedure") in VD's *Stylistics* does not work in the particular economy of Pym's scholarship, which, in the case of *Exploring Translation Theories* (2010/2014), but also in *Translation and Text Transfer* (1992/2010), contains a very thorough survey of the notion of equivalence in translation studies.

Pym comments on his translation of *équivalence* by "correspondence" in *Translation Solutions for Many Languages*, referring to it not as translation but as replacement (which perhaps points to the fact that he does not object to equivalence as a possible and accurate translation of *équivalence* in other situations): "I replace the French term '*équivalence*' with 'correspondence', since our contemporary sense of 'equivalence' would probably cover all the examples enlisted in the entire table" (23). Indeed, for Pym, equivalence has come to serve as a stand-in for the very idea of translation over the course of the history of translation studies, and is as polyvalent as the notion of translation itself.

The notion of equivalence is just as illusory for Pym as it is for Snell-Hornby. The difference is that, for Pym, equivalence is no less real for being an illusion; rather, it is a construct, a belief, much like money—which is how he sets it up in his work in *Translation and Text Transfer*, preferring to see equivalence on the model of market exchange, which I critiqued in chapter 1. According to Pym, what Snell-Hornby denounces is what he refers to as "natural equivalence," which is the idea that there is something beyond or outside, something that precedes language that is made equivalent in the transfer between the two texts. For Pym, when this idea of natural equivalence meets with what he calls "directional equivalence," which asks specifically what one is being equivalent to or for, this critique is no longer valid. In his classifying of directional equivalence, equivalence is not reversible. It is something produced through the choices translators make rather than something that exists beyond it. Equivalence is thus created in translation.

Translation also creates equivalence insofar as it is a norm (a "form" in Pym) of modern and contemporary translation in the West, not dissimilar to the norms of market value, both as concerns monetary exchange and the translation market: "As the model of exchange makes clear, equivalence is artificial, fictive, something that has to be produced on the level of translation itself. But it *must* be produced. Whether one likes it or not" (*Text Transfer* 50). In other words, just because something is a fiction does not make it untrue: this is one definition perhaps of how norms work. Pym's argument changes, evolves and is refined in the eighteen years between the first publication of *Translation and Text Transfer* and that of *Exploring Translation Theories*, but this idea of equivalence as a construct remains. In *Exploring Translation Theories*, he cites his own writing in *Translation and Text Transfer*: "Each relation of equivalence is a transitory convention, a momentary link in [a] process of potentially endless exchange [...] a fiction, a lie, a belief-structure necessary for the workings of [some] economies and the survival of [some] societies" (*Text Transfer* 47, cited in *Exploring* 37).

Instead of trying to do away with the notion of equivalence, Pym locates his analysis at its thresholds. He sets this up as a critique of the notion of quantity as it applies to translation studies: "I propose to take the simplest quantitative relations (=, ≠, ≈, >, <) and see how far they can reveal categories of ideal and less-than ideal equivalence, thus hopefully making translations talk about what it is to be a translation" (*Text Transfer* 72). Grass would call this "performative translation." It is one of my fantasy projects to push Pym's idea of equivalence thresholds embodied in mathematical symbols to the creation of a series of translation experiments based on different mathematical symbols, and the original version of this chapter included subsections for each of the mathematical signs in Pym's analysis. For space reasons, I've had to restrict this to two: = and ≠. In other words, what happens when experimental translation tries to reproduce the exact = of the injunction to equivalence, and what happens when it does the opposite of that?

=

I'd like to briefly return to homophonic translation, and the way that it calculates meaning. In Jonathan Stalling's *Yingelishi*, English phrases, transliterated into Chinese characters for the purposes of a language-learning manual, are translated back into English according to the meaning of the characters used for the transliteration. Transliteration between the Roman alphabet and Chinese characters makes hypervisible the way that copying the material of words produces a surplus of meaning: you cannot copy words without producing new, palimpsested meanings out of the characters themselves. This represents a potential to double down on meaning that does not exist in (or rather, exists differently, to a lesser extent) in phonetic writing scripts. For example, the original transliteration of Coca-Cola as 蝌蚪啃蜡, literally "bite the wax tadpole," was later rewritten as 可口可乐 "allowing the mouth to rejoice" to serve advertising interests (Kelly and Zetzsche 122). Song Hwee Lim does a fascinating read of the translation of the word "queer" in the Taiwanese context as 酷小孩 or "cool kids." Yunte Huang's *Shi* (1997) is an important precursor to Stalling's experiment and an early, foundational example of experimental translation. *Shi* unfolds classic Chinese poetry by layers, dissecting the characters through calque, commentary, explanations and what Huang calls "radical" and "diagnostic" translations that dissect the Chinese meanings, flaying open the Chinese characters for readers, all while critiquing the orientalist impulses of Pound's "etymosinological approach," which was inspired by this same potential in Chinese writing.

Stalling's book pushes this polyvalent character of Chinese characters to the extreme by using the raw material of the homophonic translations provided by the language-learning manual. Stalling does not produce homophonic translations himself, but rather carries forward the impulse inherent in these homophonic translations to produce new meanings. He does this by translating the meaning of the original Chinese characters transliterated into pinyin found in the language-learning manual. He does this with travel phrases, greetings, phrases of gratitude and also, numbers:

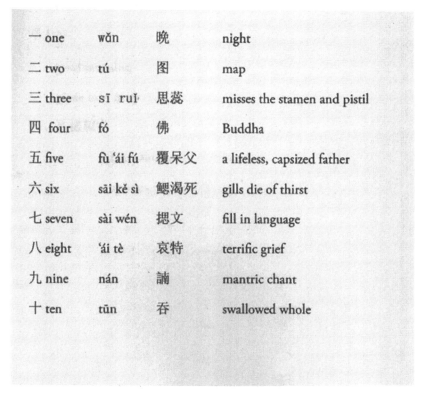

一 one	wǎn	晚	night
二 two	tú	图	map
三 three	sī ruǐ	思蕊	misses the stamen and pistil
四 four	fó	佛	Buddha
五 five	fù 'ái fù	覆呆父	a lifeless, capsized father
六 six	sāi kě sì	鳃渴死	gills die of thirst
七 seven	sài wén	摁文	fill in language
八 eight	'ái tè	哀特	terrific grief
九 nine	nán	諵	mantric chant
十 ten	tūn	吞	swallowed whole

Fig. 10. Stalling's Sinophonic translation of numbers 1–10 (*Yingelishi* 35).

Numbers, more so than proper names, should give us the absolute equivalence embodied in the = sign. What is more perfectly translatable than the number one? How could there possibly be any ambiguity, untranslatability, excess or lack in something as ideal as an abstract quantity represented in the mathematical sign? Isn't this the very modus operandi of the dream of machine translation? Problem: numbers are also words. And if numbers are words, they are also signs and sounds, and those signs and sounds have meanings, especially when they encounter another language. Stalling's translation of the sounds of numbers into meaning functions as a kind of critique, interrogation and resistance—an experimental translation, in other words, of the notion of quantity and equivalence in translation.

So we see that when experimental translation tries to translate exact quantities, these exact quantities get exploded in the material act of translation itself. But are there practices of experimental translation that *do* respect the = of absolute equivalence? That do try to keep the quantities exact? And what happens then?

All translations are judged to a certain extent on quantity, on the equivalence between the number of words in the departure text and the arrival text. Text expansion and contraction are one of the principal ways that translations are evaluated in the professional sphere. In anagrammatic translations, such as those in de la Torre's *Repetition Nineteen* or in Noel's *Transversal*, this respect of quantitative equivalence is taken to the extreme, and eclipses the equivalence of meaning—much like in a homophonic translation. For example, in the first line of de la Torre's "T23: Anagrammatic translation permutating all of the letters in the original Spanish into English-language words" (72), "u enter an abode, a silo, or an asylum" (55), all the letters of the of the first line of the Spanish original are maintained: "Uno. Un silencio, una llamarada." Only the punctuation changes, from full stops to commas, but the quantity is also maintained. I am reminded again of Emmerich commenting on her translation contract cited in chapter 1: "neither omit anything from the original text nor add anything to it," even though "*all* the words are added, *all* the words are different" (3). De la Torre hijacks the letter of the translator contract, translating it as it were, by the letter.

This is an example of an experimental translation that translates the quantity of letters exactly, thus hijacking the paradigm of equivalence as well as the paradigm of the translation of sense, and the paradox of impossibility that emerges between the two. But what about words?

A recent unpublished project of the Outranspo spearheaded by Baillehache, "€21 Folios," pokes fun at the tabulation of meaning in the translator paycheck. The idea behind the project begins with an originally authored text of 1,150 characters, produced by a translator, describing a tool used during translation that costs about what you might make translating the very description of that object. To quote Baillehache's project description from the shared Outranspo Google Drive folder: "It can be a very cheap bookstand, a crappy desk lamp, a lousy pen, a non-memory foam cushion, or a specific brand of Roubaud-standard coffee, cigarettes, or eyedrops, etc. that you use when translating, and that can highlight a specific aspect of your experience as a translator."

The next step to the project, once the original text has been produced, is to translate it, twice. Once with a 1,500-character (with spaces) French translation, and another with a 3,000-character (with spaces) French translation. The translation thus expands on two levels, by number of variants and character count, while it also diminishes: the title "21€ Folios" represents a regular amount of money a translator is paid per 1,150 characters. However, after "social security contributions and tax payments" (Baillehache, project description), this comes to about 14€, which is the limit price of the object the translator is tasked to describe. The experiment is thus tailored not to an equivalence of sense, sound or letter, but to the monetary existence of the translator.

What all the above examples do is adopt the = of equivalence, the idea that equivalence "must be produced" and that a translation must be equivalent to its source text, and push it to the extreme, to show its breaking point. We might call this a kind of *metaequivalence*, interrogating presuppositions by adopting their own logic. This is one way of attacking the problem. But what about experimental translations that do the opposite and carry out *counterequivalence* and try to be as inequivalent as possible?

≠

In Outranspo, a polytranslation is a translation toward multiple target languages. A heterotranslation is when there are multiple translators translating toward the same language. A countertranslation is a translation written against another translation of the same text. Retranslation translates a translation, and retrotranslation translates a translation back into the language of its original (this is also known as back-translation). These are practices that are used all the time in translation and translation scholarship and teaching. But in experimental translation, these practices used as procedures are pushed to the extreme and used for creative outputs that not only challenge the idea of equivalence, but explode the very idea of text.

The work of Sawako Nakayasu uses all of the Outranspian procedures mentioned above. *Mouth: Eats Color* is a work of "translation, anti-translation and originals" based on and in dialogue with the poems of Chika Sagawa, a poet of the Japanese Avant-Garde, whose international notoriety has grown considerably since Nakayasu's introduction of her work into English. Although maybe I shouldn't say English, but something like English+, as Nakayasu's translations are mixed with the Japanese of the original, as well as French. Nakayasu also translates translations. First, because Chika Sagawa was herself a translator, and poems by Mina Loy and Harry Crosby, translated by Sagawa, appear in the book, attributed to their authors, but translated and rewritten in what Irina Holca has called a "digested" form, with reference to the aesthetics of anthropophagy so important to the history of transcreation. Translations of translations, but also, mixtures of translation and creation. This process, as Holca shows, is not a way of appropriating Sagawa's poems but rather of prolonging a gesture that exists in them, as Sagawa's poems also take apart original poems by authors in foreign languages, and recombine them in translation to make new originals. Holca gives a thorough reading of Sagawa's decomposition/composition of Charles Reznikoff's *Jerusalem the Golden* into a poem translated (at least) two times by Nakayasu as "Gate of Snow," one time mixing Japanese and English and another time in English only.

I say "Gate of Snow" is translated "at least" twice because I don't really know, actually, how many times these poems are translated.

In *Mouth: Eats Color*, poems are staggered and dispersed, disappearing and reappearing later on in the book in a nonlinear disarrangement. This has the effect of heightening the labyrinthine web of the proliferating process of translations in serial, which is one of the guiding formal techniques of the book. The first poem in the book, "Promenade"—or at least its title—appears eighteen times in English throughout the book. Or fifteen: three of these times, it is written "Puromunaado" and placed in parentheses after the Japanese. These "Puromunaado" poems are numbered 1-9; the first six appear in parentheses after the English title, "Promenade." Twice the English title "Promenade" appears with the Japanese title in parentheses. The Google Translate app tells me that it also appears twice in Japanese only. Later in the book, the English title reappears but ordered by letters: Promenade (A), Promenade (B) and Promenade (C).

The English versions, mixed together with Japanese and sometimes French, translate the same poem each time in a different, sometimes radically different way. Other procedures are also at work decentering the play of translation: "half-translation, or translation-in-progress... machine and back translations, transliterations and so on" (Holca 385). The poems where the Japanese appears in the title, alone, in parentheses or preceding parentheses are also written in Japanese (mostly). Which one of these Japanese poems (if any) is the original? Which original gave rise to which translation, which translation to which translation? I find myself in a multi-necked Kline bottle, with translations leading to originals leading to translations leading to translations. This decentering is mimed in the editorial process, which hopscotches the different variants through the book, intersecting them with Nakayasu originals as well as originals, collaborations and translations of Nakayasu's contemporaries (Frances Chung, Miwako Ozawa, etc.).

This work of experimental translation exists in parallel to Nakayasu's more traditional translation of Sagawa's poems in *The Collected Works of Chika Sagawa*. This double-publishing follows Moure's practice of experimentally translating works that have other more faithful variants to position themselves against (countertranslation). Likewise, the translational logic of *Mouth: Eats Color* carries on into Nakayasu's originally authored publications, such as *Some Girls Walk into the Country They Are From*, which uses the play of editorial practice as creative practice by including translations by other translators, and playing with their ordering in the book. Translations can both and either precede and proceed originals in the order they appear in the book. She also continues mixing languages and experimental translation procedures like calque inlaid in parentheses, or simply pasted into the flow of the English, as in the poem "Bright Sun in the Head of Girls," which begins in Japanese, but is interpolated in English by what might be read as a commentary from a translational avatar of the author (since no translator name is given, as it is for some of the other poems not in English): "The preceding lines explain the fact that this, what you're reading, or hearing, or witnessing, is a totally irresponsible and mediocre translation of the poem from earlier, called 'Bright Sun in the Head of the Girls.' ... Strangely enough, it is only after the mediocre translator gives up on translation does anything of value ever happen" (*Some Girls* 61).

This line could be taken as a tongue-in-cheek definition of experimental translation as a whole. Nakayasu's poetic essay "Say Translation Is Art" is a kind of manifesto and manual for doing unconventional, contestatory and interrogating practices of experimental translation, by inviting the reader to "say" "translation" in different ways: each (most) line(s) begins with the word "say" and follows through syntactically or ends in translation: "Say translation as open art practice as open as matter and anti-matter" (2); "Say 'bad' translation. Say 'F' translation. Say ephemeral translation" (8); "Say how no corrupt loyalty fidelity to what translation" (19). I am reminded of Snell-Hornby's fifty-eight definitions of equivalence.

This play on seriality, on multiple and contradictory equivalence is also part of the poetics of the journal *Chain*, edited by Jena Osman and Juliana Spahr. This is important because the volume of *Chain* devoted to *Translucinación* (2003) blazed the trail for much of the work that I have been doing and talking about here. The organizational principle of the journal was conceived on the model of a chain letter. The very last entry in the volume on *Translucinación* takes the form of a one-sentence quote from Emma Goldman calling for an end to war. This was in the context of the U.S. war on Iraq. Spahr sent this sentence in English out in a letter asking over thirty translators to translate it into different languages. The final version is a collective poem in many languages, but also a collective call to end war. It is also an impressive editorial feat, given the chain-letter format, since translators had to be found for each of the very specific language pairs involved, from Esperanto to Serbian, from Igikuria to Haitian, and so on.

This volume of *Chain* also contained many examples of serial translations and translations that explode equivalence in other ways, beginning with Charles Bernstein's "test of poetry," which translates a source text based on a letter from Bernstein's Chinese translator, Ziquing Zhang, which is then translated four times into four separate languages by Haroldo de Campos, Leevi Lehto, Ernesto Livon-Grosman and the Royaumont translation collective. Grass gives this as an example of "performative translation."

But this is just the tip of the iceberg. The volume also includes a multitiered translation by A. Isadora Del Vecchio, Abdourahman Idrissa, Kiran Jayaram and Karen Ohnesorge of Michel-Rolph Trouillot's poem "Imigrayson" (2003), originally in Haitian Kréyol and translated five times, into English, French and Songhay (and many more than that if you count commentary and footnote as translations). The serial approach in this case is trying to solve for a real translational problem, seeking to do justice to the poetics of the text and the Kréyol language in spite of its relationship to the imperial languages most of the translators were working with. Mahwash Shoaib's five-part translations of Kishwar Naheed's *Sokhta Samani-e-Dil/Composition of a Scorched Heart* inspired the "blind-faith translation" procedure in the supplement to this book (you can read more about it there). The first publication of Caroline Bergvall's "Via," which gathers together forty-seven translations into English of the first tercet of Dante's *Inferno*, also appears in this volume of *Chain* (it was published many times subsequently).

And beyond *Chain*, serial translation is a recurring motif of experimental translation. Sharmila Cohen and Paul Legault's *Telephone* project, or Antoni Muntadas's OTTIP (*On Translation: The Internet Project*) are two such examples. And of course, serial translation is a favorite pastime of the Outranspo, be it in the multiple pseudotranslations of the "Lost Poem of Emily Dickinson," in Santiago Artozqui's "Waves" project, or in the "Renga-O" lead by Camille Bloomfield, translating original tercets into four languages using Outranspian procedures.[2]

Many of these serial translations adopt a collaborative praxis and aesthetics, which in some cases joins with a desire to exceed the text itself, challenging translational norms that are also social norms, as with Spahr's multilingual call for an end to war. Amira Hanafi's "ح ل ٩٩٧ (A language act)" is an act of activist translation carried out in collaboration as "an open invitation to contribute to a crowd translation of the English Language Unity Act of 2019, a piece of proposed legislation that would establish an official language for the United States."[3] Currently there is no official language in the United States. Hanafi posted the translation as a Google doc, and over time, the text was translated into several languages, after which Hanafi printed twenty-eight copies of the final project and mailed them to the Republican sponsors of the bill.

Hanafi's project overflows equivalence, not only as a unitary act of translation producing one text, or even as a sole translator working on their own, or as a transfer from one discrete language to another, but as a translational action reaching beyond the boundaries of the text. Perhaps with Hanafi I have strayed quite far from VD's original definition of equivalence as "the same situation… rendered by two texts using completely different stylistic and structural methods" (VD/Sager and Hamel 38). This is not only because VD's definition is extremely narrow, pertaining primarily to the translation of idiomatic expressions or cultural indicators or markers such as "No Smoking" signs, or calling Paris "La Ville Lumière," and I can't do much with that. It is also not only because the word "equivalence" explodes its own boundaries, meaning both everything and nothing, meaning itself, as a tautology of what proves translation (translation is equivalence and equivalence is translation), and not itself (equivalence is not equivalent to *équivalence*). I mean, it is because of those things. But it is also because VD's category of equivalence falls apart as soon as you poke it, disintegrating into modulation or adaptation, a change in perspective and a translation of an extralinguistic, cultural reality, straying from words. Because language itself, as Hanafi's translation shows us, is an extralinguistic reality (and also a linguistic reality, of course!), a set of politics and policies that embody, materially,

116th Congresso ~~116TH CONGRESS~~
Primera sesion ~~1ST SESSION~~

ح ر ٩٩٧ ~~H. R. 997~~

(Check: should be: مَجْلِس النُوّاب ٩٩٧)

Declarar o Inglês enquanto língua oficial dos Estados Unidos, يعلن اللغة الإنجليزية كلغة رسمية للولايات المتحدة ~~To declare [illegible] English Lus Askiv as the official language~~ des États-Unis ~~of the United States~~, estabelecer uma uniformidade na língua Inglesa como regra para naturalização ~~to establish a uniform [illegible] English IsiNgisi language rule for naturalization~~, e para evitar más interpretações dos textos respeitantes a leis na língua Inglesa ~~and to avoid misconstructions of the English [illegible] language texts of the laws~~ Stanów Zjednoczonych ~~of the United States~~, pursuant to Congress' ecilops~~powers to~~ provide for the general ku~~welfare~~ Stanów Zjednoczonych ~~of the United States~~ and to establish a uniform rule of naturalization under article I, section 8, of the Constitution.

NAME ~~IN THE HOUSE OF~~ Cámara de Representantes ~~REPRESENTATIVES~~

FEBRUARY 6, 2019

Iowa Kralı [illegible] ~~Mr. King of Iowa~~ (kendisi, Bay Allen, Bay Massie, Bay McClintock ve Bay Perry için ~~for himself, Mr. Allen, Mr. Massie, Mr. McClintock, and Mr. Perry~~) aşağıdaki kanunu sundu, ~~introduced the following bill; which was referred to the Committee on~~ Eğitim ve Emek koitesinde belirtilen ~~Education and Labor,~~ and in addition to the Committee on the Judiciary, for a period to be subsequently determined by the Speaker, in each case for consideration of such provisions as fall within the jurisdiction of the committee concerned

---

Fig. 11. Extract from Hanafi's "ح ر ٩٩٧ (A language act)." Reprinted with permission of Amira Hanafi.

the way that human justice and human injustice happen. To ask the question of equivalence, of equal value, is then also to ask the question of difference, of how to be equal without being the same: how to do the real work of trying to understand each other, without having to speak the same language.

Exquisite valencies

The title of this chapter is not "Equivalence," it is "Equivalencias," the Spanish equivalent for equivalence. "Equivalencias" is also the name of the original poem that provides the blueprint and the raw material for the twenty-five translations and subsequent commentaries in the core section of de la Torres's *Repetition Nineteen*, which in turn has been the road map for this book. In many ways, it is where I started. But the point of origin in de la Torre's book is dissimulated, it needs to be uncovered by detective work. The first piece in the series of twenty-five is "Interjet 2996," a prose piece that presents itself, through force of linearity (since it is the first in the series), as a block of text from which the words of the poem were culled, but into which, actually, the words of the original poem were inserted; the procedure is called "T1: Embedded translation," not "embedded original" or "extracted translation." The prose piece is presented as an artifice, a counterfeit source. The next piece in the series is the poem written bilingually, with the English and the Spanish overlapping, which suggests a simultaneous composition, as though the two were written together, neither preceding nor proceeding the other, neither translation nor original.

The poem "Equivalencias" appears once more in the book, directly preceding the third section, where the commentaries appear. It is in the commentary that the reader finds out that "Equivalencias" is "a poem I wrote in the nineties that gave rise to the slew of different translations presented here" (*Repetition Nineteen* 75). And actually, the original poem appeared in Spanish in de la Torre's first book, *Acúfenos*, written in Spanish and published in Mexico in 2006. For many years, people would ask de la Torre why she didn't translate *Acúfenos*. And so she did. But if was never published, except in bits and pieces hidden in and amongst her work like clinamen. One of those clinamen is "Equivalencies." And the twenty-five translations (and twenty-five commentaries) that come out of it.

The line in the commentary where she gives away the discrepancy between translation *fabula* and *syuzhet* (that the order in which the translation happened is not the same as the way in which it is presented) is followed by a remark about the way translations can proliferate in the misstep between language and text, as she points to the possibility that an English language translator, unfamiliar with the Spanish idiom "*cae la tarde*" might translate this as "the afternoon falls" (75), thus introducing a foreignness through literal translation that was not there in the original. This misstep is the place where equivalence comes into question, questioning the equal sign that exists de facto between a departure and an arrival text. As I've striven to show throughout the book, this misstep is not empty but is a place rife with potentiality. It is with this nugget of the proliferating tendency of translation, the creative potential in the multiplication of variants, where I will end, too quickly, this hijacking of equivalence as a translational norm, exploding and imploding out in many directions. Equivalencies as exquisite valences.

PROCEDURES

6.1 Algorithmic gladiator

This procedure (inspired by Artozqui), named after the Borghese gladiator—a sculpture supposedly made according to the measurements of an ideal man (but which in reality varies from casting to casting)—involves back-translating from a translated text into the original, either in order to try to accurately guess the original or inversely to create multiple, destabilized variants of an original that may or may not exist.

6.2 Primary care—Outranspian Renga therapy

Using evocative prompts for a starting line such as "write something your primary care giver said to you as a child which has been bothering you your whole life," players pass a sheet around in a circle, each time translating using Outranspian constraints and grammatical modifications.

6.3 Transcriduction

Using a short text for translation that has the potential to inspire conversation among players, translate collectively (a poem, for example). The workshop guide does not participate but rather notes down whatever they can of the conversation that transpires during the translation. This transcript becomes the translation.

See the supplementary *Handbook of Translation Procedures* for full, detailed instructions and creative results.

7

"Say free translation, I say it, I do translate like that and also like this but there is more to that story translation, more to that arc, art, ball in the air translation I pitch it to you still in the air translation"

—Nakayasu, *Say Translation Is Art*[1]

Katarzyna Giełżyńska's *C()n Du It* is a collection of video and sound poems influenced by Giełżyńska's textual audiovisual work on films, TV and advertising clips, which she calls "motion graphic" (Marecki and Małecka, "AS - *C()n Du It*" 2). The poems, all a minute or less, hijack the form, aesthetics and prosody of advertising and digital culture. They use strong visual imagery, collaged from symbolic or iconic images (like Albert Einstein's face collaged next to the Queen of England's), video game visuals, computer error messages, imitations of design practices intended to attract the viewer's attention, whether they would like it to be attracted or not. The images are edited to flash at the viewer in the hyperactive pace of capitalist visual stimulation and acceleration, of immediacy and speed. The visuals are accompanied by soundtracks of collaged machinic or hacked effects, sound bites, music and, often, screams. The final element is the text, which once again appropriates and hijacks the visual effects of advertising with font, movement and layout, but also in the short catchy plays on words that ironically debase the cliché morsels of advertising slogans and titling.

One problem for the English-language community, however, is that the poems are in Polish. Translating the poems poses a number of interesting problems, as the translator is faced with not only the problem of translating Polish wordplay but also of translating the relationship between words, images and sounds. This is a classic problem for audiovisual translation, or any kind of text translation that must preserve a link between text and image or other multimedia dimension.

For example, the poem "Granaty" borrows visuals from an old arcade game, and deploys a pun on the word *granaty*, which means grenades, but when cut up becomes *grana ty*, meaning, in Polish, "you are being played," conjugated for a feminine addressee. Likewise, the poem "Piekło z internetu" features a fixed image of a Google search for the word *piekło*, "hell," and its subsequent search results in a menu item list. The poem "Kastracja" contains animated text of the word *ja* stacking, proliferating and falling across the page in block letters and in brackets imitating an archaic aesthetics of computer-code writing. It is accompanied by stringent cries screaming "aaaaa!" *Ja* means "I" in Polish, and so the poetic meaning of the I screaming itself in pain is overwhelming—this sensorial, affective resonance is utterly lost on the foreign-language speaker.

In the first two examples, translators Piotr Marecki and Alexandra Małecka used experimental translation procedures to carry out a more-or-less faithful translation of the original. In the first, they reproduced the word decomposition through microtranslation, replacing "*grana ty*" by a play on "shooter": "shoot 'er." In their translation of "Piekło z internetu," "Hell from the Internet," they reproduced the constraint through transposition, replacing the Polish internet search with an English one for the word "hell." In the last example, to translate the screams of *ja*, the translators took recourse to a practice of image adaptation that can sometimes be seen in translations of animated films or series. In their technical report on their translation of *C()n Du It*, Marecki and Małecka give the example of the Japanese translation of the Pixar film *Inside Out*, where broccoli was replaced with green pepper on a child's dinner plate, in order for the disgust on the child's face to register with the viewer, since Japanese children are not familiar with broccoli as a familiar trope of a food disliked by children. In their modulated translation of "Kastracja," which they title "(m)emasculation," Marecki and Małecka replace the *ja* with the word "me," and accompany it by new sound as well to create the effect, in what they refer to as "total translation" in the title to their technical report.

However, Marecki and Małecka push the limits of this process by hijacking the translational strategy of localization. Localization is a strategy used in marketing that stretches the idea of translation until it becomes an adaptation for a target audience. Take these car ads that I give as examples in my translation master's class when I am introducing students to the idea of creative translation:

LE PLAISIR DE CONDUIRE N'ATTEND PAS.
NOUVELLE BMW SÉRIE 1 TROIS PORTES.

IMAGINE POWER.
IMAGINE TURBO POWER.
NOW DOUBLE IT.

THE ALL-NEW BMW 1 SERIES 3-DOOR.

SOMEONE'S BEEN WORKING OUT.

Introducing the bigger, four-door, all-wheel drive MINI Countryman.

MINIUSA.COM

"ELLE N'A PAS UN PEU GROSSI LA MINI?"

NOUVEAU MINI COUNTRYMAN. LA MINI POUR 5.

Fig. 12. BMW and mini car ads in French and English.

In these examples, it is not the language that is being translated, but rather the intentions of the text, its function, its goal or its purpose, to put it into dialogue with *skopos* translation theory (Reiß and Vermeer). And to carry out this translation of intended purpose, it is culture that gets translated. The cultural imaginary of pleasure (*plaisir*) in French culture translates into (or from) the English-language advertising culture of selling power, competition and domination: "imagine power, imagine turbo power, now double it." In the bottom example, the French version of the ad is profoundly gendered, first of all from the untranslatable play on the gendered pronoun *elle* for a car (*la voiture*), but also with the stereotype of women being more concerned about their weight (*elle n'a pas un peu grossi ?* = "hasn't she gained some weight?"). Both the gendering and the reference to being overweight risk alienating an English-language culture, especially in the United States, where these ads appeared. This is rendered in English with a reference to sports culture, and to that most "American" of institutions: the gym.

And so, as Giełżyńska hijacks the techniques and aesthetics of advertising and digital culture, so too do Marecki and Małecka hijack the strategies of localization for their translations of Giełżyńska's work. In the case of the translation of "Kastracja," this takes form in a second translation that changes the visuals to suit the words ("AS - C()n Du It"). In their report, they use the word "dynamic" to describe their translation, which, for readers familiar with the history of translation studies, will recall Eugene Nida's distinction between two poles of equivalence, formal and dynamic, the dynamic approaching what VD refer to as "adaptation." VD reference Nida's theories in order to establish their definition of adaptation:

Eugene Nida... demonstrated that some Indian languages have no word for brother and sister, or no word for wine because they do not know it, no word for cattle because they do not raise cattle, and as a result cannot understand certain Biblical images. In order to make them understand the Biblical images or metaphors, Nida proposes the introduction of adaptations, i.e. the translation method which retains the meaning but takes its signifiers from another area of experience. (VD/Sager and Hamel 279)

Adaptation, in VD, is the translation of a metalinguistic reality, a translation that goes beyond the bounds of what can be translated by linguistic structures in comparison, and attains *génie*. They give the example of translating "cricket" with *La Tour de France* or "tea" with *soupe* (as it refers to a meal at a certain time of day). Translating through adaptation translates the world the text is written in, beyond the boundaries of language and text, where equivalence would still be constrained, closely linked to these—although Ballard has noted that the distinction between equivalence and adaptation is far from neat,[2] like so many of VD's categories. Nida's introduction of dynamic equivalence in the context of evangelizing translations that propose to translate the Bible in a way that would most enable Indigenous populations to identify with it and encourage them to convert to Christianity finds cultural continuity in the use of the translation approach in contemporary advertising. In Outranspo, we call this pragmatranslation, a translation that aims at performing in the target culture the same goal as the source text in its own culture.

In the above example of the translation of "Kastracja" into "Castrat(I)on," the translators are careful to justify their procedure with the fact that Giełżyńska was involved in the translation process, and even in some cases, with her own desire to update and improve her originals. This mobilization of translation as a process of dynamic recreation is amplified by the fact that it is an example of "a true remake, since the artist had lost her hard drive between 2012 and 2013, and had no original files to work with" (Marecki and Małecka, "AS - C()n Du It" 6).

But Marecki and Małecka were interested in going even further into a total translation of the text as it is set into the ecology of subtitling and internet video clip translation. They did this by carrying out an experiment with what Abé Markus Nornes calls "abusive subtitling" (cited in "AS - C()n Du It" 10), a practice that comes from Japanese fansubbing culture, which overlays subtitles that intervene in the visuals and challenge the notion that subtitles should be as invisible as possible, not only in their form but also with their "unsuitable" content. In Marecki and Małecka's experiment, they asked students in comparative media studies and writing at MIT to write "abusive commentaries" on the poems, in order to imitate trolling practices. These commentaries were then layered into the originals in a final gesture of hijacking localization practices in the digital age.

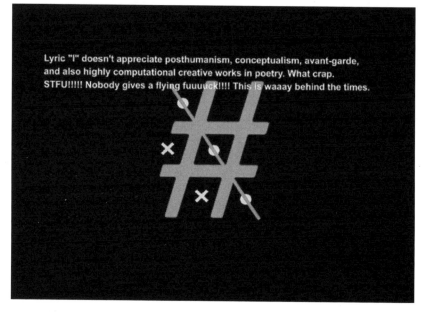

Fig. 13. Abusive subtitling in Marecki and Małecka's translation of "Kastracja"/ "Castrat(I)on." Reprinted with permission of Piotr Marecki and Aleksandra Małecka.

What do we call this? Do we call this a translation? An adaptation? A transcreation? An experimental translation? Where exactly are the lines between these notions, and where do they break?

Adapting to translational climate change

The notion of adaptation and the line between translation and adaptation exist in a mobile flux. This boundary can shift radically from one theoretical or translational context to the next and is a signpost for the way that norms of textual transfer are set up and regarded within a given culture, a given timeframe, a given ecology of the languages, texts and actors of translation. Adaptation has been used to refer to intersemiotic or multimodal shifts, adapting a book to a play or a play to the screen, for example. It has also been used to refer to generic shifts, adapting a serious work into a lighthearted, popular setting, or adapting a work for children's literature.

It has been used to refer to shifts in a text's "cultural or temporal setting" (Sanders 19). Samoyault calls this *"justesse ponctuelle,"* the punctuality of a translation, which she determines in terms of the community produced by a translation, and the adjustments translators make in relation to that potential community. She contrasts André Pézard's translation of the complete works of Dante, which, in 1965, translates the original Italian into fourteenth-century French (accompanied with many volumes of notes and commentary), to Jacqueline Risset's translation of the *Inferno*, which updates Dante's language to a contemporary readership. The English language finds a similar example in Mary Jo Bang's translation of *The Inferno*, which not only translates but adapts the language, its tone, style and register, but also the world, the extralinguistic reality and cultural references of the text in order to tailor Dante's original gesture to a new community of readers. Or Philip Terry's version that modulates *The Inferno* to the University of Essex. I am thinking here too of de Campos's transillumination of Dante, but I'll return to that in a moment.

Using the word "adaptation" to refer to a shift in a cultural or temporal setting draws attention to the boundaries of the words "translation" and "adaptation" as they move between historical periods and cultural situations. As Katia Krebs points out in a discussion of translation and adaptation in English theater, prior to Queen Victoria's copyright act of 1838, "any attempt to distinguish between translation and adaptation at that time would have been futile" (49). The instability of the terms also has to do with language, the language in which you speak the words "translation" and "adaptation," as Lawrence Raw points out in his introduction to *Translation, Adaptation and Transformation*, with relation to the Turkish language and cultural context. He uses the example of Selâmi Munir Yurdatap and Kemal Tahir's adaptations (or appropriations?) of Western figures and narratives such as Dracula or Sherlock Holmes or Mickey Spillane's Mike Hammer novels, which localize them in the post-1945 Republic of Turkey, adapting the characters, names and cultural activities of these figures with no concern for "originality" in either sense (meaning, they didn't care about being original nor did they care about protecting the integrity of the originals).[3]

At the time Yurdatap's and Tahir's works were first published, however, they were neither described as translations, adaptations, nor appropriations, but "*romanlar* [novels]"—a genre generously assigned by the publishers to short stories and novellas as well as larger works (Gürçağlar 2008: 248). In fact there is no equivalent in Turkish for "adaptation" or "appropriation"; depending on the context the words *çevirmek* (to translate) and *hazirlamak* (meaning to prepare verbally, either for spoken or written delivery) are generally employed. To "adapt" translates either as *alişmak* (to get used to), *aliştirmak* (to get accustomed to) or *uyum sağlamak* (to suit to a new purpose, as in the phrase "Adapting our native cuisine to the available food resource of a new country"). (Raw 7)

This reflection on what happens to the terminology we use to describe translation when it encounters translation, when it translates into another language, is a common trope for deconstructing translational norms, as I pointed out in the introduction with the example of the Hindi/Marathi terms *anuvad* meaning "speaking after or following" or *rupantar*, "change of form," where the words do not refer to the same norms of fidelity that can be heard in the word "translation" in its mainstream English-language definition. Here too, the distinction between translation and adaptation falls apart, or, at the very least, shifts.

For Georges L. Bastin, adaptation is not a subcategory of translation as it is for VD, but it can nevertheless overlap and fill in the gaps of translation: "Adaptation is the process of creating a meaning that aims to restore a communicational balance that would be broken by the process of translation" (Bastin, quoted in Vandal-Sirois and Bastin 24). This makes it similar to experimental translation as I have been describing it, as experimental translation also works in the places where translation breaks down—the difference being that experimental translation breaks down the process on purpose, to test its limits, see where it can break. And it also seems, keeping in mind the reflections of Raw and Palekar, that translation and adaptation themselves, as figures, currents, climates, words in translation, are places where translation breaks down.

All theories have a breaking point. They work until they do not, because they come up against the limitations of the specific context in which they were elaborated, and in which they are useful. In the case of experimental translation, the first of these limitations is the norms of translation, against which experimental translation establishes itself. If these norms change, the structures of this opposition falls apart.

In the course I teach for the professional translator training master's program at my university where I deploy procedures of experimental translation (although I call them "creative translation" in the classroom so as to not scare the students), one of the questions I get every year is: How is this any different from adaptation? Aren't we really just talking about adaptation and not translation here? The first answer to this is that there is no clear dividing line between translation and adaptation, not only because these terms change in translation, but because they often overlap (which is different than being the same or meaning the same thing).

The second answer has to do with the way that the theoretical presuppositions that we hold about translation diverge radically from the everyday common practices of translation—the very same that I am trying to train my students to master. The translation norms I have been probing throughout this book, norms like fidelity, equivalence, accuracy, productibility, predictability and navigability, are the norms that belong to machine translation. They are what machine translation does or tries to do; they are what humans have trained the machine to do. And it is through programming and training the machine, through the necessity of figuring out a set of codes and doxa in order to communicate to the machine that these norms have been reified

But these norms, like capitalism itself, undo themselves in the making, and more and more what we see as the task for the translator is linked in lived professional situations with that of the cultural mediator—what David Katan has referred to as the "transcreational turn." And in the use of the word "transcreation" by Katan and by other actors in the translation marketplace, I find another limit to experimental translation as that which opposes translational norms, because these oppositions *are* actually norms of translation practice. Current translation practice is at odds with how most people think of translation. The opposition meets that which it opposes, and gets reified into it, gets converted into norms, undoing its own opposition. Transcreation, as it was first set out by de Campos, referred to an oppositional strategy, not unlike what I have been proposing as experimental translation, seeking to challenge and break textual norms of power and domination inherited from colonial regimes, that injunction to be faithful to a source text inherited from the necessity to obey God, State and Capital. Now, it is a service translation agencies sell to clients. This is the definition of transcreation taken from the website for the translation agency Scriptis:

What is transcreation?

Great marketing copy doesn't happen overnight. It requires multiple iterations of concept testing, rewriting, and audience testing. The process becomes more difficult when you're creating content in multiple languages.

Recently, *Brand Quarterly* argued that there are only two strategies for localizing marketing messages: EITHER translate your English language materials directly, OR start completely fresh with a local advertising agency in every market you plan to reach.

Transcreation represents a middle path. You don't have to choose between a literal translation and a whole new campaign. Transcreation engages creative services to deliver high-impact communications without delaying your launch or breaking your budget. The end result of the process is internationalized copy that expresses your brand, connects with your audience, and ensures that you continue to control the message.[4]

Here we might imagine that we have strayed as far as possible from the traditional norms of fidelity, equivalence, accuracy, as de Campos invites us to do. But if we update the norms of translation to the age of algorithmic production, we see that "transcreation" in its meaning, as it has been reified in the insatiable appropriations of capitalism, now fully upholds "the productive, the predictive and the navigable" (Slater): "high-impact communications without delaying your launch or breaking your budget." The word "adaptation," in particular in Bastin's deployment of it, also refers to a biological process, of adapting to a particular ecology, of the survival of the fittest. This is what has happened to the word "transcreation"—and translation itself—as it adjusts to changing marketplace norms of translation practice. It has adapted.

So it is on this level that experimental translation strategies that use adaptation challenge the norms of marketplace transcreation: in intention, function, purpose. It is the *skopos* of experimental translation that makes it different from contemporary practices of transcreation, and also from what I teach my students in the translator training program, as my goal is to serve them, not to question the machine of the translation market (although I try to do that as well). I want them to survive in the climate changes of the current global translational ecology. But I also want them to critique the heritage of Darwinism in the instrumentalization of creative translation practices for the purposes of neocolonial and capitalist profit-driven systems of exploitation and the violence of domination that is inherent in them. There is a profound difference between de Campos's transillumination of Dante and the localizing of a BMW marketing campaign: among other things, a difference of *skopos*.

The last way in which I frame the difference between adaptation and the practices of creative translation that I teach in my class, and the practice of experimental translation that I have been writing about here, has to do with language—with the delineating of language difference in a global ecology and economy, in terms of languages as a continuum of entities existing in the politics of the nation-state, and in the limens and limits of those nation-states. And this is the same answer I give to colleagues in experimental writing who ask what the difference between experimental translation and experimental writing is—or the answer we give to Oulipians who think there is no real difference between Oulipo and Outranspo: language difference matters. Experimental translation happens in the openings and breakages, the "irreducible strangeness" (Waldrop) of languages.

On one level, this is because when you use a machine translator, you choose from a menu of languages, just as when you hire a translator, crowdsource a translator or use CAT tools. There is no option to homolinguistically translate or adapt from one language into that same language or to translate into birdsong, LandArt, dance, ritual, photography or cuisine. And this is the last of the major distinctions between translation and adaptation, in that adaptations do not require a passage from one language to another, in that sense of language as *langue*, as political entity.

Experimental translation responds to that: to the way translation happens in the algorithmic marketplace of languages, in order to oppose, respond, critique interrogate and try to understand that. Adaptation has a history of referring to practices that transfer between media and semiotic sign systems; translation does not—or if it does, it does so metaphorically in such a way that runs the risk of erasing language difference. Experimental translation is operating as a device for interrogating and challenging marketplace norms and practices of translation in the age of algorithmic production, which seem mostly to happen between spoken human languages with writing systems.

When building the corpus for this book, I operated a rather strict methodological distinction that locates experimental translation as happening between human languages. This is a somewhat strange move for me, as I usually delight in breaking down disciplinary and methodological boundaries and have an aesthetic and political disdain for the ontological status of definitions. I have operated this distinction firstly out of a concern for my own convenience. All theories have limits, otherwise they become useless in their lack of specificity; no one can know everything (nor should they), no one can write about everything (nor should they). On a practical level, I had to draw a line to separate experimental translation from adaptation and from homolinguistic and intersemiotic translation in order for the theory to hold up. If this line does not exist, there is effectively nothing to separate experimental translation from other experimental writing or other experimental art practices, from painting to dance to music and beyond.

But even to me this sounds like an excuse. And I do want to open this work more to procedures of intersemiotic, multimodal and experiential translation[5] in the future. As I write this, the Experiential Translation network is gearing up for their symposium on Performative and Experiential Translation: Meaning-Making through Language, Art and Media,[6] which is taking place at the same time as this year's Outranspo residency. And in the *Handbook of Translation Procedures*, the supplement to this book, instead of descriptions of adaptation procedures, you will find a list of potential procedures that I have not tested yet, inspired by colleagues working in this domain, that would explore the potentialities of translating beyond the boundaries of human language defined in terms of its political contours in communities, territories and nomadic itineraries. It is an insanely partial list, inspired by my own errancies in dialogue with other humans, across books and the internet, more brainstorm than inventory or encyclopedia. It is made to be critiqued, amended, expanded and tested by readers.

I have one final proviso, as a disclaimer and warning relating to my methodological decision to stick to spoken and written human languages in this book, which concerns an attention to the limits of my own linguistic knowledge and privilege. As a speaker of only colonial languages, and as a native speaker of U.S. English—that language that is *not a language*, "the language of no one" (Moure, *O Resplandor* 17), the language that is a "virus" (Raley, "Global English" 308)— it is doubly important that I pay close attention to the presumptions and blindness hiding in the limitations and global situation of dominance of my own languages. I have a great conviction to this effect, that any reflection on translation must include a reflection on one's own positionality, and the limitations of partial knowledge that incur in relation to the languages one speaks and does not speak. It is the reason for which all translation studies must practice a kind of situated knowledge: because no one speaks all the languages. And that too is the reason why experimental translation, as I have written about it here, and as I hope it will survive in other contexts, must be about the hesitations and celebrations in the breakages, catastrophes and lifelines of language difference.

Notes

Introduction

1 https://eliterature.org/.
2 https://nlp.stanford.edu/IR-book/html/htmledition/tokenization-1.html#:~:text=A%20to ken%20is%20an%20instance,containing%20the%20same%20character%20sequence.
3 https://jalammar.github.io/illustrated-word2vec/; https://blog.acolyer.org/2016/04/21/the-amazing-power-of-word-vectors/.
4 https://www.youtube.com/watch?v=L3D0JEA1Jdc.
5 "L'expérimental présente cette particularité de n'être ni moderne, ni contremporain, ni d'avant-garde, ni postmoderne.... Il est ce qui pousse l'histoire et la temporalité à bout, ce qui la teste, et ne s'en accommode pas. C'est peut-être aussi pour cette raison qu'il est impossible de stabiliser l'expérimental dans une définition permanente."
6 "Placer la langue de la traduction dans le vocabulaire du consensus démocratique ne va donc pas sans paradoxe, ni sans difficulté : cela implique de réduire, d'affaiblir, voire de nier totalement, tous les conflits qui sont inscrits en elle [...et...] s'impose au prix d'une réduction de la différence entre l'un (ou soi) et l'autre, d'une confiance sans doute assez fallacieuse dans la réciprocité et l'empathie."
7 Since Grass's book *Translation as Creative Critical Practice* is forthcoming, page numbers might be subject to change.
8 One major blind spot of this work is that it does not treat experimental sign language translation, such as in the work of Christophe Daloz, Kyra Pollitt, Olivier Schetrit or Angela Tiziana Tarantini, to give just a few examples. This is primarily out of fear of making a blunder in my ignorance of how these languages work. I would be very interested to work on this topic in the future in collaboration with someone who knows what they're doing.
9 These references, as well as their original titles, can be found in Pym's *Translation Solutions for Many Languages*.
10 Japhari Salum, "Translation of the Book Titled 'Authentification of Hadith: Redefining the Critera' from English into Swahili: An Analysis of Translation Procedures"; Vahideh Sharei, "A Comparative Study of Strategies Employed in 'Old Man and the Sea' Translated from English into Person on the Basis of Vinay and Darbelnet's Model"; Roswani Siregar, "Translation Procedures Analysis: English-Indonesian Motivational Book." And this is really just the tip of the iceberg. Google "Vinay Darbelnet seven translation procedures" and you will see just how widespread the inheritance of VD is across the globe.
11 www.outranspo.com. You can also find our work published in a special issue of the online translation journal *Drunken Boat*: https://d7.drunkenboat.com/db24/outranspo, as well as on Remue.net in French: https://remue.net/outranspo.

12 I encourage readers to consult the list of constraints and procedures on Outranspo's website as a support guide to the book: https://www.outranspo.com/classification-of-translation-constraints-procedures/.

13 https://d7.drunkenboat.com/db24/outranspo/ludivine-bouton-kelly.

1 *Emprunt*

1 https://www.nourbese.com/poetry/zong-3/.

2 I am taking this line from the translation of Shleiermacher's phrase as it appears in Rosemarie Waldrop's article "Irreducible Strangeness" in the collected volume edited by Jerrold Shiroma also titled after Schleiermacher's phrase in translation.

3 I take this citation from Bielenia-Grajewska (110), which I discuss in more detail later.

4 This is the definition given by Merriam-Webster: https://www.merriam-webster.com/dictionary/redingote.

5 https://www.youtube.com/watch?v=UTzFjw4U8eU.

6 "The word *dollar* is borrowed ultimately from German *Taler*, short for *Joachimstaler*, derived from *Joachimstal* ('Joachim's Dale'), a place in Bohemia where silver was minted in the sixteenth century" (L. Bloomfield 429).

7 See Pym (*Translation Solutions for Many Languages* 1–35) for a deeper discussion of Bally and Malblanc in their relationship to Saussure and VD.

8 For a very thorough discussion of the roots of homophonic translation, see Broqua and Weissmann, *Sound/Writing*. This list of poets is taken from Weissmann's article (195).

9 "Semble être le résultat du regard distancié qu'il [Jandl] jette sur une certaine tradition de la traduction poétique, notamment sur la hiérarchisation très répandue qui place le sens (supposé immatériel) au-dessus des aspects formels et matériels."

10 Jean-Joseph Goux does this in "Marx et Walrus." See my e-chapbook *Money, Math and Measure* for a deeper discussion of this.

11 I am taking this analysis from Maurizio Lazzarato's *La Fabrique de l'homme endetté* and *Gouverner par la dette*. Lazzarato is referring to what happens in France, but it is my understanding that the phenomenon is multi- and transnational. I am also using the address "you" here under the presupposition that the majority of readers do not belong to the 1 percent (if only because the majority of people do not belong to the 1 percent).

12 This reading of the figure of the *emprunt* is not at all confined to historical accounts but is a common occurrence in linguistic accounts in our contemporary moment as well. For example, this is Denis Jemet: "When you borrow something from someone, you are supposed to give it back, one day or another, and give it back in good condition, i.e. in the same condition as you have borrowed it. To tell the truth, this is not exactly what happens between two languages, which do not seem to be as well-behaved as human beings" ("Foreword"). I intend to show that human beings are no more well-behaved than languages.

13 Gabriel García Márquez has praised Gregory Rabassa's translation of *One Hundred Years of Solitude* as being better than the original, for example (I owe this reference to Delphine Grass and her careful and generous prepublication reading of this chapter).

14 Ferreira da Silva uses the pronoun "she" to refer to the *wounded captive body at the scene of subjugation* throughout the book, with reference to her reading of Octavia Butler's *Kindred* which scaffolds the work.

15 A full description of the project can be found in Bergvall's *Fig* (50–60).

16 "Ce retour de l'allemand dans l'anglais n'est ni une non-traduction ni un retour de l'original: c'est la réalisation d'une différence contenue dans le poème, qui est celle de l'allemand lui-même, à la fois langue de mort et langue du poète, oppression et résistance."

17 "Écrivant dans une langue souillée par le crime (ses parents sont morts dans les camps nazis, lui-même a été interné dans un camp en 1943), il cherche une écriture qui paraisse en quelque sorte traduite en allemand, singularisé à l'extrême au point de paraître parfois méconnaissable."

18 For a deeper discussion of this, see my article "The Politics of Experimental Translation."

19 https://www.nourbese.com/category/set-speaks/.

2 The Calque

1 This procedure was first practiced by Georges Perec in his "Trompe l'œil," which Bloomfield charts in her article "Homographic Translations" in *Drunken Boat*, vol. 10: https://d7.drunkenboat.com/db10/07mis/bloomfield/constraint.html.

2 "Les ressemblances… sont abominables parce qu'elles mettent le doigt sur la matérialité de l'acte de traduction, ce qui perturbe une pensée des langues en tant que systèmes de signes. Cela trouble aussi la séparation interne du signe en signifiant et signifié" (Bellomo 4).

3 This idea of translation as moving relics from one place to another does not come from nowhere; the Latin word *translatio* also designated the moving of relics or sacred objects (like a saint's remains) from one site to another in Christianity. It also referred to the transfer of power from one empire to another.

4 1. Type of mistake/solution/comment: mistakes with prepositions: missing, erroneous, superfluous/in case of doubt, put several/and if no doubt? 2. Type of mistake/solution/comment: confusion between words/dunno/win eyedowt, eyekunchik bu win eyedownt?/.3. Type of mistake/solution/comment: faulty sentence construction/allow oneself a lot of freedom so long as it remains comprehensible/break the sentence up into smaller pieces/cf. Rabelais, cf. rhythmic groups in speech (4–5 syllables)

5 http://www.outranspo.com/acts-de-fundacion/.

6 "On traduit alors mot à mot les termes étrangers pour préserver l'inattendu qu'ils ont à nos yeux français; puis par la voie de la syntaxe: on pastiche alors la structure grammaticale de l'idiome traduit; par la voie de la stylistique, et même de la métrique, enfin" (Mounin 92).

7 For a rigorous analysis of how calque is used in Chateaubriand, see Baillehache, *Désir* (13–56).

8 "My body fell like the dead fall down," in Mary Jo Bang's translation of the *Inferno* (57).

9 https://camillebloomfield.com/deep-dante/. For an English translation of Bloomfield's poem, readers are invited to plug the original Italian phrase into DeepL and create their own montage.

10 http://www.samtrainor.com/stp/.

3 Literal Translation

1 A methodology that Craig Dworkin describes as "the literalization of metaphor... a willingness to take the unintended suggestions of language as reality and to pursue a figural and subjunctive hypothesis with a quite literal, demonstrative logic" (Dworkin, "Introduction" 8). For me, this is also a kind of spelling, in the witch's sense.

2 This is a reference to Craig Santos Perez's *Unincoporated Territory* tetralogy, poems that incorporate litoral translations that bend between English and Chamorro, the native language of Guam, another "unincorporated territory" of the United States. Santos Perez writes: "My hope is that these poems provide a strategic position for 'Guam' to emerge from imperial 'redúccion(s)' into further uprisings of meaning. Moreover, I hope 'Guam' (the word itself) becomes a strategic site for my own voice (and other voices) to resist the reductive tendencies of what Whitman called the 'deformative democracy' of America" (*[Hacha]* 11).

3 "Réalité charnelle, tangible, vivante au niveau de la langue."

4 "Cache en vérité une loyauté aveugle à la lettre de sa propre langue."

5 "Des zones non-normées, des façons de parler qui, tout en étant absolument maternelles, s'écartent des normes dominantes du discours."

6 "Comme des espaces vides entre les boucles d'un filet de pêche" (85). "la traduction-de-la-lettre vise dans la langue du traducteur un cœur fait de trous" (86).

7 https://www.wokitokiteki.com/ke-kosa.html.

8 "L'oralité créole, même contrariée dans son expression esthétique, recèle un système de contre-valeurs, une contre-culture ; elle porte témoignage du génie ordinaire appliqué à la résistance."

9 "Berman la décrit tantôt à l'œuvre dans la syntaxe (inversions, rejets, déplacements), tantôt dans le lexique (néologismes, archaïsmes, usage des sens premiers ou concrets des mots), ou encore dans la sonorité (assonances, allitérations, rythmes strophiques ou libérés)."

10 https://www.tate.org.uk/art/art-terms/g/gutai.

11 Some speculation is always required with trying to figure these kind of details out since MT enterprises do not make their technology public.

12 https://e-stranger.tumblr.com/post/89970789401/you-have-to-accept-a-few-times-new-language. A video recording of the live event can be found on Abrahams's regular blog: https://aabrahams.wordpress.com/tag/kaj-mislis-s-tem/, and there is also a sound recording: https://soundcloud.com/annie-abrahams/kaj-mislis-s-tem-what-do-you-mean-final.

13 The only access I have managed to get to this is the extract printed in *Chain*, vol. 10, 116–123.

14 "Pa roule tro pre" does not appear in Michael Dash's selection of essays for his translation.

4 Transpose

1 This project has now evolved into an online course that presents the "rules" of English as a post-national hybrid language carrying traces of "place, class, crisis, trauma or displacement" in the contact between languages: https://www.englishes-mooc.org/hkw.

2 A list of her collaborators for the distorters used in *PDGN* can be found in *My Name Is Language* (17).

3 This project has also been carried out translinguistically in Anna Wierzbicka's Natural Semantic Metalanguage as Annie Abrahams kindly pointed out to me in her careful and generous rereading of this chapter. You can read more about it on Abrahams's blog: https://e-stranger.tumblr.com/post/177344059551/minimal-english.

4 "Si [une langue universelle] existait, elle éliminerait du même coup la question de la traduction."

5 "L'intensité, la mélodie ou intonation, la durée, les silences ou pauses, et en général tout ce qui est de la nature du rythme (p. ex. la répétition)."

6 Transposition ciphers actually go back much farther than that, as Martine Loekie Mariska Diepenbroek has shown in her doctoral dissertation, which trace the scytale transposition code back to the Spartans.

7 The original draft of this chapter contained a lengthy and befuddled commentary on a dispute between Katherine Hayles and John Cayley as to whether codeworks that combine human language and code by artists such as MEZ, Talan Memmott and Alan Sondheim can be considered pidgins, creoles (Hayles) or neither (Cayley), and whether porting between different systems or programming languages can be considered translation. However, many hours and many discarded pages of computer text later, I have come to the conclusion that the question of whether code is a language or not exceeds the limits of my current knowledge!

8 https://conlang.fandom.com/wiki/Ilish. This reference was gleaned from Okrent's book.

9 https://www.inform-fiction.org/index.html.

10 Published as part of a selection from the *Renderings* project associated with Montfort's Trope Tank, which sought to locate digital literary work from around the world and publish it in English: http://curamag.com/issues/2014/11/30/renderings.

11 This is the same article that is published as a report on the Trope Tank website: https://tropetank.com/reports/TROPE-12-04.pdf.

12 https://content.sakai.rutgers.edu/access/content/user/jobaille/translatingzaum/home-1.html.

13 The word "algorithm" comes from a distorted seventeenth-century transliteration of the Arabic surname of the mathmatician al-Khwarizmi, who first introduced complex mathematics, like algebra, to the West. https://www.etymonline.com/word/algebra?ref=etymonline_crossreference.

14 Noel's translation joins back in with the theme of transposition as biological or genetic code. This has been picked up by artists experimenting with something similar to what I am trying to explore here with the idea of transposition as a grammatical code. Eduardo Kac's *Genesis* project translates sentences from Genesis into Morse code and then into genetic code. Sophie Seita's *Transposition* takes many forms, as artist book, performance

and installation, etc., and is structured around seven transpositions that explode into diverse remediations to offer artistic, feminist and queer nature rituals. To do so, she leans into the definition of transposition as "horizontal gene transfers, not from parent to offspring, but either from one organism to another through copying, implanting, and inserting; or in the deletion, imbrication, and shifting positions of genetic material in a chromosome" (Seita 134).

15 Mark Parayre spoke about his experience in the round-table discussion held at the 2011 Assises de la traduction littéraire, led by Camille Bloomfield.

16 "Les traductions de textes contraints sont souvent à l'origine d'inventions qui font de la figure du traducteur l'auteur de textes susceptibles de créer un système propre, relativement indépendant du texte source, et de reformuler la relation traditionnellement verticale entre source et cible, au profit d'une relation horizontale riche d'échanges fructueux entre deux textes."

17 "Being in the 'beyond', then, is to inhabit an intervening space, as any dictionary will tell you" (Bhabha 7).

18 Edwin A. Abbott is also the author of *Flatland*.

19 See Dworkin: *Reading the Illegible* (2003), *Radium of the Word* (2020) *Nothing: A User's Manual* (2015), as well as any or most of his poetry etc.

20 I rely here on Myriam Suchet's reading (196).

21 From Moure's translation of Bueno, extracted here: https://www.asymptotejournal.com/special-feature/wilson-bueno-paraguayan-sea/.

5 Modulated

1 Entitled *Occupational Sickness* in Avasilichioaei (translated as "professional of boldness" by Sampedrín).

2 Both of the quotations are taken from resources on Erín Moure's PennSound page, the first from her "Close Listening" interview with Charles Bernstein, the second from her talk at the Kelly Writer's House. https://writing.upenn.edu/pennsound/x/Moure.php.

3 This quote is taken from "Crónica Seven" of *O Resplandor* and is attributed to Sampedrín (in Moure's essay on "the paradox of translation" that can be found on her website), but is found in *O Resplandor* in "O's notebook"—O referring to Oana Avasilichioaei. This confusion of authorship and translatorship is indicative of the play of modulation found in Moure's writing. This quote could also be attributed to Moure, the author of the *crónica*, and of *O Resplandor* (according to its cover).

4 Pessoa is also the inventor of the heteronym, as Robinson notes in *The Experimental Translator* (142).

5 As Shannon MacGuire remarks, although the name Eirin Moure appears on the cover, the spelling "Erin Mouré" appears on the copyright page "complicating the economic and symbolic registers of her gesture." MacGuire also notes that this is the last time the name "Mouré" appears on copyright pages in Moure's books.

6 "La traduction, aussi étonnant que cela nous paraisse aujourd'hui, est un gage d'authenticité. C'est pourquoi nombre de scribes médiévaux allèguent une source imaginaire : se prétendre traducteur permet d'attester la vérité d'un récit à travers le prestige d'une langue ancienne."

7 Louis Watier also gives the example of nineteenth-century poets presenting original works as poems from the Middle Ages written by troubadours, translated or found in medieval Occitan. There is a large body of work on pseudotranslation that I will not attempt to present here; Carol O'Sullivan's entry in the *Handbook of Translation Studies* provides a good short bibliography of works in English that treat the phenomenon. For readers of French, Ronald Jenn's full length monograph, *La pseudo-traduction, de Cervantès à Mark Twain*, gives a good overview in the European context. See also Douglas Robinson's entry in the *Routledge Encyclopaedia of Translation Studies*.

8 An extract can be found on the Catullus Translation Sampler on University of Pennsylvania's website: https://writing.upenn.edu/library/Catullus.html.

9 The poems of Gaius Valerius Catullus are a hotbed of experimental translation, beginning with Celia and Louis Zukofsky's semi-homophonic translations. Bernadette Mayer also published translations of Catullus that alternate between faithful renditions and playful imitations, adaptations with updated register, feminist hijackings, as well as works inspired by translation that she calls "epigrams" (*The Formal Field of Kissing*). The Catullus Translation Sampler cited above features experimental translations by poets including Charles Berstein, Richard Tuttle and Brandon Brown.

6 Equivalencias

1 I don't have space here to treat some of the very amusing examples that play with literal (in both senses of the word) translations of idiomatic expressions such as Bruno Fern, Tiphaine Garnier and Christian Prigent's *Craductions*, or the classic *Sky My Husband* by Jean-Loup Chiflet, which is also a board game. ("Sky my husband" literally translates the French expression "ciel mon mari!," which refers to a surprising situation, such as a wife being interrupted by her husband while she is with her lover.) Or de la Torre's T10: "Translation into as many idiomatic expressions as the original poem allowed."

2 All of these can be found on the Outranspo website: www.outranspo.com.

3 https://amirahanafi.com/tagged/hr997.

7

1 © Sawako Nakayasu, from *Say Translation is Art* (Ugly Duckling Presse, 2020), https://uglyducklingpresse.org/publications/say-translation-is-art.

2 "La comparaison de l' « équivalence » et de l' « adaptation » fait apparaître que ces deux catégories ne sont pas nettement distinguées" (Ballard, "A propos des procédés" 5).

3 Raw cites Turkish scholar Şehnaz Gürçağlar, *The Politics and Poetics of Translation in Turkey, 1923–1960*.

4 https://scriptis.com/what-is-transcreation/.

5 We find this term in Robinson with reference to the phenomenological experientiality of the translator. It is also the name of an AHRC project and network lead by Ricarda Vidal and Madeleine Campbell. The activities of the network as well as Ricarda Vidal and Jenny Chamarette's *Translation Games* have already come up with and tested out many ideas in this arena, translating between text, ceramic, dance, etc.: https://experientialtranslation.net/about-2/network/. The special issue of the review *Translation Matters* devoted to *Intersemiotic Translation and Multimodality* edited by Karen Bennett is also a wonderful resource.

6 https://kings.padlet.org/ricardavidal/ETN_conference.

Bibliography

Abbott, Edwin A. *How to Parse: An Attempt to Apply the Principle of Scholarship to English Grammar*. Seely, Jackson & Halliday, 1874.

Abrahams, Annie. *From Estranger to e-Stranger*. Editions +++plus+++, 2014.

Aguirre-Oteiza, Daniel. "What Politics Where Breath Fractures? (In)translation and the Poetics of Difference." *Journal of Spanish Cultural Studies*, vol. 19, no. 2, 2018, pp. 233–245.

Ahmed, Sarah. *Living a Feminist Life*. Duke University Press, 2017.

Alammar, Jay. "The Illustrated Word2vec." Jay Alammar: Visualizing Machine Learning One Concept at a Time, https://jalammar.github.io/illustrated-word-2vec/.

———. "Visualizing a Neural Machine Translation Model (Mechanics of Seq2seq Models With Attention)." Jay Alammar: Visualizing Machine Learning One Concept at a Time, https://jalammar.github.io/visualizing-neural-machine-translation-mechanics-of-seq2seq-models-with-attention/.

Alighieri, Dante. *Inferno*. Translated by Mary Jo Bang. Graywolf Press, 2013.

———. *L'Enfer*. Translated by Jacqueline Risset. Flammarion, 1985.

———. *Oeuvres completes*. Translated by André Pézard. Gallimard, 1965.

Appiah, Kwame Anthony. "Thick Translation." *Callaloo*, vol. 16, no. 4, 1993, pp. 808–819.

Arber, Solange. "Traduire 'sous verre' ou 'à la vitre': L'imaginaire de la transparence en traduction." *Itinéraires: Littérature, textes, cultures*, vol. 3, 2018, https://doi.org/10.4000/itineraires.4625.

Arrojo, Rosemary. *Fictional Translators*. Routledge, 2018.

Artozqui, Santiago. "L'Outranspo et la traduction creative." *En Attendant Nadeau*, 2017, https://www.en-attendant-nadeau.fr/2017/07/18/outranspo-traduction-creative/.

———. "Waves." Remue.net, Dossier Outranspo, https://remue.net/waves-une-forme-poetique.

Atkins, Tim. *Collected Petrarch*. Crater, 2014.

———. "Seven Types of Translation: Petrarch's Canzione." PhD diss., Roehampton University, 2011.

———. "Seven Types of Translation: Translation Tables." *English: Journal of the English Association*, vol. 69, no. 267, 2020, pp. 379–396, https://doi.org/10.1093/english/efaa029.

Baillehache, Jonathan. *Le désir de traduire: Penser la traduction selon Antoine Berman, Chateaubriand, Pound et Roubaud*. Presses Universitaires de Rennes, 2021.

———. "L'Oulipo et la traduction moderniste." *Formules*, vol. 16, 2012, pp. 279-290.

———. "The Remediation of Russian Avant-Garde Poetry." *Translating E-Literature*, 2014, https://octaviana.fr/document/COLN0011_7.

———. "Traduire la littérature à contraintes: Traduction ou transposition?" *Translating Constrained Literature/Traduire la literature à contrainte*, edited by Camille Bloomfield et al., special issue of *MLN*, vol. 131, no. 4, 2016, pp. 892-904.

———. "Translatingzaum." Translating Digitizing Avant-Garde Books, https://content.sakai.rutgers.edu/access/content/user/jobaille/translatingzaum/home-1.html.

Baker, Mona. "Corpus Linguistics and Translation Studies: Implications and Applications." *Text and Technology, in Honor of John Sinclair*, edited by Mona Baker et al. John Benjamins, 1993, pp. 233-250.

Ballard, Michel. "À propos des procédés de traduction." *Palimpsestes. Revue de traduction*, vol. 113, no. 30, 2006, pp. 113-130.

———. *Versus: La version réfléchie*. Vol. 1, *Repérages et paramètres*. Editions Ophrys, 2003.

———. *Versus: La version réfléchie*. Vol. 2, Les signes au texte. Editions Ophrys, 2004.

Bally, Charles. *Linguistique générale et linguistique française*. Editions Francke Bern, 1965 [1944].

Bassnett, Susan, and Harish Trivedi. "Introduction." *Postcolonial Translation: Theory and Practice*, edited by Susan Bassnett and Harish Trivedi. Routledge, 1999.

Bellomo, Paolo. "L'empreinte du calque: La matière reproduite dans l'imaginaire de la traduction." *Itinéraires: Littérature, textes, cultures*, vol. 3, 2019, https://doi.org/10.4000/itineraires.4965.

Bellos, David. *Is That a Fish in Your Ear? Translation and the Meaning of Everything*. Faber and Faber, 2012.

Benjamin, Walter. *Illuminations*. Translated by Harry Zohn. Schocken Books, 1969.

Bennett, Karen, ed. *Intersemiotic Translation and Multimodality*, special issue of *Translation Matters*, vol. 1, no. 2, 2019.

Bergvall, Caroline. *Drift*. Nightboat Books, 2014.

———. *Fig: Goan atom*. Salt, 2005.

Berman, Antoine. *La traduction et la lettre, ou L'auberge du lointain*. Editions du Seuil, 1999.

———. *L'Épreuve de l'étranger: Culture et traduction dans l'Allemagne romantique*. Gallimard, 1995.

Bernabé, Jean, Patrick Chamoiseau and Raphaël Confiant. *Eloge de la Créolité.* Gallimard, 1993.

Bhabha, Homi K. *The Location of Culture.* Routledge, 1994.

Bielenia-Grajewska, Magdalena. "Linguistic Borrowing in the English Language of Economics." *Lexis,* vol. 3, 2009, pp. 107–135, https://journals.openedition.org/lexis/643.

Bloomfield, Camille. "Deep Dante." *Ridondante: L'Oplepo per il Sommo.* Biblioteca Oplepiana, vol. 49, 2021. https://camillebloomfield.com/deep-dante/.

———. "Homographic Translations." *Drunken Boat,* vol. 10, https://d7.drunkenboat.com/db10/07mis/bloomfield/constraint.html.

———. "Renga-O. La forme japonaise du renga revisitée par l'Outranspo." Remue. net: Dossier Outranspo, 2020, https://remue.net/renga-o-la-forme-japonaise-du-renga-revisitee-par-l-outranspo.

———. "Poèmes pour Brexités/Poems for Brexitees." *Paris,* edited by Andrew Hodgson. Dostoyevsky Wannabe, 2019, pp. 69–80.

———."Traduire La Disparition de Georges Perec." *Vingt-Huitièmes Assises de la traduction littéraire,* 2012.

Bloomfield, Camille, and Hermes Saleda. "La contrainte et les langues (portugais, italien, français, espagnol, anglais)." *Translating Constrained Literature/Traduire la littérature à contraintes,* edited by Camille Bloomfield et al., special issue of *MLN,* vol. 131, no. 4, 2016, pp. 964–984.

Bloomfield, Leonard. *Language.* Routledge, 2015 [1933].

Bouhmid, Alison. "Creative Feedback." *On Creativity and Writing (and Teaching English as a Foreign Language),* blog, January 24, 2019, http://www.alisonbouhmid.com/creative-feedback.

———. "Diversity in Creative Writing Workshops: The Case of Undergraduates Studying English as a Foreign Language." *Recherches et pratiques pédagogiques en langues de spécialité, Cahiers de l'Apliut,* vol. 38, no. 1, 2019, https://doi.org/10.4000/apliut.7006.

bpNichol. *Translating Translating Apollinaire: A Preliminary Report.* Membrane Press, 1979.

Brand, Carina. "'Feeding Like a Parasite': Extraction and Science Fiction in Capitalist Dystopia." *Economic Science Fictions,* edited by William Davies. Goldsmiths Press, 2018, pp. 95–142.

Briggs, Kate. *This Little Art.* Fitzcarraldo Editions, 2020.

Broqua, Vincent. "La traduction de poésie expérimentale comme *Translucinación.*" *La main de Thôt,* vol. 5, 2017, http://revues.univ-tlse2.fr/lamaindethot/index.php?id=671.

———. "Temporalités de l'expérimental." *Miranda,* vol. 16, 2018, https://doi.org/10.4000/miranda.11342.

Broqua, Vincent, and Dirk Weissmann, eds. *Sound/Writing: Traduire-écrire entre le son et le sens—Homophonic Translation—Traducson—Oberflächenübersetzung.* Editions des archives contemporaines, 2019.

Brown, Brandon. *The Poems of Gaius Valerius Catullus.* Krupskaya, 2011.

Bueno, Wilson. *Paraguayan Sea.* Translated by Erín Moure. Nightboat Books, 2017 [1992].

Bürger, Peter. *Theory of the Avant-Garde.* Translated by Michael Shaw. University of Minnesota Press, 1984.

Cage, John. *Silence.* Wesleyan University Press, 2013.

Campana, Andrew. "Seika No Kôshô." *Curamag, Renderings*, vol. 14, 2014, http://curamag. com/issues/2014/12/3/renderings-seika-no-ksh.

Carr, Angela. "One More Word: The Translator's Archive in *Secession with Insecession.*" *Sillages Critique*, vol. 23, 2017, https://doi.org/10.4000/sillagescritiques.5517.

Catullus, Gaius Valerius. *Catullus (Gai Valeri Catulli Veronensis liber).* Translated by Louis Zukofsky and Celia Zukofsky. Cape Goliard Press, 1969.

Cayley, John. *Grammalepsy: Essays on Digital Language Art.* Bloomsbury Academic, 2020.

———. *Translation.* http://programmatology.shadoof.net/, https://collection.eliterature. org/1/works/cayley__translation.html [originally published on www.shadoof.net, 2004].

———. "The Translation of Process." *Translation-Machination*, edited by Christine Mitchell and Rita Raley, special issue of *Amodern*, vol. 8, 2018, https://amodern.net/article/the-translation-of-process/.

Cecire, Natalia. *Experimental: American Literature and the Aesthetics of Knowledge.* Johns Hopkins University Press, 2019.

Césaire, Aimé. *Soleil cou coupé.* Editions K, 1948.

Cheyfitz, Eric. *The Poetics of Imperialism: Translation and Colonization from the Tempest to Tarzan.* University of Pennsylvania Press, 1997.

Chiflet, Jean-Loup. *Sky My Husband! Ciel mon mari! The Intégrale: Dictionary of the Running English; Dictionnaire de l'anglais courant.* Points, 2016 [1985].

Chuquet, Hélène, and Michel Paillard. *Approche linguistique des problèmes de traduction anglais-français.* Editions Ophrys, 2002.

Clarke, Chris. "The Impact of Constraint Visibility on the Translation of Constraint-Based Writing." *Translating Constrained Literature/Traduire la literature à contrainte*, edited by Camille Bloomfield et al., special issue of *MLN*, vol. 131, no. 4, 2016, pp. 877–891.

———. "The Strain of Constraint: Loyalty, Elasticity, and Feasibility in Translation." *Francosphères*, vol. 10, no. 2, 2021, pp. 265–282.

———. "Tlönslation: From Desnos to English via Uqbarian Literature." Remue.net, Dossier Outranspo, 2020, https://remue.net/tlonslation-from-desnos-to-english-via-uqbarian-literature.

Collins, Sophie, ed. *Currently & Emotion: Translations*. Test Centre, 2016.

Colyer, Adrian. "The Amazing Power of Word Vectors." *the morning paper: a random walk through Computer Science research*, 2016, https://blog.acolyer.org/2016/04/21/the-amazing-power-of-word-vectors/.

Corbett, John, et al. "Week 2: Indigenous Programming (Main thread)." critical code studies, http://wg20.criticalcodestudies.com/index.php?p=/discussion/70/week-2-indigenous-programming-main-thread.

Cronin, Michael. *Translation in the Digital Age*. Routledge, 2013.

Dante, Emma. *Moi, Personne et Polyphème*. Translated by the collective La Langue du bourricot. Presses Universitaires du Midi, 2016.

Das, S. "Namkaran: The Traditional Ritual of Naming a Baby." *Sanskriti Magazine*. https://www.sanskritimagazine.com/namkaran-the-traditional-ritual-of-naming-a-baby/.

Davies, William "Introduction to *Economic Science Fictions*." *Economic Science Fictions*, edited by William Davies. Goldsmiths Press, 2018.

De Campos, Haroldo. *Novas: Selected Writings*. Northwestern University Press, 2007.

De la Torre, Mónica. *Acúfenos*. Taller Ditoria, 2006.

———. "Doubles." *Words without Borders*, 2006, https://wordswithoutborders.org/read/article/2006-02/doubles/.

———. *Public Domain*. Roof Books, 2009.

———. *Repetition Nineteen*. Nightboat Books, 2020.

———. *Talk Shows*. Switchback Books, 2007.

Derrida, Jacques. "'This Strange Institution Called Literature': An Interview with Jacques Derrida." Translated by Geoffrey Bennington and Rachel Bowlby. *Acts of Literature*, edited by Derek Attridge, Routledge, 1992, pp. 33–75.

Diepenbroek, Martine Loekie Mariska. "Myths and Histories of the Spartan Scytale." PhD diss., University of Bristol, 2020.

Doris, Stacy. *Cheerleeder's Guide to the World: Council Book*. Roof Books, 2006.

———. *Conference*. Potes and Poets Press, 2001.

———. *Paramour*. Krupskaya, 2000.

———. *Parlement: Une cométragédie*. P.O.L, 2005.

Dworkin, Craig. *Dictionary Poetics*. Fordham University Press, 2020.

———. "extract from *DEF*." *Paris*, edited by Andrew Hodgson. Dostoyevsky Wannabe, 2019, pp. 9–16.

———. "Introduction: Against Metaphor (construye en lo ausente)." *Architectures of Poetry*, edited by Craig Dworkin. Rodopi, 2004.

———. *Nothing: A User's Manual*. Information as Material, 2015.

———. *Parse*. Atelos, 2008.

———. *Radium of the Word*. University of Chicago Press, 2021.

———. *Reading the Illegible*. Northwestern University Press, 2003.

Eco, Umberto. *The Search for the Perfect Language*. Translated by James Fentress. Blackwell Publishers 1997 [1995].

Efthymiades, Yiannis. "9/11 or Falling Man." Translated by Karen Van Dyck. *Currently & Emotion*, edited by Sophie Collins. Test Centre, 2016, pp. 321–326.

Emmerich, Karen. *The Making of Originals*. Bloomsbury, 2017.

Felstiner, John. *Paul Celan: Poet, Survivor, Jew*. University of Illinois Press, 2011.

Fenton, Sabine, and Paul Moon. "The Translation of the Treaty of Waitangi: A Case of Disempowerment." *Translation and Power*, edited by Maria Tymoczko and Edwin Gentzler. University of Massachusetts Press, 2002, pp. 25–44.

Fern, Bruno, Tiphaine Garnier, and Christian Prigent. *Craductions*. Les Impressions Nouvelles, 2015.

Ferreira da Silva, Denise. *Unpayable Debt*. Sternberg Press, 2022.

———. "Unpayable Debt: Reading Scenes of Value against the Arrow of Time." *Documenta 14 Reader*, edited by Quinn Latimer and Adam Szymczyk. Asia Art Archive, 2017.

Formigari, Lia. *Signs, Science and Politics: Philosophies of Language in Europe, 1700–1830*. Translated by William Dodd. John Benjamins, 1993.

Gaddis-Rose, Marilyn. *Translation and Literary Criticism: Translation as Analysis*. St. Jerome, 1997.

Galvin, Rachel. "For Has Its Reasons: Translation and Copia." *Translating Constrained Literature/Traduire la literature à contrainte*, edited by Camille Bloomfield et al., special issue of *MLN*, vol. 131, no. 4, 2016, pp. 846–865.

———. "Poetry Is Theft." *Comparative Literature Studies*, vol. 51, no. 1, 2014, pp. 18–54.

Gayraud, Irène. "Pour une traduction comme risque et désir: Potentialisations de l'original." *Itinéraires*, vol. 3, 2019, 10.4000/itineraires.4846.

Gellé, Albane. *Si je suis de ce monde*. Translated into sign language by Christophe Daloz. Directed by Anne de Boissy. Production by Les Trois-Huit at the NTH8/Nouveau Théâtre du 8e, Lyon.

Gibbs, Anna. "Fictocriticism, Affect, Mimesis: Engendering Difference." *Text: Journal of the Australian Association of Writing Programs*, vol. 9, no. 1, 2005, http://www.textjournal.com. au/april05/gibbs.htm.

Giełżyńska, Katarzyna. "*C()n Du It.*" *korporacja ha!art*, http://archiwum.ha.art.pl/ gielzynska/menu_static.html.

Ginsberg, Samuel. "Sonic Modernity and Decolonizing Countersounds in the Poetry of Urayoán Noel." *Latin American Research Review*, vol. 54, no. 1, 2019, pp. 135–150, https:// doi.org/10.25222/larr.335.

Glissant, Edouard. *Caribbean Discourse*. Translated by Michael Dash. University Press of Virginia, 1992.

———. *Le discours antillais*. Gallimard, 1997.

Gómez Capuz, Juan. "El tratamiento del préstamo linguistico y el calco en los libros de texto de bachillerato y en la obras divulgativas." *Revista de estudios filologicos*, vol. 17, 2009, http://www.tonosdigital.com/ojs/index.php/tonos/article/viewFile/294/203.

———. "Towards a Typological Classification of Linguistic Borrowing." *Revista Alicantina de Estudios Ingleses*, vol. 10, 1997, pp. 81–94.

Goux, Jean-Joseph. "Marx et Walrus: Un déplacement éthique." *L'Argent*, edited by Marcel Drach. Editions La Découverte, 2004, pp. 131–138.

Grass, Delphine. *Translation as Creative Critical Practice*. Cambridge University Press, forthcoming.

Grass, Delphine, and Lily Robert-Foley, eds. *The Translation Memoir*. Routledge, forthcoming.

Greaves, Sara, and Marie-Laure Schultz. "Dissociating Form and Meaning in Bilingual Creative Writing and Creative Translation Workshops." *E-rea*, vol. 9, no. 2, 2012, https://doi. org/10.4000/erea.2601.

Greenough, James B., and George L. Kittredge. *Words and Their Ways in English Speech*. Beacon Press, 1965.

Grimaldi-Donahue, Allison. "Welcome to the 2nd Queer Translation Issue." *Queen Mob's Teahouse*, 2018, https://queenmobs.com/2018/06/welcome-to-the-2nd-queer-translation-issue/.

Gürçağlar, Şehnaz. *The Politics and Poetics of Translation in Turkey, 1923–1960*. Rodopi, 2008.

Haugen, Einar. "The Analysis of Linguistic Borrowing." *Language*, vol. 26, no. 2, 1950, pp. 210–231.

Hawkey, Christian. *Ventrakl*. Ugly Duckling Presse, 2010.

Hayles, N. Katherine. *How We Became Posthuman: Virtual Bodies in Cybernetics*. University of Chicago Press, 1999.

———. *My Mother Was a Computer: Digital Subjects and Literary Texts*. University of Chicago Press, 2010.

———. *Writing Machines*. MIT Press, 2002.

Hejinian, Lyn. "Barbarism." *The Language of Inquiry*. University of California Press, 2000, pp. 318–336.

Hermans, Theo. "Norms and the Determination of Translation. A Theoretical Framework." *Translation, Power, Subversion*, edited by Román Álvarez and M. Carmen-África Vidal. Multilingual Matters, 1996, pp. 25–52.

Hodge, Siobhan. "Time That Travels Sings Concurrently to the Path of Letters: Translation in Padcha Tuntha-obas' Composite. Diplomacy." *Colloquy: Text, Theory, Critique*, vol. 32, 2017, pp. 4–36.

Hofstadter, Douglas. "The Shallowness of Google Translate." *The Atlantic*, January 2018, https://www.theatlantic.com/technology/archive/2018/01/the-shallowness-of-google-translate/551570/.

Hokenson, Jan Walsh, and Marcella Munson, eds. *The Bilingual Text: History and Theory of Literary Self-Translation*. St Jerome Publishing, 2007.

Holca, Irina. "Sawako Nakayasu Eats Sagawa Chika: Translation, Poetry, and (Post)Modernism." *Japanese Studies*, vol. 41, no. 3, 2021, pp. 379–394, 10.1080/10371397.2021.2008236.

Holmes, James S. "The Name and Nature of Translation Studies." *Indian Journal of Applied Linguistics*, vol. 13, no. 2, 1987, pp. 9–24.

Hsia, Yü. *Pink Noise (Fenhongse zaoyin)*. Garden City, 2007.

Huang, Yunte. *Shi: A Radical Reading of Chinese Poetry*. Roof Books, 1997.

Jakobson, Roman. "On Linguistics Aspects of Translation." *Language in Literature*, edited by Krystyna Pomorska and Stephen Rudy. The Belknap Press of Harvard University Press, 1987 [1959].

Japhari, Salum. "Translation of the Book Titled 'Authentication of Hadith: Redefining the Critera' from English into Swahili: An Analysis of Translation Procedures." *International Jounnal of Linguistics, Literature and Translation*, vol. 2, no. 4, 2019, pp. 130–136.

Jamet, Denis. "Foreward." *Borrowing*, edited by Aurélia Paulin and Jennifer Vince, special issue of *Lexis*, vol. 3, 2009, https://doi.org/10.4000/lexis.623.

Jenn, Ronald. *La pseudo-traduction, de Cervantes à Mark Twain*. Peeters, 2013.

Joyce, James. "Anna Livia Plurabelle" (*Finnegan's Wake*). Translated by Ludivine Bouton Kelly and Tiphaine Samoyault. *Drunken Boat*, vol. 24, "Dossier Para-Outranspo," https://d7.drunkenboat.com/db24/outranspo/ludivine-bouton-kelly.

Katan, David. "Translation at the Cross-Roads: Time for a Transcreational Turn?" *Perspectives*, vol. 24, no. 3, 2015, pp. 365–381.

Kelly, Nataly, and Jost Zetzsche. *Found in Translation*. Tarcher Perigee, 2012.

Kennedy, George. *Comparative Rhetoric: An Historical and Cross-Cultural Introduction*. Oxford University Press, 1998.

Kilpi, Volter. *Gulliver's Voyage to Phantomimia*. Transcreated by Douglas Robinson. Zeta Books, 2020.

Kirey-Sitnikova, Yana. "Prospects and Challenges of Gender Neutralization in Russian." *Russian Linguistics*, vol. 45, 2021, pp. 143–158, https://doi.org/10.1007/s11185-021-09241-6.

Krebs, Katja. "Translation and Adaptation—Two Sides of an Ideological Coin." *Translation, Adaptation and Transformation*, edited by Lawrence Raw. Bloomsbury, 2012, pp. 42–53.

Laiti, Outi. "Ethnoprogramming: An Indigenous Approach to Computer Programming: A Case Study in Ohcejohka Area Comprehensive Schools." Master's thesis, University of Lapland, 2016, https://lauda.ulapland.fi/handle/10024/62624.

Larizgoitia, Xabier Alberdi. "A Typology of Calques: The Calquing Mechanism in Contemporary Basque." *ELUA. Estudios de Lingüística Universidad de Alicante*, vol. 24, 2010, pp. 13–35.

Larsonneur, Claire. "The Disruptions of Neural Machine Translation." *spheres* 5 (2019), https://spheres-journal.org/contribution/the-disruptions-of-neural-machine-translation/.

Lazzarato, Maurizio. *Gouverner par la dette*. Les Prairies ordinaires, 2014.

———. *La Fabrique de l'homme endetté: Essai sur la condition néolibérale*. Editions Amsterdam, 2011.

Lim, Song Hwee. "How to be Queer in Taiwan: Translation, Appropriation, and the Construction of a Queer Identity in Taiwan." *AsiaPacifiQueer: Rethinking Gender and Sexuality*, edited by Peter Jackson et al. University of Illinois Press, 2007, pp. 235–250.

Littau, Karin. "First Steps toward a Media History of Translation." *Translation Studies*, vol. 4, no. 3, 2011, pp. 261–281.

———. "Translation and the Materialities of Communication." *Translation Studies*, vol. 9, no. 1, 2014, pp. 1-15, 10.1080/14781700.2015.1063449.

———. "Translation in the Age of Postmodern Production: From Text to Intertext to Hypertext." *Forum for Modern Language Studies*, vol. 33, no. 1, 1997, pp. 81-96.

———. "Translation's Histories and Digital Futures." *International Journal of Communication*, vol. 10, 2016, pp. 907-928.

Liu, Lydia. "Introduction." *Tokens of Exchange: The Problem of Translation in Global Circulations*, edited by Lydia H. Liu. Duke University Press, 1999, pp. 1-12.

———. "The Question of Meaning-Value in the Political Economy of the Sign." *Tokens of Exchange: The Problem of Translation in Global Circulations*, edited by Lydia H. Liu. Duke University Press, 1999, pp. 13-44.

Lutz, Theo. "Stochastische Texte." *Augenblick*, vol. 4, 1959, pp. 3-9. Translated by Helen MacCormac, 2005. https://www.stuttgarter-schule.de/lutz_schule_en.htm.

MacGuire, Shannon. "Parasitic Poetics: Noise and Queer Hospitality in Erín Moure's *O Cidadán.*" *Canadian Literature*, no. 224, 2017, pp. 47-63.

MacLeod, Scott. *Tales of the OOtd War.* Extracted in *Translucinación*, edited by Jena Osman and Juliana Spahr, special issue of *Chain*, vol. 10, 2003 [1999]), pp. 116-123.

Manning, Chris. "Stanford CS224N: Natural Language Processing with Deep Learning." Stanford Online, 2021, https://www.youtube.com/playlist?list=PLoROMvodv4rOSH 4v6133s9LFPRHjEmbmJ.

Marecki, Piotr, and Aleksandra Małecka. "AS - C()n Du It by Katarzyna Giełżyńska—A Case of a Total Translation of an Electronic Literature Work." *Miranda*, vol. 12, 2016, https://doi.org/10.4000/miranda.8371.

———. "Hyper-Constrained: Translating Nick Montfort's Textual Generators." *Word and Text*, vol. 4, 2014, pp. 83-97.

———. "Renderings: Translating Literary Works in the Digital Age." *Digital Scholarship in the Humanities*, vol. 32, no. 1, 2017, pp. 184-191, https://academic.oup.com/dsh/article-pdf/32/suppl_1/i84/17751533/fqx010.pdf.

Martín Ruiz, Pablo. "Ways to Start Looking at Potential Translation." *Translating Constrained Literature/Traduire la literature à contrainte*, edited by Camille Bloomfield et al., special issue of *MLN*, vol. 131, no. 4, 2016, pp. 919-931.

Mauranen, Anna, and Pekka Kujamäki. *Translation Universals: Do They Exist?* John Benjamins, 2004.

Mayer, Bernadette. *The Formal Field of Kissing: Translations, Imitations and Epigrams.* Catchword Papers, 1990.

McCance, Dawn, and Erín Moure. "Crossings: An Interview with Erín Moure." *Mosaic*, vol. 36, no. 4, 2003, pp. 147-161.

Meriläinen, Lea, Helka Riionheimo, Päivi Kuusi and Hanna Lantto. "Loan Translations as a Language Contact Phenomenon: Crossing the Boundaries between Contact Linguistics, Second Language Acquisition Research and Translation Studies." *Philologia Estonica Tallinnensis*, vol. 1, no. 1, 2016, pp. 104–124.

Mitchell, Christine. "Translation and Materiality: The Paradox of Visible Translation." *Translating Media*, vol. 30, no. 1, 2010, pp. 23–29.

Mitchell, Christine, and Rita Raley, eds. *Translation-Machination*, special issue of *Amodern*, vol. 8, 2018, https://amodern.net/issues/amodern-8-translation-machination/.

Molnár, Katalin. *Quant à je (kantaje)*. POL, 1996.

Montfort, Nick, and Natalia Fedorova. "Carrying across Language and Code." *Trope*, vol. 12, no. 4, 2012, http://dspace.mit.edu/bitstream/handle/1721.1/78889/TROPE-12-04.pdf?sequence=1&isAllowed=y.

Mounin, Georges. *Les belles infidèles*. Presses Universitaires de Septentrion, 1994.

Moure, Erín. "Elisa Sampedrín and the Paradox of Translation, or the Intranslatable." *Zat-So Productions*, 2021, https://erinmoure.mystrikingly.com/#es-and-the-paradox-of-translation-or-the-intranslatable-pdf.

———. *Little Theatres: Poems*. House of Anansi Press, 2011.

———. *O Cidadán: Poems*. House of Anansi Press, 2002.

———. *O Resplandor*. House of Anansi Press, 2010.

———. *Sheep's Vigil by a Fervent Person: A Transelation of Alberto Caeiro/Fernando Pessoa's O guardador de rebanhos*. House of Anansi Press, 2004.

———. *Unmemntioable*. House of Anansi Press, 2012.

Mukherjee, Sujit. *Translation as Discovery: And Other Essays on Indian Literature in English Translation*. Orient Longman, 2006.

Muntadas, Antoni. *On Translation: The Internet Project*. http://www.adaweb.com/influx/muntadas/.

Murphy, Amanda. "Poétiques hétérolingues: Le queering des Langues? L'exemple de Katalin Molnár." *De Genere—Rivista Di Studi Letterari, Postcoloniali E Di Genere*, vol. 5, 2019, pp. 73–87, https://www.degenere-journal.it/index.php/degenere/article/view/112/104.

Nabokov, Vladimir. "Problems of Translation: *Onegin* in English." *Partisan Review*, vol. 22, 1955, pp. 498–512.

Naheed, Kishwar. *Sokhta Samani-e-Dil/Composition of a Scorched Heart*. Translated by Mahwash Shoaib. Extracted in *Translucinación*, edited by Jena Osman and Juliana Spahr, special issue of *Chain*, vol. 10, 2003, pp. 149–165.

Nakayasu, Sawako. *Mouth: Eats Color: Sagawa Chika Translations, Anti-translations and Originals*. Rogue Factorial, 2011.

———. *Say Translation Is Art.* Ugly Duckling, 2020.

———. *Some Girls Walk into the Country They Are From.* Wave Books, 2020.

Newmark, Peter. *Approaches to Translation.* Pergamon Press, 1981.

———. *A Textbook of Translation.* Prentice Hall, 1988.

Niranjana, Tejaswini. *Siting Translation: History, Post-structuralism, and the Colonial Context.* University of California Press, 1992.

Noel, Urayoán. *Hi-Density Politics.* Blazevox, 2010.

———. *Transversal.* University of Arizona Press, 2021.

Okrent, Arika. *In the Land of Invented Languages.* Random House, 2010.

Osman, Jena, and Juliana Spahr, eds. *Translucinación,* special issue of *Chain,* vol. 10, 2003.

O'Sullivan, Carol. "Pseudotranslation." *Handbook of Translation Studies,* vol. 2., edited by Yves Gambier and Luc van Doorslaer. John Benjamins, 2011, pp. 123–125.

Outranspo. "Classification of Translation Constraints & Procedures." Outranspo.com, 2020, http://www.outranspo.com/classification-of-translation-constraints-procedures/.

———. "Dossier Outranspo." Remue.net, 2021, https://remue.net/outranspo.

———. "Outranspo." *Drunken Boat,* vol. 24, 2016, https://d7.drunkenboat.com/db24/outranspo.

Pailthorpe, Baden. "Eighty-Four Doors." Art exhibit *Lingua Franca.* Firstdraft Gallery, Sydney, 2012, https://www.sullivanstrumpf.com/assets/Uploads/Cntrl-z.net-Lingua-Franca-Pailthorpe-Baden.pdf.

Palekar, Shalmalee. "Re-mapping Translation: Querying the Crossroads." *Queer in Translaion,* edited by B. J. Epstein and Robert Gillet. Routledge, 2017, pp. 8–25.

Parrish, Allison. "Experimental Writing with the Vectorized Word." Strange Loop, 2017, https://www.youtube.com/watch?v=L3D0JEA1Jdc.

Pato, Chus. *Secession with Insecession.* Translated and echolated by Erín Moure. Book Thug, 2014.

Philip, M. NourbeSe. "Considering the Dystranslation of *Zong!*" Interview with Barbara Ofosu-Somuah. *Violent Phenomena,* edited by Kavita Bhanot and Jeremy Tiang. Tilted Axis Press, 2022, pp. 287–304.

———. "Outline of Events Related to the Unauthorised Translation of *Zong!* as Told to the Author by Setaey Adamu Boateng by Renata Morresi and Benway Series Press." Blog category "set speaks," Noubese.com, 2021, https://www.nourbese.com/category/set-speaks/.

———. *She Tries Her Tongue, Her Silence Softly Breaks.* Wesleyan University Press, 1989.

———. *Zong!* Silver Press, 2023 [2008].

Poibeau, Thierry. *Babel 2.0: Où va la traduction automatique?* Odile Jacob, 2019.

Pollitt, Kyra Margaret. "Signart: (British) Sign Language as Poetry as Gesamtkunstwerk." PhD diss., University of Bristol, 2014.

Pym, Anthony. *Exploring Translation Theories.* Routledge, 2014 [2010].

———. *On Translator Ethics.* John Benjamins, 2012.

———. *Translation and Text Transfer: An Essay on the Principles of Intercultural Communication.* Tarragona: Intercultural Studies Group, 2010 [1992].

———. *Translation Solutions for Many Languages: Histories of a Flawed Dream.* Bloomsbury Academic, 2016.

———. "What Technology Does to Translating." *Translation and Interpreting*, vol. 3, no. 1, 2011, pp. 1-9.

Quéma, Anne. "Engendering Biopoetics of Testimony: Louise Dupré, Chus Pato, and Erin Moure." *Canadian Jewish Studies/Etudes juives canadiennes*, vol. 32, 2021, pp. 143-161.

Queneau, Raymond. *Hitting the Streets.* Translated by Rachel Galvin. Carcanet, 2013.

Rafael, Vincente L. *Motherless Tongues: The Insurgency of Language Amid Wars of Translation.* Duke University Press, 2016.

Raguet-Bouvart, Christine, ed. *Inscrire l'altérité: Emprunts et néologismes en traduction.* Palimpsestes 25. Presses Sorbonne Nouvelle, 2012.

Raley, Rita. "Algorithmic Translation." *CR: The New Centennial Review*, vol. 16, no. 1, 2016, https://escholarship.org/uc/item/9p08q4wq.

———. "Machine Translation and Global English." *Yale Journal of Criticism*, vol. 16, no. 2, 2003, pp. 291-313.

Ramayya, Nisha. *States of the Body Produced by Love.* Ignota, 2019.

Raw, Lawrence. "Introduction: Identifying Common Ground." *Translation, Adaptation and Transformation*, edited by Lawrence Raw. Bloomsbury, 2012, pp. 1-20.

Reiß, Katharina, and Hans Vermeer. *Toward a General Theory of Translational Action: Skopos Theory Explained.* Translated by Christiane Nord. St. Jerome Publishing, 1984.

Ribeiro Pires Vieira, Else. "Liberating Calibans: Readings of Antropofagia and Haraldo de Campos' Poetics of Transcreation." *Postcolonial Translation: Theory and Practice*, edited by Susan Bassnett and Harish Trivedi. Routledge, 1999, 95-113.

Robert-Foley, Lily. *Money, Math and Measure.* Essay Press, 2016, https://issuu.com/essaypress/docs/robert-foley_pr_pages/11.

———. "The Politics of Experimental Translation: Potentialities and Preoccupations." *English: Journal of the English Association*, vol. 69, no. 267, 2020, pp. 401–419.

———. "To Erre Is Calque: The Uses and Abuses of Calque in Avant-Garde Translation." *Avant-Garde Translation*, edited by Alexandra Lukes. Brill, forthcoming.

Robertson, Lisa. *Cinéma du présent*. Translated by Pascal Poyet. Théatre Typographique, 2015.

———. *Cinema of the Present*. Coach House Books, 2014.

Robinson, Douglas. *The Experimental Translator*. Palgrave, 2023.

———. *The Last Days of Maiju Lassila: A Pseudotranslation by Douglas Robinson*. Atmosphere Press, 2022.

———. *Translationality*. Routledge, 2017.

———. *Who Translates? Translator Subjectivities Beyond Reason*. State University of New York Press, 2001.

Romero, Amilcar. "Poem 21." *Curamag, Renderings*, 2014, http://curamag.com/issues/2014/12/3/renderings-poem-21.

Rudolf, Michał "Poet." Translated by Aleksanda Małecka and Piotr Marecki. Port to JavaScript by Nick Montfort. *Curamag, Renderings*, 2014, http://curamag.com/issues/2014/12/3/renderings-poet.

Rutherford, Jonathan, and Homi K. Bhabha. "The Third Space: Interview with Homi K. Bhabha." *Identity: Community, Culture, Difference*, edited by Jonathan Rutherford. Lawrence and Wishart, 1990, pp. 207–221.

Sagawa, Chika. *The Collected Works of Chika Sagawa*. Translated by Sawako Nakayasu. Canary Books, 2011.

Sakai, Naoki. "Translation and the Figure of the Border: Toward the Apprehension of Translation as a Social Action." *MLA Profession*, 2010, pp. 25–33.

Samoyault, Tiphaine. *Traduction et violence*. Seuil, 2020.

Sanders, Julie. *Adaptation and Appropriation*. Routledge, 2005.

Santos Perez, Craig. *[Hacha], from Unincorporated Territory*. Omnidawn, 2017.

Saro-Wiwa, Ken. *Sozaboy (Pétit minitaire)*. Translated by Samuel Millogo and Amadou Bissiri. Actes Sud, 2003.

Saussure, Ferdinand de. *Cours de linguistique générale*. Payot & Rivages, 1995 [1916].

———. *Course in General Linguistics*. Translated by Wade Baskin. McGraw Hill, 1959.

Scheunemann, Dietrich. "From Collage to the Multiple. On the Genealogy of Avant-Garde and Neo-Avant-Garde." *Avant-Garde/Neo-Avant-Garde*, edited by Dietrich Scheunemann. Rodopi, 2005, pp. 15–48.

Schilling, Derek. "Translation as a Total Social Fact and Scholarly Pursuit." *Translating Constrained Literature/Traduire la literature à contrainte*, edited by Camille Bloomfield et al., special issue of *MLN*, vol. 131, no. 4, 2016, pp. 841–845.

Seita, Sophie. "Transposition: Nature." *Queenzenglish.mp3: Poetry, Philosophy, Performativity*, edited by Kyoo Lee. Roof Books, 2020, pp. 132–134.

Sekiguchi, Ryoko. *Calque*. P.O.L, 2001.

Shakespeare, William. *Jambonlaissé*. Translated by L'Indéprimeuse. Directed by Justine Camille-Carette. Théâtre de Ménilmontant, Paris, 2018.

Sharei, Vahideh. "A Comparative Study of Strategies Employed in 'Old Man and the Sea' Translated from English into Person on the Basis of Vinay and Darbelnet's Model." *Theory and Practice of Language Studies*, vol. 7, no. 4, 2017, pp. 281–286.

Sharpe, Christine. *In the Wake: On Blackness and Being*. Duke University Press, 2016.

Shetrit, Olivier, and Sale Petit Bonhomme. "Concert en langue des signes." Translated/performed by Olivier Shetrit, Carré Bleu, Poitiers, April 8–9, 2011, https://www.dailymotion.com/video/x2gi4m6.

Shinonome, Nodoka. "Contemporary Japanese Poetry Generator." Translated by Andrew Campana. *Curamag, Renderings*, 2014, http://curamag.com/issues/2014/12/3/renderings-contemporary-japanese-poetry-generator.

Shiotsuka, Shuichiro. "Deux romans lipogrammatiques en japonais: La traduction de *La Disparition* et *Mettons du rouge à lèvres sur l'image rémanente* de Yasutaka Tsutsui." *Oulipo@50*, edited by Camille Bloomfield et al., special issue of *Formules*, vol. 16, 2012, https://www.ieeff.org/f16shiotsukaok.pdf.

Simon, Sherry. *Translating Montreal Episodes in the Life of a Divided City*. McGill-Queen's University Press, 2006.

Siregar, Roswani. "Translation Procedures Analysis: English-Indonesian Motivational Book." *IOSR Journal of Humanities and Social Science*, vol. 21, no. 5, 2016, pp. 51–57.

Slater, Avery. "Crypto-Monolingualism: Machine Translation and the Poetics of Automation." *Translation-Machination*, edited by Christine Mitchell and Rita Raley, special issue of *Amodern*, vol. 8, 2018, https://amodern.net/article/crypto-monolingualism/.

Smith, May. *The Influence of French on Eighteenth-Century Literary Russian: Semantic and Phraseological Calques*. Peter Lang, 2006.

Snell-Hornby, Mary. *The Turns of Translation Studies: New Paradigms or Shifting Viewpoints?* John Benjamins, 2006.

Spivak, Gayatri. "The Politics of Translation." *Outside in the Teaching Machine*. Routledge, 1993, pp. 200–225.

Stalling, Jonathan. *Yingelishi*. Counterpath, 2011.

Starhawk. *Dreaming the Dark: Magic, Sex and Politics*. Beacon Press, 1988 [1982].

Suchet, Myriam. *Outils pour une traduction postcoloniale*. Archives Contemporaines, 2009.

Talab Jaafar, Shurooq, Dipima Buragohain and Harshita Aini Haroon. "Differences and Classifications of Borrowed and Loan Words in Linguistics Context." *International Languages and Knowledge—Learning in a Changing World*, edited by Ina Suryani and Dipima Buragohain. UniMAP Press, 2019, pp. 95-112.

Terry, Philip. *Dante's Inferno*. Carcanet Press, 2014.

———. "Extract from *Exercises in Translation*." *English: Journal of the English Association*, vol. 8, no. 267, 2020, pp. 397-400.

Thomason, Sara G. *Language Contact: An Introduction*. Edinburgh University Press, 2022 [2001].

Tiziana Tarantini, Angela. "When Accessibility Becomes Performance: Sign Language Interpreting in Music and Live Concerts as 'Performative Rewriting.'" Conference paper, *Performative and Experiential Translation: Meaning-Making through Language, Art and Media*, organized by Ricarda Vidal, Madeleine Campbell, Heather Connelly and Joanna Kosmalska, King's College, London, July 13-15, 2022.

Toury, Gideon. *Descriptive Translation Studies and Beyond*. John Benjamins, 1995.

Trainor, Samuel. "*Cinema Skopos:* Strategic Layering and Kaleidoscopic Functionality in Screenplay Translation." *Palimpsests*, vol. 30, 2017, pp. 15-46, https://doi.org/10.4000/palimpsestes.2393.

———. "Retracing Transparency: Calques and Creativity in Modernist Translation." *Traductologie, traduction: Travail et creation*, 2014, https://hal.archives-ouvertes.fr/hal-01465446.

———. "Synoptic Translation Prototype for *Sir Gawain and the Green Knight*," http://www.samtrainor.com/stp/.

Trouillot, Michel-Rolph. "Imigrayson." Translated by A. Isadora Del Vecchio, Abdourahman Idrissa, Kiran Jayaram and Karen Ohnesorge. *Translucinación*, edited by Jena Osman and Juliana Spahr, special issue of *Chain*, vol. 10, 2003, pp. 213-227.

Tuhiwai-Smith, Linda. *Decolonizing Methodologies: Research and Indigenous Peoples*. Zed Books, 2012 [1999].

Tuntha-obas, Padcha. *Composite Diplomacy*. Tinfish, 2005.

———. *Trespasses*. O Books, 2006.

Van Harskamp, Nicoline. *My Name Is Language*. Scriptings and Archive Book, 2020.

———. "The New International Phonetic Alphabet School." Englishes MOOC, https://www.englishes-mooc.org/hkw.

Vandal-Sirois, Hugo, and Georges L. Bastin. "Adaptation and Appropriation: Is There a Limit?" *Translation, Adaptation and Transformation*. Bloomsbury, 2012, pp. 21–52.

Vinay, Jean-Paul, and Jean Darbelnet. *Comparative Stylistics of French and English: A Methodology for Translation*. Translated by Juan C. Sager and M.-J. Hamel. John Benjamins, 1995.

———. *Stylistique comparée du français et de l'anglais*. Didier, 1958.

Venuti, Lawrence. *The Translator's Invisibility: A History of Translation*. Routledge, 2018 [1995].

Von Flotow, Luise. "Feminist Translation: Contexts, Practices and Theories." *TTR*, vol. 4, no. 2, 1991, pp. 69–84.

Wagner, James. *Trilce*. Calamari Press, 2006.

Waldrop, Rosemarie. "Irreducible Strangeness." *towards a foreign likeness bent: translation*, edited by Jerrold Shiroma. Poetics 1. Duration, 1999, pp. 106–110.

Watier, Louis. "L'imaginaire philologique de la traduction: Pseudotraduction et redefinition de la fiction au XVIe siècle." *Les Imaginaires de la traduction*, special issue of *Itinéraires*, vol. 2-3, 2018/2019, https://doi.org/10.4000/itineraires.4726.

Weaver, Warren. "Translation." *Machine Translation of Languages*, edited by William Locke and A. Donald Booth. MIT Press, 1955, pp. 15–23.

Weightman, J. G. "Translation as a Linguistic Exercise." *English Language Teaching*, vol. 3, 1950, pp. 69–76.

Wright, Chantal. *Portrait of a Tongue*. University of Ottawa Press, 2013.

Yoshihara, Jirō. "Gutai Art Manifesto." Translated by Reiko Tomii. *Gutai Splendid Playground*, edited by Ming Tiampo and Alexandra Munro. Guggenheim Museum Publications, 2013, pp. 18–19, http://web.guggenheim.org/exhibitions/gutai/data/manifesto.html.

Youdale, Roy. *Using Computers in the Translation of Literary Style: Challenges and Opportunities*. Routledge, 2020.

Index

Abbott, Edwin A., 162–163
Abrahams, Annie, 4, 129–131
Accents, 41, 69–71, 82, 91, 125
Acrostics, 154, 156, 166
Adair, Gilbert, 156
Adaptation, 25, 26, 33–34, 205–217
Addition/subtraction of material, 57
Adobe, 151–152
Advertising and marketing, 16, 207, 214–217
Affect, 33, 71, 168, 180
Ahmed, Sara, 20
Algorithmic translation
   and adaptation, 216
   algorithms as procedures, 154
   based on habit, 23
   calque, 90
   Englishes (Van Harskamp), 136
   literal translation, 114, 115–118
   machine translation and meaning, 124–125
   sexism, 149
   transcreation, 17
Alignment between languages, 115–117
Alphabets, 100, 147, 151–152, 156, 191
Anagrams, 193
Anaphora, 1, 148, 149, 150
Annotations, 176
Aporia, 162, 163
Appiah, Anthony, 178
Applied translation studies, 15
Appropriation, 45, 112, 184, 195, 211
Arber, Solange, 88, 89
Arp, Jean, 90
Art, 129–131
Artificial Intelligence (AI), 116, 117
Artozqui, Santiago, 10, 198, 203
Assimilation, 48
Atkins, Tim, 10, 36
Aubergines, 79, 82
Audiovisual translation, 16
Auge, 41, 51
Autocorrect, 4, 127
Automatic writing, 5
Autotheoretical experiments, 33, 177–178
Avant-Garde, 8–10, 53, 89, 94, 126, 132–133, 183, 195
Avasilichioaei, Oana, 167, 170–171

Back translations, 77, 85, 128, 156, 195
Baillehache, Jonathan, 16, 109, 110, 112, 123, 125, 151, 152, 157, 194
Baker, Mona, 159

Ballard, Michel, 26, 33, 47, 51, 81, 101, 209
Bally, Charles, 141–142
Bang, Mary Jo, 211
Barbaric likenesses, 80–83
Basic English, 138, 158
Baskin, Wade, 52, 55
Bastin, Georges L., 212, 214
Baudelaire, Charles, 9
Beck, Cave, 139
Bellomo, Paolo, 80, 81, 83, 89
Bellos, David, 1, 4, 122, 123–124
Benabou, Marcel, 53
Benjamin, Walter, 7, 8, 88, 152, 159
Bergvall, Caroline, 68–69, 70–71, 72, 198
Berman, Antoine, 13, 109, 112, 123, 125, 146–147
Bernabé, Jean, 119
Bernstein, Charles, 198
Bhabha, Homi K., 7, 180
Bielenia-Grajewska, Magdalena, 59
Bilingual corpora, 115–116, 117, 124–125, 133
Binary code, 12, 21, 107, 114, 120, 139–140, 145, 150, 160
Bissiri, Amadou, 36, 164
Bloomfield, Camille, 4, 77–78, 87, 90, 132–133, 157, 199
Bloomfield, Leonard, 84–85, 86, 87, 91
Borges, Jorge Luis, 122, 123–124, 164
Borrowings
   accents, 69
   calque, 80
   emprunt, 30, 44, 45–49, 50, 51
   fixed versus individual translator choice, 26
   linguistic accounts of, 50
   monetary metaphors, 56
   semantic change, 77
   as theft, 56, 60
   as trade, 59
Bouhmid, Alison, 83
Bouton-Kelly, Ludivine, 36, 79
bpNichol, 9, 22–23
Brand, Carina, 118
Breath, 64, 74
Briggs, Kate, 58
"Bright Sun in the Head of Girls," 197
Broqua, Vincent, 10, 11, 14, 18, 183
Brown, Brandon, 32, 180–182, 183
Bueno, Wilson, 165
Buragohain, Dipima, 46
Bürger, Peter, 9–10

Cage, John, 18, 155
Caiero, Alberto, 173
Calque, 17, 24, 26, 31, 46, 77-105, 197
Campana, Andrew, 146-147
Canada, 9, 187
Capitalism, 11, 12, 17, 22, 44, 53, 55, 64, 118, 129, 138, 213, 215
Carson, Anne, 178, 179, 180
Catallus, Gaius Valerius, 53, 180, 181, 182-183, 225n9
"Catallus 101," 179, 180
Cayley, John, 152-154, 155, 156, 159, 161
Cecire, Natalia, 18, 144
Celan, Paul, 73
Cervantes, 175
Chain, 197-198
Champs en fleurs, 83-87
"Change in perspective," 32-33
Characteristica universalis, 139-140, 142
Chateaubriand, François-René de, 88-89
Cheyfitz, Eric, 109, 110, 112, 115, 132
Chinese poetry, 153-154, 191-192, 198
Chiotis, Thodoros, 147
Chuquet, Hélène, 47, 54
Ciphers, 142-143
Citations, 171
Clarke, Chris, 158, 164
Clinamen, 201
C()n Du It (Giełżyńska), 205-206, 208
CNRTL (Centre National de Ressources Textuelles et Lexicales), 50
Codes
    binary code, 12, 21, 107, 114, 120, 139-140, 145, 150, 160
    computer code, 145
    grammar as, 143-144
    literal translation, 114, 115, 124
    music, 142
    transposition, 32, 136, 146, 148, 158
Code-switching, 121, 127, 128
Coding, 21, 129, 144-145, 146
Cohen, Sharmila, 198
Cole, Norma, 66
Collaborative translations, 33, 199
Collage, 16, 31, 78, 90, 93, 94, 97, 205
Collins, Sophie, 74, 159
Colonialism
    appropriation, 17
    calque, 101
    debt, 54, 59
    English, 67, 68, 99
    fidelity, 13
    foreignization, 97
    literal translation, 112
    naming, 101-102
    and oral traditions, 118-119
    privilege of colonial languages, 129
    in publishing, 75

"Rotten English," 164
Sanskrit, 99
standardization, 143
translational norms, 14-15
universals, 12
Colors, 8
Commentary, translation as, 182, 197, 209
Competence, linguistic, 130
Composite Diplomacy (Tuntha-obas), 97
Computer-assisted translation (CAT), 29, 59, 90
    (see also machine translation)
CONA (Institute for Contemporary Arts Processing), 129-131
Concours d'agrégation, 15
"Concrete Perl," 147, 151
Concrete poetry, 125, 147
"Confusion," 82-83
Constraint-based writing, 32, 156-164
Context-free grammar, 147-148, 155
Contracts, translation, 55, 57, 125, 193-194
Copyright, 13, 116, 171, 211
Corbett, Jon, 144
"Correctness," 15, 90
Correspondence, 189 (see also equivalence)
Counterequivalence, 194-195
Creative-critical approaches, 15, 18, 28, 170, 177, 178, 179, 183, 202
Cree#, 144
Creoles, 68-69, 112, 113, 119, 198
Criticism, translation as, 182
Crónicas, 170-171
Cronin, Michael, 12, 59, 97
Crowd-sourced translation, 29, 199
Cryptography, 22
"Cult of transparency," 12
Culture, 16, 51, 60, 205-209
Cyber-punk, 152
Cyrillic, 147, 151-152

Dada poetry, 53, 127, 128, 143
Daguerrotypes, 89
Dante, 4-5, 90, 132-133, 198, 211
Dante, Emma, 36
Darbelnet, Jean. See VD (Vinay/Darbelnet)
Dash, Michael, 111, 113
Data mining, 118, 119, 129, 133
Davies, William, 53
Debt, 30-31, 44, 45, 55, 56-64, 74
De Campos, Haroldo, 10, 16-17, 182, 198, 211, 213
Decoding, 22, 115, 116, 124, 143
Decolonial practice, 112, 188
"Deep Dante" (Bloomfield, 2021), 4, 90, 132-133
DeepL, 2, 4, 19, 90, 132, 133, 149, 188
Deep structures, 22, 32, 147
Delak, Maja, 130
De la Torre, Mónica, 4, 17, 64-67, 73, 83-84, 92, 121-128, 184, 193, 201
Delisle, Jean, 47, 51

De Man, Paul, 7
Departure/arrival languages, 34
Derrida, Jacques, 12, 38
Dialects, 69
Dibbel, Julian, 32
Dick, Jennifer K., 36
Dictionaries, 4, 29, 98-99, 123, 158, 179
Diction err, 99-103
Didi-Huberman, Georges, 83
Digital technology, 30-31, 114, 118,
    119-120, 152 (see also computer-assisted
    translation (CAT); Google Translate; machine
    translation)
Dimitrakakis, Christos, 147
Directionality of translation, 46-47, 190
"Discourse on the Logic of Language"
    (Philip), 67-68
Discrete entities, languages as, 58, 62, 80, 128
La Disparition (Perec), 156
Distortion, 88, 136-137
"Doing justice," 34-35, 52
"Dollar," 51-52
Dominican Republic, 68
Don Quixote, 175
Doris, Stacy, 37
"Doubles" (de la Torre), 83-84
Douglas, Stan, 43
Drift (Bergvall), 70-71
Dutch, 129
Dworkin, Craig, 142, 162-163
"Dystranslation," 59, 64, 74, 75

Echolation, 169-170
Éclairage/lighting/perspective, 167-168, 178
Eco, Umberto, 139-140, 145
Economic values, 51, 52, 56-64 (see also
    capitalism; debt)
Efthymiades, Yiannis, 158-159
Eighty-Four Doors (Pailthorpe), 4, 132
Electronic Literature Organization (ELO), 5
Elgin, Suzette Haden, 137
Emails, 183
Embodiment, 119-120, 126, 167-168, 177-183
Emmerich, Karen, 57, 193
Emprunt, 24, 26, 30, 39-76, 86
Empty signifiers, 53-54
English
    as additional language, 135-136
    advertising and marketing, 207-208
    Anglo-Saxon, 65, 71, 122
    Basic English, 138, 158
    Bloomfield's poetry, 77-79
    calque, 84, 85
    coding, 21, 129, 144
    colonialism, 15, 59, 67, 68, 99
    e-lit translations, 152
    emprunt, 39-45, 67

equivalence, 195-196
false cognates, 77
foreignization, 97
French/Latin vocabulary, 49
Global English, 20-21, 113, 129
    as global language, 20
    hegemony of, 20-22, 67, 100, 129, 138
    homolinguistic translation, 162
    imperialism, 129
    as intermediary language, 129
    modulation, 168
    national character of, 169
    non-standard forms of, 135-136
    politics of, 130
    "servitude," 48
    as universal, 22
Englishes (Van Harskamp), 136
Enlightenment, 16, 60, 61, 63, 86, 115, 139,
    140, 143
Equivalence, 15, 16, 25, 26, 33, 52, 61-62, 108, 169,
    187-202
"Equivalencies/Equivalencias" (de la Torre), 4, 92,
    127, 201
Equivalents (Stieglitz), 126
"Equivocation" (de la Torre), 127
Erring/errors, 14, 70, 78, 81-85, 125, 137, 174
Eshelman, Clayton, 121
Essentialism, 26, 27, 75, 137
E-stranger to estranger, 128-133
"Étonnante Athena" (Bloomfield), 79
Etymologies, shared, 36, 77-78, 99-100, 125, 179
Expanded Translation Network, 36
"Experimental translation," choice of
    terminology, 18-19
Experimental writing, 18
Exquisite valencies, 201-202
External referents, 52, 55, 62 (see also signifier/
    signified)
Extralinguistic material, 26, 33

False cognates/false friends, 11, 77-78, 81, 83,
    88, 121
Fan-based translation, 29, 173
Fedorov, Andrei, 24
Fedorova, Natalia, 146, 147, 148, 149-150
Felstiner, John, 73
Fentress, James, 139, 140
Ferreira da Silva, Denise, 61, 62, 63, 65, 68
Fidelity, 10, 13-16, 33-34, 35, 69, 147,
    150-151, 157
Figurativeness, 109
Finnegan's Wake, 36, 91
Footnotes, 40, 95, 96, 174, 176, 177, 178-179
"Foreign" as enemy, 143
Foreignization, versus domestication, 110
"Foreign" vs "native," 47, 48-49, 69, 70-71, 81, 128
Formigari, Lia, 52

French
  adaptation, 207-208
  Bloomfield's poetry, 77-79
  calque, 36, 48, 80, 89, 91
  Canada, 27, 187
  e-lit translations, 152
  equivalence, 196
  experiment, 11
  French vocabulary in English, 49
  gender (grammatical), 148-149
  imperialism, 112, 113
  Katalin Molnár, 69
  and Latin, 62
  modulation, 168
  national character of, 169
  pidgins, 164
  politics of, 130
  snob poem, 77-78
"Frenglish," 165
Frequency, 49, 133
Functional correspondence, 52
Functions of location in an utterance, 123

Galician, 170, 171, 187
Galley, Michel, 147-148
Galvin, Rachel, 17, 86, 161
"Gate of Snow," 195-196
Gayraud, Irène, 10
Gender (grammatical), 148-149, 208
Generic shifts, 210-211
Geographic modulation, 172, 173, 183
German, 46, 73, 85, 152, 188
Ghost in the machine, 126, 127-128
Gibbs, Anna, 142
Giełżyńska, Katarzyna, 205-206,
  208, 209
Ginsberg, Samuel, 119-120
Glissant, Edouard, 74, 75, 111, 112, 115, 119,
  132-133, 135
Global English, 20-21, 113, 129
Global translatability, 54
Globish, 138
Glossaries, 41, 48
Godard, Barbara, 29
Goldman, Emma, 197
Gonguly, Avishek, 137
Google Translate, 4, 65, 122, 124, 125, 126, 127,
  129, 131, 132
Grammar, 32, 70, 85, 96, 125, 135-165, 166
Grapheme-level borrowings, 50
Grass, Delphine, 10, 15, 28, 33, 170, 177, 178,
  191, 198
Greaves, Sara, 83
Greek, 82, 86, 109, 147, 183
Greenough, James B., 59
Gregson v. Gilbert, 39, 40, 44, 62,
  68, 75

Grimaldi-Donahue, Allison, 10
Gulliver, Lemuel, 173
Gulliver's Voyage to Phantomimia, 173, 176-177
Gutai, 125-126

Hamel, M.-J. *See* Sager, Juan C. and Hamel, M-J.
Hanafi, Amira, 199, 200
Haroon, Harshita Aini, 46
Haugen, Einar, 46, 48-49, 56, 57, 60, 69, 84, 85, 86
Hayles, N. Katherine, 28, 30, 145
Hejinian, Lyn, 82
Hermans, Theo, 14, 177
Heteronyms, 173-176, 179, 181
Hi-Density Politics (Noel), 119-120, 121
Hijacking, logic of, 17, 122, 128, 133, 194
Hindi, 14
Hinge languages, 21
Hodge, Siobhan, 97
Hofstadter, Douglas, 1, 148
Hokenson, Jan Walsh, 52, 53
Holca, Irina, 195, 196
Holmes, James S., 15, 54
Homologue loans, 86
Homophony, 43, 48, 53-54, 56, 62, 65-70, 72, 86,
  191-192
Hoover, Paul, 184
Hsia Yü, 4
Huang, Yunte, 191-192
Hungarian, 69, 70, 130
Hybridity, 7, 17, 138

I Ching, 140
Identity, 101, 172
Idiomatic expressions, 33, 78, 199, 202
Image translation, 206
"Imigrayson" (Trouillot), 36, 198
Imperialism, 82, 112, 113, 115, 120, 129, 183
Impropriety, 81
Incomprehensibility, 71
Indexes, creative, 159
Indigenous programming languages, 144
Indirect speech, 177
Inform 6, 145-146
Installations, 68
Intentionality, 3-4
Interactive fiction, 146
Interference, 81, 82
Interpretation, 126-127
Interruptions, 74
Intersemioticity, 20, 34, 210-211, 216
Intertextuality, 6, 91, 171, 181
Intonation marks, 97
Intralinguistic translation, 23, 162
Introduction, translator's, 174, 177
Invented languages, 36, 137-139,
  164-165, 166
Invention, 32, 80, 157

Invisibility, translator, 19–20
Italian, 36, 74, 80, 130, 211
Italics, 41, 68, 73, 159

Jakobson, Roman, 23
Jambonlaissé (2018), 4
Jamet, Denis, 46
Japanese, 125–126, 146–147, 156, 195, 196, 197
Javascript, 146–147, 152
Johnson, Barbara, 12
Joyce, James, 91
Justice, 34–35, 74, 157, 200

Kac, Eduardo, 223n14
Kant, Emmanuel, 62
Karounwi, Anuoluwapo, 144
Katan, David, 17, 213
Kelly, Nataly, 191
Kennedy, George, 145
Kilpi, Volter, 173, 174
Kirey-Sitnikova, Yana, 149
Kislov, Valéri, 156
Kittredge, George L., 59
Krebs, Katia, 211
Kujamäki, Pekka, 14

Láaden, 137, 164
Lacunae in arrival languages, 50–51, 53, 60, 155
Laiti, Outi, 144
La Langue du bourricot, 36
Language contact, 49, 59, 81
Language difference, 1, 4, 10, 19–23, 28, 40, 54, 71, 168–169
Language learning classrooms, 47, 78, 81, 83, 94
Language mixing, 121, 138, 164–165, 197
Language policies, 13–14, 81
Larsonneur, Claire, 1, 116, 118
Last Days of Maiju Lassila, The (Robinson), 175–177, 179
Latin, 48, 49, 62, 162, 179
Lazzarato, Maurizio, 219n11
Legault, Paul, 198
Leibniz, Gottfried Wilhelm, 139–140, 142
Le Lyonnais, François, 53
Letters, 40, 41–43, 100, 109, 123, 151, 193–194
Likeness, 83
Liminal spaces, 173–174
L'Indéprimeuse, 4
Lingua Franca exhibition, 132, 133
Lipograms, 156
Literal translation, 24, 31–32, 78, 80, 107–134, 147, 157
Litoral translations, 108, 112, 114, 118, 119–120
Littau, Karin, 29, 89
"Little Mothers," 100
Liu, Lydia, 52, 54–55, 57, 59

Loans, 30, 44, 45–48, 51, 56, 60, 84–85
(*see also emprunt*)
Localization, 51, 206–207, 209
Logic, 61–62, 110, 115, 128, 140, 143
Logopandecteision, 139
Loh Dian-yang, 24
"Lost" in translation, 57–59
Lull, Raymond, 140
Lutz, Theo, 5

MacGuire, Shannon, 173
Machine learning, 55, 118 (*see also* algorithmic translation)
Machine poetry, 5
Machine translation, 1–6 (*see also* Google Translate; neural machine translation (NMT); statistical machine translation (SMT))
Abrahams live conversation, 131
and adaptation, 215
in arts, 129–132
Basic English, 138
capitalism, 118
changing politics and poetics of translation, 114–115
ciphers, 143
direct translation, 122
early systems, 9
empty signifiers, 53–54
English as invisible language of, 21
equivalence, 188
experiments, 18
intermediary coding, 124
literal translation, 32
modulation, 168
as "neutral," 132
norms of, 213
of numbers, 193
pronoun ambiguity, 148
rule-based MT, 22–23
sexism, 149
and the 'sign,' 7
training, 21, 58–59, 115–116, 117, 124
translation of meaning, 123–124
"uncouthness," 132–133
universals, 159
MacLeod, Scott, 131
Maher, Ciarán, 69
Małecka, Aleksandra, 147, 155, 205, 206–207, 208–209
Manning, Chris, 148
Marathi, 14
Marecki, Piotr, 147, 155, 205, 206–207, 208–209
Martín Ruiz, Pablo, 10, 159–161
Marx, Karl, 54, 57, 63

Materiality
  ancestral bones, 64
  of books, 91
  calque, 80, 88-89
  danger of translation, 74
  de la Torre poetry, 65
  elementa, 63
  emprunt, 45, 51, 54, 57, 62
  of history, 65, 71, 73
  language-text disruption, 153
  machine translation, 124
  "material turn," 29
  networks of materiality, 55-56
  non-linear poetics, 153
  of the signifier, 71-72
  tournant sensible ("sensitive turn"), 30
  zaum poetry, 151
Mathematical values, 66, 117, 139-140, 141,
  159-161, 188, 190-191
Matrices, 89, 90-91, 143
Mauranen, Anna, 14
MacSweeney, Christina, 178
Meaning (*see also* signifier/signified)
  and algorithms, 183
  and authority, 116
  colonialism, 13
  created rather than found, 55-56
  dual foreign and local meanings, 51
  empty signifiers, 53-54
  essentialism, 26
  excess/surplus, 66-67
  expansions of, 86, 93, 188
  hierarchization of, 54
  human somatic relationship to, 183
  imported, 50
  literal translation, 121-128
  matrices, 89-91
  meaningful tokens, 51-56
  metaphor as motor for, 57
  non-symmetrical, 188
  political economics, 54
  presumption of sense, 13
  signifier as motor of new meanings, 87
  surplus of, 62-63, 191
  in-between texts, 128
  translation as transparent transfer of, 11
  universals, 49, 139
  and value, 63-64
  vector space, 8, 123
Memory, 39-40, 44-45
Mercanton, Jacques, 91
Meriläinen, Lea, 84
Mesostics, 155-156
Mess(e), 76
Metacommentary, 68, 162
Metaequivalence, 194-195
Metaphor, 30, 52-53, 56, 59, 60, 88, 92, 109

Metaphysics, 12, 100
Metareflection, 15, 29, 158, 163
Metonymy, 57, 59
Migration, 44, 65, 67
Militaristic concepts, 22, 34, 115, 143
Millogo, Samuel, 36, 164
Mimesis, 8-9, 72-73, 88, 90, 142, 180
Modernism, 16, 45, 92
Modernity, 18
Modernization of language, 211
Modulation, 24, 32, 167-185, 187
Molnár, Katalin, 69-70, 72, 82-83, 85, 91
Monetary metaphors, 52-53, 54-55, 56-64, 188,
  190, 194
Monier-Williams, Monier, 99, 100, 101
Monolingualism, 19, 22, 66, 69, 80
Montage, 89
Montalvo Center, 65
Montfort, Nick, 145-146, 147, 148, 149-150,
  151, 152
Morphology, 50, 78, 97
Mounin, Georges, 88
Moure, Erín (Eirin), 10, 19, 32, 165, 167, 168,
  169-172, 173, 178, 179, 187, 216
Mourning, 179-180
Mouth: Eats Color, 195-196
Multilingualism, 47, 121
Multimodal translation, 20, 34, 210-211, 216
Munson, Marcella, 52, 53
Muntadas, Antoni, 198
Murphy, Amanda, 10, 69-70, 72
Music, 141-142, 143
My Name is Language (Van Harskamp), 101-103,
  135-136

Nabokov, Vladimir, 178
Naheed, Kishwar, 198
Nakayasu, Sawako, 195-196, 197, 205
Names, 40, 41, 83, 101-103, 127, 173
National entities, languages as, 62, 80, 98, 102, 120,
  129, 130, 143, 168-169, 170
Nation-states, 10, 13, 20, 58, 69, 108, 120
"Native" vs "foreign," 47, 48-49, 69, 70-71, 81, 128
Natural language processing (NLP) matrices, 2
Navajo, 137
Neddam, Martine, 129-130
Negative accumulation, 61, 62, 68
Nelson, Graham, 145-146
Nerrière, Jean-Paul, 138
Neural machine translation (NMT)
  ciphers, 143
  external fixed reality, 55
  frequency, 133
  functions of location in an utterance, 123
  imperialism, 129
  "loss," 58-59
  matrices, 89-90

modulation, 168
more than decoding, 23
and the 'sign,' 7
syntagmatic translation, 125
training, 117, 124
transcription, 116–117
values, 2
Neural nets, 21, 116–117, 129, 147
Newmark, Peter, 28
N-gram translation, 166
Nicknames, 102
Nida, Eugene, 24, 208
Niranjana, Tejaswini, 12
Nodoka, Shinonome, 146–147
Noel, Urayoán, 32, 107–108, 113–114, 115,
    118–119, 121, 126, 156, 193
Non-contradiction, principle of, 61–62
Nonequivalence, 188
Non-language sign systems, 20
Nonsense poetry, 53, 128, 151
Non-translation, as strategy, 73–74, 95, 108, 182
Normalization practices, 70
Nornes, Abé Markus, 209
Nox (Carson), 179
Numbers, 32, 193
Nüshu, 137–138

Oblique translation strategies, 24, 141, 168
Obsolescence, 17, 149
Occlusion, 72–75
Ogden, Charles, 138, 158
Okrent, Arika, 137, 138–139, 141, 143
Old Norse, 71
"Olvido Mortel," 145–146
One-to-one correspondence, 188
Onomatopoeia, 67
Opacity, 37–38, 65, 71, 73, 74, 75
Oppositions, 60
Oraliture, 113
Oral traditions, 29, 32, 41, 66–67, 112–113, 118–119
O Resplandor (Moure), 19, 168, 170, 171, 172,
    179, 216
Original-translation relationship, 58, 73, 79, 84, 88,
    107, 147, 175, 178, 197
Orthography, 41, 70–71, 100, 113, 156, 173, 191
Osman, Jena, 197
OTTIP (On Translation: The Internet Project), 198
Oulipo, 5, 23, 53, 124, 143, 156, 160, 215
Outranspo, 35, 53, 79, 83, 86, 93, 157, 160, 161, 162,
    185, 194, 195, 198, 209, 215, 216
Overliteralness, 41, 146–147
Ownership of translations, 13

Paillard, Michel, 47, 54
Pailthorpe, Baiden, 4, 132, 133
Palekar, Shalmalee, 212
"Paradox" (Moure), 167

Paradox of authorship, 174
Parallel texts, 123, 196
Paratextual phenomena, 174, 176–184
Parrish, Allison, 8
Parse (Dworkin), 162–163
"Pastiche," 88
Pato, Chus, 169–170, 172, 187
PDGN (Van Harskamp), 135–137, 138, 144–154
Perec, Georges, 156, 221n1
Performative and Experiential Translation, 216
Performative translations, 177, 191, 198
Periodicity, 11, 18–19
Pézard, André, 211
Phelan, James D., 65
Philip, M. NourbeSe, 17, 31, 39–45, 51, 62, 63, 64,
    67–68, 72, 74–75
Philosophy, 12, 61, 140, 141
Phonemes, 40, 50
Photography, 8–9, 10, 89, 126
Photoshop, 31, 89
Pidgins, 145, 158, 164
Pink Noise (Hsia Yü), 4
"Pint," 57
Place names, 59–60
Pneumatic functions, 64, 74
"Poem 21" (Romero), 146
"Poems for Brexitees" (Bloomfield), 77, 78, 79
Poetry
    adaptation, 205
    bilingual poetry, 66
    calque, 77, 83–84, 90, 94–98, 99–103
    concrete poetry, 125, 147
    emprunt, 39–45, 68
    as engineering, 153
    equivalence, 195–196
    Google software, 65
    homophonic translation, 53
    literal translation, 107, 121–128
    machine translation, 4–5, 6, 9
    modulation, 179, 180, 184
    nonsense poetry, 53, 128, 151
    polyphony, 87
    racism, 65
    "test of poetry," 198
    translation norms, 16
    transposition, 152–161
Poibeau, Thierry, 1, 5, 9, 21, 22, 138
Polish, 205–206
Political economics, 54, 55, 60, 66
Polyglottal mash-ups, 127
Polylingual resonance, 69
Polyphony, 69, 87, 90
Portrait of a Tongue (Tawada), 179
Portunhal, 165
Postcoloniality, 7, 21, 59
Poststructuralism, 54
"Potential translation," 160–161

Power, 46, 55, 59, 60, 69, 71, 74
Poyet, Pascal, 159
Preface, translator's, 174, 177
Prestige, 113
Printing, 29, 72, 80
Privilege, 20–21, 60, 65, 129
Programming languages, 21, 144–145, 147,
    154–155
Pronouns, 148–150, 177, 208
Proper nouns, 95, 101, 127
Prosody, 15
Proteus text-to-speech (TTS), 131
Proust, Marcel, 152
Pseudotranslation, 175–176, 177, 184, 198
Psychoacoustic sound environments, 68–69
Publishing, 74, 75
Puerto Rico, 108
Punctuality, 211
Punctuation, 95–96, 193
Purity norms, 27, 31
Pym, Anthony, 26, 27, 29, 30, 33, 34, 45, 58, 176,
    177, 180, 188, 189, 190–191

Quant à je, 69, 82
Quantitative equivalence, 193
Queer translation, 49–50, 70, 87, 91, 93, 178
Queneau, Raymond, 158

Race, 60–61, 65, 74, 75
Raley, Rita, 7, 21, 22, 32, 129, 132, 133, 138, 216
Ramayya, Nisha, 99–103, 179
Raw, Lawrence, 211–212
Recouperation, 76
Redingote, 50
Register, 68, 164
Reiß, Katharina, 207
Repetition Nineteen (de la Torre), 64–67, 122,
    193, 201
Resistance, 112–121, 130
Retranslation, 161, 174, 195
Retrotranslation, 161, 195
"Reversal of terms," 180
Reverse engineering, 158, 161
Rhetoric, 109, 145, 183
Ribeiro Pires Vieira, Else, 17
Ricardo Reis (Saramago), 179
Richards, Carol, 155
Richards, I. A., 138
"RIP Motivation: entente cordiale poem"
    (Bloomfield), 78–79
Robertson, Lisa, 159
Robinson, Douglas, 6, 9, 13, 22, 32, 33, 37, 150,
    173–174, 175–176, 177, 178, 179
Romanian, 167, 171, 172
Romero, Amílcar, 146
"Rotten English," 164
Roubaud, Jacques, 160

Rudolf, Michael, 147
Russian, 148–149, 150, 151–152, 156

Sagawa, Chika, 195, 196
Sager, Juan C. and Hamel, M-J., 26, 27, 30, 34, 45,
    47, 48, 49, 50, 60, 80–81, 85, 108–109, 122, 123,
    141, 167, 168–169, 187, 189
Sakai, Naoki, 13, 58
Saleda, Hermes, 157
Samoyault, Tiphaine, 11–12, 30, 35, 36, 73, 211
Sampedrín, Elisa, 32, 167, 168, 170–172, 179
Sanders, Julie, 211
Sanskrit, 99–100
Santos Perez, Craig, 222n2
Saro-Wiwa, Ken, 36, 164
Saussure, Ferdinand de, 52, 54, 55, 57, 60, 63, 123
"Say Parsley" (Bergvall), 68–69
"Say Translation is Art" (Nakayasu), 197, 205
Scheunemann, Dietrich, 8
Schilling, Derek, 157
Schultz, Marie-Laure, 83
Screenplay translation, 92
Seafarer (Bergvall), 71, 72
Secession/ Insecession (Moure), 169–172, 179, 187
Seita, Sophie, 223n14
Self-translation, 107, 122, 156
Semantic calque, 85–86, 93 (*see also* meaning)
Semantic change, 77, 80, 86, 109
Sense-for-sense translation, 29
"Sensitive turn," 30
Sentience, 3–4
Separability, 62–63, 64, 65, 83
Serial translations, 33, 66, 152, 180–181, 196, 197,
    198–199, 201
"Servitude," 48, 49–50, 51, 60, 109
Sharp, Granville, 40
Sharpe, Christina, 44, 63, 72, 75
Sheep's Vigil of a Fervent Person (Moure), 173
Shiotsuka, Shuichiro, 156
Shoaib, Mahwash, 198
Signifier/signified
    "abomination of the mirror," 83
    abstract values, 58
    and algorithms, 114
    calque, 80
    emprunt, 30–31, 49–50, 52, 53–54, 55, 60, 62
    history of translation studies, 6
    machine translation, 124–125
    neural machine translation (NMT), 7–8, 117
    philosophy, 12, 13
    signifier as motor of new meanings, 87
    signs of value, 65–72
Sign language translation, 219n8
Silicon Valley, 65
Simon, Sherry, 10
Siri, 127
Situatedness, 60

Skopos translation theory, 207, 215
Skoulding, Zoë, 36
Slater, Avery, 5–6, 16, 21, 22, 97, 115, 116, 118, 140, 214
Slavery, 39–40, 44, 61, 63, 67, 68
Slovenian, 129, 130
Smartphones, 114, 119–120
Snell-Hornby, Mary, 188, 190, 197
Snob poem, 77
Songhay, 198
Song Hwee Lim, 191
Sonotranslation, 36, 53, 121, 152, 185
Soubira, Jacob-Abraham, 158
Source/target language (terminology of), 34
Sozaboy (Saro-Wiwa), 36, 164
Spaces between words, 64, 74
"Spacey emptiness," 23
Spahr, Juliana, 197, 199
Spanish
    calque, 84, 92
    emprunt, 67, 73
    equivalence, 193
    "Equivalencies/Equivalencias" (de la Torre), 201
    gender (grammatical), 148–149
    language mixing, 165
    lipograms, 156
    literal translation, 107, 112, 119, 121, 125, 126, 127
    transposition, 146
Spivak, Gayatri, 23
Spoken languages, focus on, 20–21
Stalling, Jonathan, 191–192, 193
Standardization, 71, 98, 102, 110, 113, 116, 117, 129, 133, 143
Stănescu, Nichita, 167, 170, 171
States of the Body Produced by Love (Ramayya), 99–103
Statistical machine translation (SMT), 2, 115–116, 124, 125
Stephenson, Neal, 143
Stieglitz, Alfred, 126
Stochastische Texte (Lutz, 1959), 5
Stories/narratives, 86, 87, 126, 149–150
Strangeness and beauty, 122, 124, 125, 131, 133, 163, 215
Stromajer, Igor, 131
Structural linguistics, 5, 23, 28–29, 54, 143, 148
Stylistic effects, 47, 60
Subjectivity, translator's, 89, 176, 178–179, 180
Subtitling, 209
Suchet, Myriam, 73
Swift, Jonathan, 173–174
Syllables, 97
Synonyms, 93
Synoptic hypothesis, 91–92
Synthetic metacalques, 92

Tahir, Kemal, 211–212
Tales of the OOtd War (MacLeod), 131
Talk Shows (de la Torre), 184
TAUM-METEO, 9
Tawada, Yoko, 179
Technical resistance, 112–121
Technical translation, 15–16, 122
Technology, 89, 92, 114–115, 126 (*see also* digital technology; machine translation; photography; printing)
Telephone project, 198
Temporality, 11, 14, 63, 86, 87, 122, 168, 170–172, 174, 179
Terry, Philip, 37, 211
"Test of poetry," 198
Text-to-speech, 131
Thai, 94–98
"The Two" poetry generator, 148
Third languages, translation through, 125, 129, 159, 162, 164
Thomason, Sara, 49
"Tlönslation" (Clarke), 164
Tokens, 7–8, 23, 51–56, 89, 114
Toury, Gideon, 13–14, 15
"Tower of Anti-Babel," 115, 116, 138
Traduit Partouze ("translation orgy"), 76
Trainor, Samuel, 87–88, 91, 92
Transcreation, 10, 16–17, 28, 173, 174, 176, 195, 213–217
Transcription, 73, 116, 131, 156
Transduction, 160
Translating Constrained Literature, 151, 157, 159, 161
Translating E- Literature, 148, 150, 151
Translational norms
    and adaptation, 212–213
    challenging, 11–15, 16–17, 21, 110
    changing over time, 181
    codification of, 23–24
    collaborative translations, 199
    colonialism, 14–15
    experimenting with, 150–151
    machines affirm, 123
    machine translation, 133
    navigability, 97
    transcreation, 214–217
"Translation" as term, 212
"Translation in Six Steps: Thai to English," 94–98
Translation Memoir, The (Grass and Robert-Foley), 170
"Translation memoirs," 177
Translation memory (TM), 90
Translation of "translation," 14
Translations of translations, 195

Translation studies
  calque, 87
  emprunt, 54, 57, 58
  formal/dynamic, 208
  literal translation, 109
  metaphor, 31
  non-symmetrical meaning, 188
  norms, 13-14, 23
  privilege of English, 20
  structural linguistics, 6, 54, 58
  theory/practice divide, 15
  transcendentalism, 6
  and Vinay-Darbelnet procedures, 27, 28-29
Translator positionality, 89, 176-184
Translator voice, 19-20
Transliteration, 73, 91, 94-98, 100, 191, 192, 196
Translucinación, 197
Transparency, 11-12, 16, 50, 54, 62, 73, 87-88, 96, 115
Transparent I, 62
Transposition, 24, 32, 135-165, 168, 206
Transversal (Noel), 110-111, 112, 119, 193
Trilce (Vallejo), 121
Trope Tank, 145-146, 150
Trouillot, Michel-Rolph, 36, 198
Tuntha-obas, Padcha, 94-98
Typographical art, 151

Uncanniness, 80, 163
Uncouthness, 122, 131, 132, 133, 163
United States, 199, 208
Universals, 14, 22, 49, 115, 117, 138-140, 159
Unmemntioable, The (Moure), 172
Unreadability, 71, 73, 162
Untola, Algot, 175, 179
Untranslatability, 6, 73, 75, 108, 146, 156

Vallejo, César, 121
Van Dyck, Karen, 158-159
Van Harskamp, Nicoline, 22, 101-103, 135-137, 138, 154
Vassilikos, Vassilis, 57
VD (Vinay/Darbelnet)
  adaptation, 208-209
  calque, 80-81, 84, 85
  emprunt, 47-48, 50, 52, 60
  equivalence, 187, 189, 199
  hijacking logic, 17
  literal translation, 108-109, 121, 122, 123

machine translation, 5
modulation, 167, 168-169, 170, 172
procedures, 24-34
transposition, 141, 143
Vectors, 7-8, 55, 89, 116, 123
Venuti, Lawrence, 13, 16, 20, 88, 96
Vermeer, Hans, 207
"Via" (Bergvall), 198
Vicari, Eliana, 185
Viedma Peláez, Andrés, 145-146
Voice production software, 131
Voice recognition, 4, 32, 121, 125, 126

"Wake work," 44-45, 63-64, 75
Waldrop, Rosemarie, 4, 215
Watier, Louis, 175
Weaver, Warren, 1, 5, 22, 115, 116, 117, 122, 138, 143
Weightman, J. G., 168
Weissmann, Dirk, 54
Wells, H. G., 138
Whitney, W. D., 46
Wilkins, John, 139, 141
Wokitokiteki.com, 107, 112, 114, 115, 126
Women's language, 137-138
Word as unit, 78
Word-for-word translation, 29, 108-109
Words Without Borders, 84
Word vectors, 89, 139, 140, 166
"Word windows," 7-8
Work-on-the-letter, 109
Wright, Chantal, 178, 179
"Wrong" translation, 90

Yingelishi (Stalling), 191
Yorlang, 144
Yoruba, 41, 43, 144
Yoshihara Jirō, 126
Youdale, Roy, 1
"Your turn" (de la Torre), 125
Yurdatap, Selâmi Munir, 211-212

Zaum poetry, 151-152, 157
Zetzsche, Jost, 191
Zhang, Ziquing, 198
"Zone," 9
Zong! (Philip), 39-45, 62, 63, 64, 67, 72, 74-75
Zukofsky, Celia and Louis, 16, 53